God's Unruly Friends

God's Unruly Friends

DERVISH GROUPS
IN THE ISLAMIC LATER MIDDLE PERIOD
1200–1550

Ahmet T. Karamustafa

ONEWORLD
OXFORD

A Oneworld Book

Published by Oneworld Publications 2006

rst published in the United States of America by the University of Utah Press

A CIP record for this title is available
From the British Library

ISBN-13: 978-1-85168-460-1
ISBN-10: 1-85168-460-3

Cover design by Liz Powell
Printed and bound in India by Thomson Press (India) Ltd.

Oneworld Publications
185 Banbury Road
Oxford OX2 7AR
England
www.oneworld-publications.com

TO FATEMEH

Gözüm canım efendim sevdiğim devletli sultanım

Contents

Acknowledgments

I first met the deviant dervishes in earnest when I read Vāḥidī's *Menāḳıb-i Ḫvoca-i Cihān ve Netīce-i Cān* in 1983. During the following three years, I tried to trace the history of these enigmatic figures and incorporated the initial results of my research into my doctoral dissertation in the form of one long chapter. While I continued to gather information on the dervishes after this point, it was only in the summer of 1991 that I returned to them with renewed interest. The present work is largely the outcome of my efforts during the past two years to understand and explain dervish piety.

I have accrued many debts in the process of working on this project. The Library of the School of Oriental and African Studies, the Library of the Institute of Ismaili Studies, the British Library (all in London), the Library of the Institute of Islamic Studies (Montreal), Süleymaniye Kütüphanesi (Istanbul), and İstanbul Üniversitesi Kütüphanesi gave me easy access to their collections, for which I am grateful. The Institute of Islamic Studies of McGill University and the Department of Asian and Near Eastern Languages and Literatures of Washington University in St. Louis gave me unfailing institutional support, the former in the form of academic guidance and financial assistance throughout my graduate studies and the latter by providing me with ideal working conditions in an admirable atmosphere of collegiality for the past six years. I feel privileged to be associated with these fine institutions.

Many colleagues and friends have contributed to this book. It is a pleasure to thank them here for their interest, time, and invaluable criticism and simultaneously to absolve them of any responsibility for the final outcome. Gerhard Böwering of Yale University, J. T. P. De Bruijn of the University of Leiden, Jamal Elias of Amherst College, Carl W. Ernst of the University of North Carolina, Gary Leiser, Michel M. Mazzaoui of the University of Utah, James W. Morris of Oberlin College, and Azim Nanji of the University of

Florida have all read and commented upon different versions of the manuscript in its entirety. My colleagues and friends at Washington University, Engin D. Akarlı, Cornell H. Fleischer (now at the University of Chicago), and Peter Heath, in addition to exercising their customary critical acumen on the manuscript, offered me constant support and encouragement. Beata Grant, also of Washington University, saved me from many an infelicity of expression by smoothing my style.

To Hermann Landolt of McGill University, my teacher and friend, I owe a special debt of gratitude. He was involved in the project from its inception and guided it to maturation for over a decade in his inimitable style. His unflagging support has been a safe haven for a fledgling scholar.

Finally, I am happy to acknowledge my incalculable debt to Fatemeh Keshavarz of Washington University, my wife, friend, and colleague. She has been the mainstay of this research project and more over the past several years, and it is to her that this book is lovingly dedicated.

Usage

Arabic and Persian titles, technical terms, and personal names have been transliterated according to the Library of Congress transliteration systems for these languages, while the transliteration of names and terms in Ottoman Turkish follows, with some deviations, the system proposed by Eleazar Birnbaum, "The Transliteration of Ottoman Turkish for Library and General Purposes: Ottoman Turkish Transliteration Scheme," *Journal of the American Oriental Society* 87 (1967): 122–56. The choice of transliteration system was guided by context (thus, *tekbīr* rather than *takbīr* in transliterating from Ottoman Turkish), though the transliteration of certain often-used words (Qalandar, *zāwiyah, ḥadīth*) has been rendered uniform throughout the manuscript in order not to confuse the reader.

Dates are given in both the Islamic lunar and Common Era years, separated by a slash. I have used the conversion tables supplied by F. R. Unat, *Hicrī Tarihleri Milādī Tarihe Çevirme Kılavuzu* (Ankara: Türk Tarih Kurumu Yayınları, 1984). Islamic solar dates, primarily used in Persian publications, are represented by the addition of the letters "sh" (for *shamsī*) to the date.

Unless otherwise noted, all translations are my own.

CHAPTER ONE

Introduction

In the mid-sixth/twelfth century, a peculiar-looking ascetic visited the palace of the Ghaznavid ruler Muʿizz al-Dawlah Khusraw Shāh (r. 547–55/1152–60) in Ghazna in eastern Afghanistan to ask for alms. He had bare feet and was dressed in a black goat's skin. On his head he wore a cap of the same material, ornamented with horns. In his hand he carried a club adorned with rings, pierced ankle-bones, and small round bells. Khusraw Shāh responded favorably to the ascetic's request and received his blessings.[1]

More than a century and a half later, ascetics of very similar appearance are recorded to have gathered around Barak̡ Baba (d. 707/1307–8) in Asia Minor and Iran. Barak̡ Baba arrived in Syria in the year 706/1306 at the head of a group of about one hundred dervishes, naked except for a red cloth wrapped around his waist. He wore a reddish turban on his head with a buffalo horn attached on either side. His hair and his moustache were long, while his beard was clean-shaven. He carried with him a long pipe or horn (*nafīr*), as well as a dervish bowl. He did not accumulate any wealth. His disciples were of similar appearance, carrying long clubs, tambourines and drums, bells, and painted ankle-bones, with molar teeth attached to strings suspended from their necks. Wherever they went, the disciples played and Barak̡ Baba danced like a bear and sang like a monkey. It is reported that Barak̡ Baba had control over wild animals, as he demonstrated by scaring a ferocious tiger and riding a wild ostrich on two different occasions. Apparently, he exercised similar control over his disciples, whom he forced to perform the prescribed religious practices on pain of forty blows of the bastinado. Nonetheless, his dervishes were renowned for their antinomian ways, which included failure to observe the ritual fast and consumption of legally objectionable foods and drugs. The Mamlūk sources also accuse them of belief in metempsychosis and denial of the existence of the hereafter, while to Barak̦ himself is imputed an excessive love of ʿAlī, which he supposedly viewed as the sole religious obligation.[2]

A century after Barak̦ Baba's visit to Syria, on 25 May 1404, the Spanish traveler Ruy Gonzales de Clavijo passed through a place called Delilarkent ("city of madmen," present-day Delibaba) in the vicinity of Erzurum in eastern Anatolia. He reported that the whole village was inhabited by dervishes:

> These Dervishes shave their beards and their heads and go almost naked. They pass through the street, whether in the cold or in the heat, eating as they go, and all the clothing they wear is bits of rag of the torn stuff that they can pick up. As they walk along night and day with their tambourines they chant hymns. Over the gate of their hermitage is seen a banner of black woollen tassels with a moon-shaped ornament above; below this are arranged in a row the horns of deer and goats and rams, and further it is their custom to carry about with them these horns as trophies when they walk through the streets; and all the houses of the Dervishes have these horns set over them for a sign.[3]

The lone ascetic dressed in goat's skin in Afghanistan, the tumultuous crowd of mendicant disciples around Barak̦ Baba in Syria, and the naked dervishes of Delibaba in Asia Minor represent a kind of renunciation that emerged and spread in Islamdom during the Later Middle Period (ca. 600–900/1200–1500).[4] This new movement differed from previous versions of Islamic renunciation in significant ways. On one hand, the new renouncers elevated the ascetic principles of mendicancy, itinerancy, celibacy, and self-mortification to unprecedented heights through a radical interpretation of the doctrine of poverty. On the other hand, they welded asceticism with striking forms of social deviance in such a way as to render deviant behavior the ultimate measure of true renunciation. In their zeal to reject society and to refuse to participate in its reproduction in any fashion, the new renouncers embraced such anarchist and antinomian practices as nudity or improper clothing, shaving all bodily and facial hair, and use of hallucinogens and intoxicants as the only real methods of renunciation. The avoidance of gainful employment, family life, and indeed all forms of social association was not sufficient. Withdrawal from society had to be accompanied by active rejection and destruction of established social custom. More than anything else, it was in their deliberate and blatant social deviance that the new renouncers differed from their previous counterparts in Islamic history.

The new renunciatory movement was not homogeneous. Its various manifestations forged the features of poverty, mendicancy, itinerancy, celibacy, self-mortification, and other forms of social deviance into distinct combinations with varying degrees of emphasis on the eremitic and cenobitic options. The solitary mendicant, the wandering group of disciples, and the partially settled dervish community of the reports presented above reflect these different manifestations of the new dervish piety. Uncompromising eremiticism based on radical poverty, usually characteristic of the initial phase of the renunciation movement, was everywhere followed by a cenobitic reaction. While mendicancy and itinerancy remained the norm, the attraction of community life dampened the anchoritic zeal inherited from the ascetic virtuosi of the previous generations. The original ascetic mandate was further attenuated when renouncers began to practice mendicancy and itinerancy on a part-time, mostly seasonal, basis. Wandering and begging in a state of extreme poverty most of the year, these renouncers returned to their hospices the rest of the year, where they enjoyed the relative comfort of settled life. Despite such diversity, however, social deviance always remained constant.

Although the new renunciatory piety was already in evidence during the sixth/twelfth century, its first clear manifestations in the form of identifiable social collectivities emerged around the turn of the seventh/thirteenth century. They took the form of two widespread movements: the Qalandarīyah, which first flourished in Syria and Egypt under the leadership of ethnically Iranian leaders, most notably Jamāl al-Dīn Sāvī (d. ca. 630/1232–33), and the Ḥaydarīyah, which took shape in Iran as a result of the activities of its eponymous founder Quṭb al-Dīn Ḥaydar (d. ca. 618/1221–22). Both movements rapidly spread from their respective places of origin to India and to Asia Minor.

Already before the end of the seventh/thirteenth century, other dervish groups similar to the mendicant Qalandars and Ḥaydarīs began to appear in different regions of Islamdom. The followers of Barak̦ Baba in newly conquered Asia Minor and western Iran were the earliest and most prominent representatives of this wave of locally contained religious renunciation. During the following two centuries, many more groups appeared alongside the still effective Qalandars and Ḥaydarīs, notably Abdāls of Rūm, Jāmīs, Bektāşīs, and Shams-i Tabrīzīs in Asia Minor and Madārīs and Jalālīs in Muslim India.

The definitive establishment of the great regional empires of the Ottomans, Ṣafavids, Üzbeks, and Mughals during the tenth/sixteenth century led to tighter organization of the deviant dervish groups. The loose social collectivity of the Later Middle Period was either transformed into a new Sufi order or assimilated into an older one. In Ottoman Asia Minor and the Balkans, the Bektāşīye emerged as a major new order that carried the legacy of the earlier Qalandars, Ḥaydarīs, and Abdāls of Rūm, while in India Qalandars infiltrated the socially respectable Sufi orders (*ṭarīqahs*), which led to the emergence of suborders like the Chishtīyah-Qalandarīyah. Similar processes must have been operative in the formation of the Khāksār in Iran, which probably came into being through a merger of different movements such as the Ḥaydarīyah and Jalālīyah. Not all of the earlier dervish groups survived into this later period; some simply disappeared altogether, as evidenced by the case of the Jāmīs in the Ottoman Empire.

HISTORIOGRAPHY

The deviant dervish groups that constituted the new renunciatory movement have received varying degrees of scholarly attention.[5] The Qalandars have been the subject of several studies, while the Ḥaydarīs, Abdāls of Rūm, and the others remain largely unexplored.[6] Even in the case of the Qalandars, however, scholars have, as a rule, restricted the scope of their research to a specific region and period and have not attempted to trace the history of the group in Islamdom as a whole.

At present, there exists no comprehensive study of new renunciation.[7] The phenomenon is not even acknowledged as a distinct phase in the historical development of Islamic modes of piety. This lack of analytical depth and focus is patently visible in the inability of previous scholarship to produce a satisfactory explanation for the emergence and enduring appeal of deviant renunciation. Indeed, the reasons for the formation, spread, and flourishing of new movements of renunciation during the Later Middle Period have remained obscure. This is hardly surprising. Dervish piety has not normally been viewed as the manifestation of a new mode of religiosity. Instead, it has been subsumed under the larger and seemingly permanent category of "popular religion." The operative assumption here has been that there was a watertight separation in premodern Islamic history between high, normative, and official religion of the cultural elite on the one hand and low, antinomian, and popular religion of the illiterate masses on the other hand. Dervish religiosity has generally been viewed as one, and only one, feature of the sphere of popular religion. Conceived as a static mixture of ill-defined beliefs and practices, however, popular religion is immune to historical change. The illiterate common people of the premodern periods are thought to have clung tenaciously to their ancient religious lore and ritual behavior, resisting the manipulative pressures of the "literate" religious tradition. Submerged in the sea of unchanging popular religious practice, socially deviant renunciation is thus stripped of its historical specificity and rendered impervious to historical explanation.

The relegation of anarchist dervishes to the sphere of popular religion and low culture has deep historical roots. The cultural elite of medieval Islamdom consistently identified the dervishes as the riffraff of society and readily decried them as impostors and ignoramuses. Within the decade of their appearance in the Arab Middle East, the Qalandars and the Ḥaydarīs, for instance, were portrayed as shameless charlatans by ʿAbd al-Raḥmān al-Jawbarī in a book that he wrote between 619/1222 and 629/1232 to unveil the tricks perpetrated by numerous classes of beggars and swindlers of the underworld.[8] A few decades later, the eminent scholar Naṣīr-al-Dīn Ṭūsī (d. 672/1274) did not hesitate to take an actively hostile attitude toward the dervish "rabble." In 658/1259–60, a group of Qalandars presented themselves in Ḥarrān, Syria, to the Mongol ruler Hülegü (r. 654–63/1256–65). When the ruler wanted to know who these people were, Naṣīr al Dīn's comment, "[They are] the excess of this world," prompted Hülegü to order the summary execution of all the Qalandars.[9] The puritanic Muḥammad al-Khaṭīb, who wrote a whole treatise to denounce the irreligious practices of Qalandars in 683/1284–85, emphatically commended the non-Muslim Mongols for their harsh treatment of the Qalandars.[10] In a similar vein, such prominent Sufis as Ibrāhīm Gīlānī (d. 700/1301), the preceptor of the better-known Ṣafī al-Dīn Ardabīlī (d. 735/1334), and the Chishtī Muḥammad Gīsū'darāz (d. 826/1422) warned their followers against mixing with the Qalandars.[11]

Clear condemnation of mendicant dervishes remained a consistent feature of elite intellectual life throughout the Later Middle Period. Vāḥidī (fl. first half of the tenth/sixteenth century), the outspoken Ottoman Sufi critic of deviant renunciation, for instance, was vehement in his rejection of the dervishes as shameless hypocrites and impostors who traded in the religious sensibilities of the naturally ignorant and credulous common people. Vāḥidī denounced them as false Sufis, utterly lacking in any sincere religious sentiments, and as such definitely worse than infidels:

> Even the infidel comes to the fold of the faithful, but not the heretic dervish; the infidel has receptivity but not him.
>
> He is out of the sphere of hope while the infidel is in the circle of fear of God,
>
> by God, the infidel is far superior to him.[12]

Vāḥidī's contemporary Laṭīfī (d. 990/1582), the biographer of poets, harbored the same sentiments toward deviant dervishes, whom he decried as partners of the devil.[13] Interestingly, much the same approach toward the scandalous dervishes and their audience is found in the European counterparts of these cultured Ottoman gentlemen. The particular set of assumptions that governed elite views of new renunciation is fully displayed in the following colorful account of the Qalandars by Giovan Antonio Menavino, a well-informed and keen European observer of the Ottoman society of the late fifteenth and early sixteenth centuries:

> Dressed in sheepskins, the *ṭorlaḳ*s [read Qalandars] are otherwise naked, with no headgear.[14] Their scalps are always clean-shaven and well rubbed with oil as a precaution against the cold. They burn their temples with an old rag so that their faces will not be damaged by sweat. Illiterate and unable to do anything manly, they live like beasts, surviving on alms only. For this reason, they

> are to be found around taverns and public kitchens in cities. If, while roaming the countryside, they come across a well-dressed person, they try to make him one of their own, stripping him naked. Like Gypies in Europe, they practice chiromancy, especially for women who then provide them with bread, eggs, cheese, and other foods in return for their services. Amongst them there is usually an old man whom they revere and worship like God. When they enter a town, they gather around the best house of the town and listen in great humility to the words of this old man, who, after a spell of ecstasy, foretells the descent of a great evil upon the town. His disciples then implore him to fend off the disaster through his good services. The old man accepts the plea of his followers, though not without an initial show of reluctance, and prays to God, asking him to spare the town the imminent danger awaiting it. This time-honored trick earns them considerable sums of alms from ignorant and credulous people. The *ṭorlaḳ*s . . . chew hashish and sleep on the ground; they also openly practice sodomy like savage beasts.[15]

This passage transports us to the strange yet familiar landscape of "popular religion." Menavino's detailed tableau of the Qalandars is drawn against a dark and somewhat hellish landscape that is peopled with ignorant and credulous masses and the equally ignorant and thoroughly fraudulent group of false saints that the masses venerate. If they are not total idiots, the impostor saints exploit the religious sensitivities of the simple folk and extract material benefits from them. This inversion of the flow of blessings and compassion from saintly figures to the common people is accompanied by a thorough distancing of the popular scene through the addition of features that render the landscape strange and almost bestial. In all this, Menavino is closely followed by his later counterparts, whose general attitude to the dervishes is epitomized by the following sentences of E. W. Lane, the scholarly observer of early nineteenth-century Egyptian society:

> That fancies such as these [that is, believing in *jinn*s] should exist in the minds of a people so ignorant as those who are the subject of these pages cannot reasonably excite our surprise. But the Egyptians pay superstitious reverence not to imaginary beings alone: they extend it to certain individuals of their own species; and

> often to those who are justly the least entitled to such respect. . . . Most of the reputed saints of Egypt are either lunatics, or idiots, or impostors.[16]

To the "enlightened" cultural elite of both medieval Islamdom and Christendom, then, the antinomian dervish was the symbol par excellence of the religion of the vulgar. It is remarkable that this specific set of assumptions and the particular view of religion and human culture of which it is symptomatic have been operative since the Middle Ages and that they still inform the historiographical discourse within which research on the history of the Islamic region is conducted. In a ground-breaking article that returned the issue of popular religion to the agenda of historical research, Mehmed Fuad Köprülü (d. 1966) wrote about the deviant dervishes in the following terms:

> If we consider that these men were in general recruited from the lower classes and were incapable of [comprehending] some very subtle mystical observations and experiences, it becomes quite obvious that their undigested "pantheistic" beliefs would naturally lead to beliefs such as incarnation and metempsychosis and, in the final analysis, to "antinomianism." . . . As a general principle, beliefs that could only be digested by people who possess a [high degree] of philosophical capacity and who are susceptible to mystical experience always lead to consequences of this sort among people of feeble intellect.[17]

Closer to our own day, Fazlur Rahman (d. 1989) was even more vehement than Köprülü in his denunciation of popular religion. Referring to the seventh/thirteenth and eighth/fourteenth centuries, he wrote:

> This phenomenon of popular religion very radically changed the aspect of Sūfism even if it did not entirely displace its very ideal. For practical purposes Islamic society underwent a metempsychosis. Instead of being a method of moral self-discipline and elevation and genuine spiritual enlightenment, Sūfism was now transformed into veritable spiritual jugglery through auto-hypnotic transports and visions just as at the level of doctrine it was being transmuted into a half-delirious theosophy. . . . This, combined with the spiritual demagogy of many Sūfi Shaykhs, opened the way for all

> kinds of aberrations, not the least of which was charlatanism. Ill-balanced *majdhūbs* . . . , parasitic mendicants, exploiting dervishes proclaimed Muhammad's Faith in the heyday of Sūfism. Islam was at the mercy of spiritual delinquents.[18]

It is small wonder that scholars have not taken any substantial interest in the culture of the "feeble-minded" masses and in the practices of "parasitic . . . spiritual delinquents." Significantly, Köprülü himself never published his monograph on the Qalandars, although he repeatedly announced its forthcoming appearance in several of his publications. Since the "vulgar" was nothing but a repository for distorted and contaminated versions of the subtle and pure beliefs of "high" religion, it simply made better sense to tap the original sources directly and consign "low" religion to where it belonged, in "the bosom of the vulgar."

There are serious problems with this "two-tiered" model of religion. The assumption of an unbridgeable separation between high, normative and low, antinomian religion serves to obscure rather than clarify the true nature of the deviant dervish groups and the process of their emergence in the aftermath of the Mongol invasions. While it may conceivably serve a heuristic purpose in other contexts, in the case of the dervish groups of the Later Middle Period the creation of a catch-all category of popular or low religion only confounds the researcher. Such a move strips this particular mode of dervish religiosity of its specific features and renders it immune to analysis by suggesting that it is essentially indistinct from the "popular" versions of other religious trends such as millenarianism and messianism. These mentally and sociologically distinct religious attitudes are thus reduced to the presumed common denominator of "popularity."[19]

The detailed historical examination of deviant dervish groups undertaken in the present work, however, yields results that seriously challenge the application of the two-tiered model of religion in the study of new renunciation. Such close scrutiny reveals that the movements in question formed a distinct religious phenomenon that differed radically from other purportedly popular religious phenomena such as millenarianism, messianism, and saint veneration. Dervish piety stood apart from all other modes of Islamic religiosity through its relentless emphasis on shocking social behavior and its open contempt for social conformity. More significantly, it was not restricted in either social origin or appeal to "lower" social strata. It is not easy to determine the social composition of the dervish groups, but, contrary to the received view that the rank and file of the movements in question must have been composed of the illiterate and the ignorant, there is certainly sufficient evidence to establish that these movements frequently recruited from the middle and high social strata. The socially deviant way of renunciation was attractive enough to produce converts from several social strata of medieval Islamic society. Most telling in this connection is the fact that the cultural elite that consisted of the literati in the widest sense of the term lost some of its members, either temporarily or permanently, to the dervish cause. To judge by the presence of poets, scholars, and writers of a certain proficiency among their numbers, the anarchist dervishes were not always the illiterate crowd their detractors reported them to be. Instead, socially deviant renunciation exercised a strong attraction on the hearts and minds of many Muslim intellectuals.

Furthermore, dervish religiosity was, naturally, a distinct religious phenomenon that developed in a historically specific social and cultural context. Surely, its sudden appearance and rapid spread during the seventh/thirteenth and eighth/fourteenth centuries require an explanation. It is a measure of the methodological poverty of the two-tiered model of religion that it not only fails to generate such an explanatory analysis but even obscures the obvious need for one by denying popular religion a historical dimension. The vulgar, it is understood, is timeless. Reliance on a dichotomous view of Islamic religion thus opens the way for the preponderance of externalistic explanations such as "survival of non-Islamic beliefs and practices under Islamic cover." Indeed, the ascendancy of popular religious practice during the Middle Periods is usually, if at all, explained through recourse to the time-honored "survival" theory. In this view, popular Islam took shape in the Near East during the Early Middle Period through large-scale conversions of the masses of unlettered peoples to Islam. As a result of this expansive process of conversion, "Islam, originally the religion of a political and urban elite, became the religion and social identity of most Middle Eastern peoples."[20] Outside the Near East, the process continued into the Later Middle Period through the conversion of nomadic Turks in

Central Asia (as well as in Iran and Asia Minor), Hindus of low caste in India, and Berbers and black peoples of Africa. The halfhearted and in most cases merely nominal Islamization of these masses barely in touch with high literate traditions, the argument runs, led to the introduction of non-Islamic, especially shamanistic and animistic, beliefs and practices into Islam. The ensuing revitalization of "popular culture," when coupled by the concomitant attenuation of Islamic high culture in the aftermath of the destructive wave of Mongol conquests, made possible the emergence and speedy diffusion of saint veneration in general and deviant mystic movements in particular in the heartlands of Islam.[21]

Applied to socially deviant renunciation, the theory of non-Islamic survivals would suggest that the emergence of new renunciation in medieval Islamdom should be understood in terms of the continuation of "primitive" non-Islamic belief patterns in imperfectly Islamized cultural environments. However, it is misleading to see deviant renunciation solely as a survival of pre-Islamic beliefs and practices. That there was a substantial degree of continuity between pre-Islamic and Islamic religious belief and practice in all the relevant cultural spheres is itself not in dispute here. Many components of dervish piety, especially in costume and paraphernalia such as the dervish staff or ankle bones and molar teeth, may well have had their origins in pre-Islamic or contemporary non-Islamic contexts.[22] Yet their reconfiguration into a visibly Islamic mode of religiosity occurred as a result of social dynamics internal to Islamic societies. Neither "survivals" nor "traces," these originally extraneous beliefs and practices became the building blocks of a new Islamic synthesis. Therefore, the explanation for the emergence and entrenchment of this mode of Islamic piety should be located within, rather than without, Islamic societies.

CHAPTER TWO

Renunciation Through Social Deviance

Dervish piety can be described as "renunciation of society through outrageous social deviance." This mode of religiosity was predicated upon complete and active rejection of society that was expressed through blatantly deviant social behavior. To the anarchist dervish, religious salvation was incompatible with a life led within the orders of society, since social life inevitably distanced humanity from God. Salvation could be found only in active, open, and total rejection of human culture, and the deviant dervish did not withdraw into the wild nature to lead a life of seclusion but created for himself a "social wilderness" at the heart of society where his fiercely antisocial activity functioned as a sobering critique of society's failure to reach God. Cautious not to become part of the "master narrative," the dervish carefully carved out his own space on the margins of that narrative, where he inscribed his boisterous commentary in a most conspicuous fashion.

It would, therefore, be correct to describe new renunciation as a movement based on rejection of society. The dervishes defined themselves through calculated defiance of the social order and proceeded to construct an intensely antiestablishment protest movement. They did not aim to replace the existing social order by a rival one, nor did they seek to reform society; they simply negated all cultural norms and structures. The negative, reactive nature of renunciation manifested itself in the form of blatant social deviance, which became the hallmark of dervish piety. In order to implement their anarchist agenda, the dervishes adopted numerous deviant practices. These can be subsumed under the two general categories of asceticism and antinomianism.

ASCETICISM

Social deviance was manifested primarily in the form of an intense and permanent asceticism that was flaunted by the dervishes in their attempt to secure salvation through active renunciation of human social institutions. Their ascetic practices, which without exception all negated basic institutions of Islamic societies of the Middle Period, can be identified as poverty, mendicancy, itinerancy, celibacy, and self-inflicted pain.

Voluntary rejection of all property was perhaps the most prominent feature of dervish piety. It is well known that the very term *darvīsh* means "poor" or "indigent" in Persian (Arabic equivalent, *faqīr*).[1] The ascetic dervishes lived in absolute indigence, and their possessions were reduced to the bare minimum. The characteristic accoutrements of each dervish group included one or more of the following items: woolen or felt garment or animal hide, distinctive cap, begging bowl, pouch, spoon, club, belt, bell, hatchet, lamp or candle, razor, needle, flint stone, and musical instruments (commonly tambourine, drum, and pipe). The founding masters themselves appear to have practiced absolute poverty by rejecting even these minimal possessions. Jamāl al-Dīn Sāvī, Quṭb al-Dīn Ḥaydar, and Otman Baba are all known, for instance, to have worn no clothing at all for long periods during their dervish careers.[2] Actualized in practice, voluntary poverty was also a well-articulated part of dervish ideology. The Qalandars, who had an elaborate discourse of poverty, rested their case on the example of the Prophet Muḥammad, who, they argued, chose poverty over the two worlds.[3] The Abdāls of Rūm, for their part, professed to be following in the footsteps of the Prophet Adam, who was almost completely naked and free of possessions when he was expelled from Paradise.[4]

The rule against owning property was accompanied by the injunction against gainful employment. The ascetic dervishes openly refused to participate in the economic reproduction of society. This is most conspicuous in the lives of the founding masters: Jamāl al-Dīn Sāvī, Quṭb al-Dīn Ḥaydar, and Otman Baba all turned to nature for their sustenance and carefully avoided even physical contact with the property of others. They categorically rejected all kinds of alms. In Otman Baba, who consistently likened property, especially money, to feces and reacted violently to any offer of alms, this unwillingness to accept alms went so far as to become an almost psychological repulsion.

For the majority of ascetic dervishes, however, the disdain for gainful employment meant continuous dependence on the generosity of others, especially for food. Begging and alms-taking, at times fairly regulated, became the rule. Due to lack of information, it is not possible to trace the evolution of the attitude of different groups toward mendicancy, yet it appears that if they had qualms about accepting gifts and donations to begin with, at least some Qalandars and Abdāls gradually discarded them. This relaxation of originally more stringent standards was most visible in the appearance of Qalandarī and Abdāl hospices, veritable institutions dependent upon carefully managed economic surplus and subject to political control. Even in such cases, however, belief in the efficacy and necessity of begging was never abandoned, and compromise solutions were found, such as living on the revenue of the hospice during winter months and begging for the rest of the year, as in the lodge of Seyyid Ġāzī in northwest Asia Minor.

Homeless wandering was another trait shared by all ascetic dervish groups. Voluntary poverty and mendicancy easily led to renunciation of settled life. This was the case even when itinerancy did not play a major role in the careers of exemplary ascetics themselves. Although he developed a penchant for traveling before his conversion to extreme asceticism, Jamāl al-Dīn later came to prefer seclusion in cemeteries over wandering. Similarly, Quṭb al-Dīn Ḥaydar seems to have spent all his adult life in the small town of Zāvah in northeast Iran. Nevertheless, their examples did not prevent their followers from adopting a life of itinerancy. In the case of the Abdāls, by contrast, the master himself, Otman Baba, was a homeless wanderer. In all cases, itinerancy, like begging, functioned both as the ultimate proof of and the best control over absolute poverty. The truly poor ones, except the formidable masters who survived either in the wilderness (like Quṭb al-Dīn) or in "cities of the dead" (like Jamāl al-Dīn), could not lead settled lives without compromising the principle of poverty. Unavoidably dependent upon the generosity of others, yet wary against reliance on any single source of sustenance for any length of time, the voluntary poor naturally turned to homeless wandering as the only consistent solution.

It is beyond doubt that conversion to any one of the dervish paths entailed the rejection of marriage and the acceptance of celibacy. The importance given to the renunciation of all sexual reproduction is most pronounced in the case of the Qalandars and Ḥaydarīs. Both Jamāl al-Dīn and Quṭb al-Dīn clearly viewed all sexual activity as a grave threat to a life of complete devotion to the sacred. According to some reports, the former owed his conversion to the Qalandarī path at least partially to his endeavor to remain chaste in accordance, it would seem, with the example of the Qurʾānic Yūsuf.[5] For his part, Quṭb al-Dīn must have been equally wary of his sexual powers, if, as seems likely, his followers' practice of suspending iron rings from their genitals was fashioned after the example of their master. In Quṭb al-Dīn Ḥaydar's case, it may well be that his habit of immersing himself for long periods in cold water was, among other things, also a method of dampening the sexual instinct.[6] Even though similar feats are not recorded for the commonality of ascetic dervishes, celibacy as a corollary of absolute poverty clearly remained the rule among them.

Bodily mortification was a continuous feature of the life of an ascetic dervish. At the very least, all dervishes voluntarily subjected themselves to constant exposure by rejecting the comforts of settled life such as regular diet, shelter, and clothing. This basic condition of helplessness was exacerbated by additional mortifying practices such as shaving all bodily hair, wearing iron chains, rings, collars, bracelets, and anklets, and self-laceration. In all likelihood, these acts of self-denial were perceived by the dervishes not as self-inflicted pain but as the natural result as well as the confirmation of voluntary death before actual biological death. Complete devotion to the Divine entailed utter disregard for worldly existence, both physically and mentally. Active courting of physical death was a common component of dervish piety.

Several other ascetic practices—silence, seclusion, sleep-deprivation, and abstinence from food—are attested in the sources for the careers of the ascetic virtuosi who came to be venerated as founding fathers by their followers, yet it is impossible to know to what extent these additional methods of self-discipline continued to be used by the dervish groups. In the absence of evidence to the contrary, one can only surmise that they were never completely abandoned.

Defined as rejection of property, gainful employment, social station, sexual reproduction, and bodily health, dervish asceticism seriously conflicted with the established social life of medieval Islamdom. Asceticism in itself was not, however, tantamount to social deviance. Practiced only by a negligible minority, the option of severe ascetic flight from society could be easily tolerated and even condoned by most Muslims, including the cultural elite. After all, asceticism had become a highly visible and much cherished component of Sufi piety several centuries before the Later Middle Period.[7] Moderate and permanent asceticism was prescribed for all Sufis, while intense forms were used as temporary measures of spiritual discipline on the Sufi path. Even severe asceticism on a continuous basis could be accommodated through recourse to the doctrine of divine attraction (*jadhbah*), whereby the Sufi was thought to be drawn out of society toward God without regard for the social consequences of such attraction. The divinely pulled ones (*majdhūbs*) could practice extreme forms of asceticism through the grace and will of God, even if this meant operating in shady areas of the religious law (*sharīʿah*).[8]

Dervish piety, however, had as its core an uncompromising rejection of society. For the anarchist dervish, asceticism was only a tool, albeit indispensable, in the struggle to shatter the shackles that social life placed on true religiosity. The religious perils of human interaction could not be avoided through an ascetic flight from society. The dervish did not abandon his social station in order to lead the life of a recluse. Only an active nihilism targeted directly at human society could sever him from his social past and lead him to the proximity of salvation. His religious struggle had a chance to succeed only if he combined his asceticism with anarchist practices that allowed him to test his spiritual stamina in action. Thus, the other face of dervish piety was an uncompromising antinomianism.

ANTINOMIANISM

Deviant dervishes were thoroughly antinomian in appearance and behavior. They violated all social norms with equal ease and indifference and deliberately embraced a variety of unconventional and socially liminal practices.

Perhaps the most potent antinomian feature of new renunciation, certainly the most often cited and criticized, was open disregard for prescribed Islamic ritual practices. The extent to which different groups at different times neglected to fulfill their ritual obligations is impossible to ascertain. Nevertheless, there is little reason to question the accuracy of the reports contained in many sources, hostile and friendly, to the effect that deviant dervishes neither prayed nor fasted. In this context, silence on this issue in sympathetic texts is particularly telling. In Jamāl al-Dīn's sacred biography, for instance, there are only two casual references to ritual prayer, while the hagiography of Otman Baba fares only slightly better in this respect.[9] For its part, the report that Barak̦ Baba's disciples were required to perform prescribed religious practices on pain of forty blows of the bastinado itself reveals the difficulty of enforcing these practices on the dervishes.[10] Moreover, it appears that at least some groups replaced ritual prayer in particular with utterance of simple formulaic expressions. Such was the case with the Qalandars and Abdāls of Rūm, among whom the utterance of the formula "God is the Greatest" (*takbīr*) clearly had a ritual function and may have come to replace the daily ritual prayer.[11] The dervishes' disregard for daily prayer and fasting presumably also carried over to the religious duties of legal charity and pilgrimage. The former was not binding on the propertyless dervishes, while the lack of reports on anarchist dervishes wandering toward Mecca suggests that the ritual pilgrimage was not on the agenda of renunciation.

In addition to eschewing ritual obligations, the dervishes further contravened the *sharīʿah,* in spirit if not always in letter, by adopting patently scandalous and antisocial practices. Foremost among these, on account of its conspicuous nature, was the cultivation of a bizarre general appearance. The coiffure, apparel, and paraphernalia of the dervishes were all shockingly strange. In a social setting where external appearance functioned as an unfailing marker of social identity, the refusal to adopt socially and legally sanctioned patterns of costume and their deliberate replacement by outrageous dress codes clearly signified protest and rejection of social convention.

In dress, the dervishes set themselves off from all social types in a variety of ways. Some went completely naked, while others wore only a simple loincloth. Still other dervishes adopted the time-honored garment of social withdrawal, the woolen or felt cloak, though blue, the Sufi color, was avoided in favor of black or white. The Qalandars of Jạmāl al-Dīn's times wore plain woolen sacks and thus were known as Jawlaqs or Jawlaqīs. The Abdāls of Rūm, in an innovative antisocial move, donned animal hides as their sole garment. The dervishes also registered their protest in headgear, either by not wearing any or by designing distinctive hats. Most dervishes seem to have gone barefoot.[12]

The most radical measure in coiffure was the fourfold shave called the "four blows" (*chahār ẕarb*): shaving off the hair, beard, moustache, and eyebrows. The fourfold shave was the distinctive mark of the Qalandars and was also adopted by the Abdāls of Rūm, Bektāşīs, and Shams-i Tabrīzīs and Jalālīs. For their part, the Ḥaydarīs and Jāmīs shaved their beards but let their moustaches grow long. Both of these practices were clear departures from the example of the Prophet Muḥammad (*sunnah*), which enjoined the wearing of beards and moustaches.[13] They also contravened established social custom in medieval Islamic societies, in which the loss of hair symbolized loss of honor and social status.[14] In a typical renunciatory move, the dervishes adopted the socially reprehensible practice of the "clean shave" and thus charged it with a new, positive meaning.[15]

The equipment of the dervishes was also peculiar. Apart from the standard begging bowl and the dervish club, they also possessed outlandish paraphernalia. The Ḥaydarīs had a predilection for iron rings, collars, bracelets, belts, anklets, and chains. The Abdāls of Rūm carried distinctive hatchets, leather pouches, large wooden spoons, and ankle-bones. While the ideological and practical significance of some of these accoutrements can be reasonably reconstructed (iron equipment, for instance, clearly stood for strict control over the *nafs* or animal soul), the meaning of others (like ankle-bones) remains obscure.

Besides the careful cultivation of a scandalous external appearance, the dervishes violated social and legal norms by adopting legally suspicious and unconventional practices. Perhaps the most conspicuous was the use of intoxicants and hallucinogens. The use of cannabis leaves is clearly documented in the case of all three dervish groups. The very "discovery" of the use of hashish as a hallucinogen was attributed to both Quṭb al-Dīn Ḥaydar and Jamāl al-Dīn Sāvī, while there are repeated reports that demonstrate the significance of hashish for both the Qalandars and Abdāls of Rūm.[16] Although it is quite possible that consumption of cannabis leaves had assumed the proportions of ritual among the dervishes, this presumption cannot be substantiated due to lack of detailed information on this subject.[17] That open recourse to hallucinogens and intoxicants (reports suggest that at least some dervishes such as the Jāmīs and Shams-i Tabrīzīs also consumed alcohol) was sufficient to place the dervish groups beyond the pale of social respectability, however, cannot be doubted.[18]

In a similar vein, ascetic renouncers also offended social sensibilities through their conspicuous elevation of music and dance to the status of ritual practice. Though largely domesticated by Sufism, the use of music and dance in religious contexts remained, in legal terms, a suspicious practice in Islamic societies in the Early Middle Period.[19] As was their custom, the dervishes did not hesitate to indulge in radical behavior in this regard as well. They apparently carried tambourines, drums, and horns at all times and incorporated singing and dancing in ceremonies conducted in public. The Abdāls of Rūm and Jāmīs in particular were notorious for their large-scale gatherings in which music and dance occupied a prominent place, though the same practice is also recorded for the Qalandars and Ḥaydarīs.

Another antisocial dervish practice, particularly inscrutable from a modern perspective, was self-laceration and self-cauterization. The Abdāls of Rūm displayed excessive zeal in carving names and figures on their bodies, a practice not recorded for the other dervish groups. This may presumably be explained by the fervent Shīʿism of the Abdāls. Whatever the religious and psychological motives behind such behavior, it manifestly deviated from established religious custom in Ottoman Anatolia and the Balkans and increased the distance between Abdāl piety and social convention.

On a different front, the detractors of the Qalandars and Abdāls of Rūm in particular accused them of reprehensible forms of sexual libertinism, especially sodomy and zoophilism. While such trite accusations should be taken with a grain of salt, they cannot be discarded altogether. Rejection of marriage, or even of the female sex, does not entail complete abstinence from sexual activity. Celibacy, in this context, meant primarily the refusal to participate in the sexual reproduction of society and did not exclude unproductive forms of sexual activity. It is likely, therefore, that antisocial ways of sexual gratification came to be included in the deliberately rejectionist repertoire of some dervishes. The existence of a distinct group of youths known as *kōçeks* (from Persian *kūchak*, "youngster") among the Abdāls is certainly suggestive in this regard.[20]

The penchant of the dervishes for distancing themselves from the established social and religious order is also visible in their adoption of controversial and extremist beliefs and doctrines. The strategy of the dervishes here was to apply radical interpretations to central religious, in particular mystical, concepts such as passing away of the self (*fanāʾ*), poverty (*faqr*), theophany (*tajallī*), and sainthood (*walāyah*). Indeed, the very antinomianism of their practices was viewed by the anarchist dervishes themselves as the natural result of the "correct" interpretation of these concepts. Thus, deviant renunciation was often justified by passing away of the self, which was expressed in the language of death. The dervish was one who voluntarily chose death and "died before dying." The alleged *ḥadīth* (saying of the Prophet Muḥammad) *mūtū qabla an tamūtū*, "die before you die," supplied the prophetic sanction for this attitude.[21] Technically, the dervish considered himself to have the status of a dead person. He often demonstrated the utter seriousness of this conviction physically by dwelling in cemeteries.[22] The implication, significantly, was that he was not bound by social and legal norms. The latter applied to "legal persons" of clear social standing. The dervish, having shattered the confines of society, had no social persona: he functioned in a territory that was above and beyond society.

Similar renunciatory interpretations of the concepts of poverty, theophany, and sainthood always yielded the same rejectionist conclusion. Poverty literally meant absolute poverty. Theophany implied the presence of God in all his Creation, and thus the meaninglessness of legal prescriptions and proscriptions. Sainthood meant the existence of saints, the dervishes themselves, who were exempt from social and legal regulations. The underlying message was always the same: the dervish had to implement an absolute break with his social past and to devote his future solely to God by means of radical renunciation.

It is, therefore, not surprising that the anarchist dervishes adopted "heretic" views with ease, probably in order to strengthen their rejectionist agenda. Such was the case with the fervent Shīʿism of the Abdāls of Rūm and Jalālīs, which the dervishes displayed ostentatiously in the heavily Sunnī cultural areas they inhabited. Also remarkable in this context was the belief, common especially among the dervishes who practiced the fourfold shave, that the human face reflected divine beauty. This was clearly a continuation of the well-attested Sufi practice of "looking at beardless boys," a "dangerous" practice much criticized by Sufis themselves.[23] At the same time, the adoration of the human face may also reflect the influence of Ḥurūfiyah, a new religious movement that came into being toward the end of the eighth/fourteenth century in Iran and Asia Minor, since according to Ḥurūfī tenets the human face was the locus par excellence of the continuous theophany of the Divine in human beings.[24]

In summary, the severely ascetic and cheerfully antinomian practices of the dervishes assume their real meaning only when viewed in their proper context: rejection of society. The synthesis of the ascetic principles of poverty, mendicancy, itinerancy, celibacy, and bodily mortification with the antinomian features of disregard for religious duties, outrageous external appearance, adoption of legally suspicious and unconventional practices, and appropriation of extremist beliefs resulted in the emergence of a new mode of religiosity along the axis of renunciation. The basis of this new renunciatory piety was open and deliberate rejection of the social order. The dervishes negated the existing social structure in all its dimensions. This negation was most conspicuous in the conflict between the adamantly individualistic dervish piety and the normative legal system constructed by religious scholars and accepted, albeit with serious qualifications, by the Sufis. Dead to society, the dervishes were also impervious to legal sanctions. They cheerfully proceeded to replace the prescriptive and proscriptive injunctions of the *sharīʿah* by another code of behavior, in which deliberate eschewal of the religious law played a key role. Thus, they abandoned observation of the ritual and other legal obligations almost completely and freely violated socially sensitive legal proscriptions and prescriptions.[25]

The dervishes did not, however, stop at negation of society pure and simple. The life of a hermit in the wilderness, for instance, equally built on rejection of society, failed to appeal to them. Anchoritism was never a serious option. Instead, the dervishes had to test the salvational efficacy of their renunciatory spirituality through action within the world. Rejection of society functioned as an effective mode of piety only when it was conspicuously and continuously targeted at society. For the individual dervish, this meant radical conversion to and permanent preservation of the option of renunciation through blatant social deviance.

CHAPTER THREE

Renunciation, Deviant Individualism, and Sufism

The purpose of this chapter is to provide a broad context for the study of renunciation in Islam and to locate points of articulation between the mode of dervish piety displayed by world-denying dervish groups of the Later Middle Period on the one hand and previous or contemporary modes of Islamic religiosity on the other. The argument throughout is that renunciatory dervish piety emerged from within Sufism as a new synthesis of two of its most powerful subcurrents: asceticism and anarchist individualism.

RENUNCIATION

A pivotal conflict in the development of Islamic religiosity during the first two centuries of Islam was the confrontation between world-embracing and world-rejecting attitudes.[1] A powerful tendency to reject the world, inherent in the conception of a supramundane God and the postulate of an "other" world, was everywhere opposed by an equally strong tendency to embrace the world by rendering salvation conditional on morally correct behavior in society. Significantly, the sources of the Islamic religion—the Qur'ān and the "example of the Prophet Muḥammad" (*sunnah*)—lent themselves to both this-worldly and other-worldly constructions. The Qur'ān supplied Muslims with many unequivocally renunciatory verses that called believers to eschew this world and to turn their gaze firmly toward the other world.[2] Other Qur'ānic verses, equally numerous and clear in meaning, plunged the believers into the quagmire of mundane affairs, leaving no doubt that other-worldly salvation was contingent upon acceptable performance in the social arena.[3] The *sunnah,* a fluid reality throughout this period, was subject to the same ambiguity. If it was possible to activate the essentially renunciatory core of the *sunnah* to challenge world-embracing Muslims, it remained equally possible to respond by carefully grooming the image of the Prophet Muḥammad to endorse a world-embracing mode of religiosity.[4] The result was a deep structural tension within the religion that set adrift conflicting attitudes toward the world, any one of which could, nevertheless, be Islamically legitimized on the basis of clear Qurʾānic verses and sound *ḥadīth*-reports.

Although it is difficult to ascertain the relative weight of affirmative and renunciatory approaches to the world in early Islamic history, there is little doubt that world-embracing tendencies gained a major impetus with the establishment of an international Islamic empire in the the Near East. The conquests that laid the foundation for this empire, insofar as they reflected the religious duty of securing the supremacy of Islam in the world (*jihād*), were themselves concrete proof that most Muslims had accepted such military action as legitimate salvational activity on earth.[5] The activism inherent in the doctrine of *jihād* rapidly crystallized into clearly articulated this-worldly political agendas, a process that eventually culminated in the hegemony of political activism on the level of political ideology. Even though quietism was also prominently represented in the form of the Murjiʾī movement, it stopped short of denying the world, motivated as it was by an "anti-sectarian emphasis on the community at large."[6] The concern with the unity and worldly supremacy of the community assured the ascendancy of world-embracing ideas in the realm of politics.

A similar process was at work in the domain of economic activity. The accumulation of enormous economic power in Muslim hands, in itself a sign of this-worldly orientation, greatly facilitated the entrenchment of economic attitudes favorable to the world. This is most clearly visible in the key role that merchant capital played in the emergence and unfolding of High Caliphal Islamic society.[7] Gradually, and not without considerable opposition, a world-embracing economic ethnic became normative.

Political and economic affirmation of the world, however, had to be legitimized in religious terms. Here the most impressive achievement of Muslims who viewed human society as the true arena of salvational activity was the development of a formidable legal apparatus, the *sharīʿah,* designed to facilitate salvation by the regulation of social life within a soteriological normative framework. Perhaps the clearest indicator of world-affirmation in the *sharīʿah* was the development of the doctrine of "consensus" (*ijmāʿ*). This doctrine expressed the binding nature of the consensus of the community of believers (*ummah*); it embodied in effect the recognition of the community as the sole legitimate religious authority within the Sunnī sphere. Expressed somewhat differently, the doctrine of *ijmāʿ* acknowledged the community as the only proper receptacle, bearer, and dispenser of the Qur'ān and the *sunnah,* the sole point of contact, albeit indirect, with God.[8] The identification of the community of believers as the third source of legal authority after the Qur'ān and the *sunnah* necessitated a consistent emphasis on the communal as opposed to the private in religious life. In practice, this emphasis meant the primacy of public ritual and religiously sanctioned norms (the *sharīʿah*) over private religiosity and morality. In all areas of the sacred in society, the exoteric (*ẓāhir*) was privileged over the esoteric (*bāṭin*); aspects of private piety that were not susceptible to public scrutiny automatically became suspect as being potentially anticommunal. Not only could the private disrupt communal homogeneity by opening the door to blameworthy innovation (*bidʿah sayyiʾah*) and antinomianism, but it would in the long run also violate the primacy of the community through its propensity to generate claims of personal proximity to God. In the eyes of the "people of the community," therefore, the community's need to safeguard the core of religion overrode the equally urgent need to develop modes of piety that could satisfy the demands of the individual believer for a direct relationship with God.[9]

No matter how efficacious, however, the community-oriented argument that rested on the solid bed of *ijmāʿ* and drew strength from the political and economic achievements of the Muslim community could not dampen, let alone extinguish, the salvational anxieties of believing individuals. The latter could be placated only by a mode of piety that placed individual conscience at its heart. Thus, simultaneously with, and no doubt primarily in reaction to, the rising tide of this-worldliness in the Muslim community, ascetic tendencies of world renunciation (*zuhd*) rose to the surface.

Renunciation was a pious religious attitude that foregrounded the effort of the individual Muslim to establish a private rapport with God. The critique of renouncers was built on the God-humanity axis of religiosity and took the human individual, after God himself, to be the single most important variable in the religious equation. This critique went right to the heart of every pious Muslim believer. No one could deny that Islam, as a religion, had individual conscience at its core. In the final analysis, the helpless and weak believer had to face the absolute Master alone.

The motive force of renunciation was originally the fear of God, or deep anxiety for one's fate in the afterlife. Its dominant characteristic was strong aversion to the world, which was viewed as a barrier to godly piety and eternal salvation. Such a negative valuation of the world led to the adoption of characteristically ascetic principles such as celibacy, solitude, excessive fasting, vegetarianism, poverty, rejection of economic activity, indifference to public opinion, and even withdrawing to cemeteries for ascetic exercises.[10] "Wool-wearing" renouncers everywhere personified the troubled religious consciences of pious Muslim individuals.

The conflict between world-affirmers and renouncers reached a culmination during the first half of the third/ninth century. While the former were busy putting the finishing touches to their community-based legal system (witness the activity of al-Shāfiʿī, 150–205/767–820), the latter took renunciation to its height with the doctrine of "complete reliance on God" (*tawakkul*). The privileging of the doctrine of reliance, which first surfaced in the thought of Shaqīq Balkhī (d. 194/809–10) and remained prevalent until the mid-third/ninth century, involved a subtle yet extremely significant shift of emphasis from negative rejection of the world to positive and exclusive orientation toward God. Fear of God and concern for the afterlife were replaced by complete surrender to God's will. Some features of the ascetic period, such as continence, began to disappear in the "*tawakkul* era," though rejection of gainful employment remained as the central practical manifestation of true *tawakkul*.[11] Significantly, it was in this period that probing legal treatises on the question of gainful employment, such as the *Kitāb al-kasb* of Muḥammad al-Shaybānī (d. 189/804), were written, largely "to overcome deep-seated religious prejudices against making money, convictions made popular by mendicant ascetics."[12] It is also likely that many of the well-known antiascetic *ḥadīth* were put into circulation at this time in response to the trenchant critique of worldly involvement contained in the striking ascetic feats of prominent renouncers.[13] In addition, the detractors seem to have utilized the similarities between the ascetics and Christian monks to their own benefit in their polemic.[14] In spite of all the strong criticism against it, the ascetic option clearly continued to captivate especially the cultural elite, as evidenced by the emergence at this time of *zuhdīyāt*, a poetic genre defined by the theme of asceticism.[15] The rift between the two approaches had reached alarming levels.

It was at this juncture that Sufism emerged as a new mode of piety that bridged the abyss between individualist renunciatory piety and community-oriented legalist world-affirmation. It did so by means of a creative synthesis, which represented, to all indications, a powerful reinterpretation of the doctrine of unity (*tawḥīd*). The "this world/other world" dichotomy of the early asceticism was first gradually displaced by the antithesis "God/all other than God," which then led to a positive evaluation of the latter through the application of the doctrine of unity. Whatever God created, in particular this world, had to be accepted. This was an extremely productive maneuver that, with one stroke, neutralized ascetic devaluation of the world and brought God into the reach of the individual. As a creation of God, the world was essentially divested of its negative features and became the legitimate arena of salvational activity. Life in society was now seen not as an evil snare that had to be shunned at all cost but as a challenge, admittedly formidable but not insurmountable, on the path that led humanity to God. In some sense, this world too, like the other world, was infused with the Divine, which rendered God accessible to the individual living in society. The theoretical elaboration of this view took several centuries and reached its zenith in the thought of Ibn al-ʿArabī (d. 638/1240) only after the fertilization of Sufi theorizing by the philosophical tradition. The flower was, however, already present in the seed that gave birth to it, and the impact of the creative synthesis of the classical phase of Sufism was felt in all aspects of Islamic culture from mid-third/ninth century onward. "Inner-worldly mysticism" became a real force within Islam.[16]

The positive evaluation of worldly existence dealt a heavy blow to asceticism as an independent mode of piety, as evidenced by a new contempt for practical *tawakkul*. Sufis, themselves mostly gainfully employed, generally disapproved of rejection of economic activity.[17] Other principles of asceticism, such as seclusion (*khalwah, ʿuzlah*), abstinence (*jūʿ*), and silence (*samṭ*), were transformed into mere techniques of spiritual discipline.[18]

Slowly, but surely, Sufism and mainstream religiosity blended. The coalescence of Sufism with Sunnī communalism was not the work of Sufi propagandists alone, but came about as the result of an alliance. On one hand, Sufis recognized the need to smooth the rough edges of their erstwhile individualistic piety, a task which they took very seriously, to judge by the number and prominence of communalistic Sufi manuals produced during the fourth/tenth and fifth/eleventh centuries. On the other hand, "the people of the *sunnah* and the community," represented most prominently by Shāfiʿīs and Ḥanbalīs in Iraq, came to realize the rich potential of Sufism to absorb the threat posed by the uncompromisingly individualistic piety of other-worldly asceticism. In this context, it is likely that the capacity inherent in Sufism to preempt the Shīʿī option due to the affinity between the two modes of piety was not lost on the communalists. The result was a powerful coalition of forces that was to preserve its efficacy even when transported outside its land of origin, Iraq, to another region of Islamdom that played a key role in the development of Islamic piety, Khorasan.

The conflict between world-affirmers and renouncers came to a head in Khorasan roughly one century later than in Iraq, in the mid-fourth/tenth century. Here the renouncers wielded tremendous social and religious power. The Karrāmīyah, as the ascetic movement in Khorasan and eastern Iran was known, appeared to have the upper hand throughout this region. The movement was well organized and in time developed a distinctive institution, the hospice (*khānqāh*), that later spread within Islamdom under a transformed Sufi affiliation.[19] The antisocial tendencies of the Karrāmīyah, epitomized in aversion to gainful employment, were countered locally by the this-worldly practices of the Malāmatīyah, also an indigenous movement. The Malāmatīyah had as its basis the belief that piety and godly devotion should not be reduced to a single vocation out of many in social life but should instead infuse its every aspect. Such thorough suffusion of human life in this world with pure religiosity was possible only through concealment of one's inner spiritual states, for their manifestation would ineluctably lead the individual to claim the prerogatives of a religious specialist and would therefore result in the establishment of separate religious tracks in social life, which was anathema. This clear affirmation of communal life translated, on the level of the individual, to the rule to earn one's own livelihood: the Malāmatīs, who probably had organic links with artisans and urban "young-manliness" (*futuwwah*) organizations, had no tolerance for the parasitic social existence of the Karrāmīs.[20]

The nature of the confrontation between the other-worldly Karrāmīs and inner-worldly Malāmatīs was transformed by the introduction and gradual ascendancy of Iraqī Sufism in Khorasan during the fourth/tenth and fifth/eleventh centuries. Through the efficacy of its powerful synthesis of individualist and communalist tendencies, Sufism disenfranchised both the Karrāmīyah and Malāmatīyah by sapping them of their spiritual thrust and absorbing their institutional features. From the former, it adopted the institution of the *khānqāh*; from the latter, it inherited the *futuwwah* lore and practices. In the process, the Karrāmīyah, also vehemently opposed by mainstream Sunnīs, was gradually relegated to an obscure role as a historical sect in heresiographies, while the Malāmatīyah was transformed into a subcurrent in the rich sea of Sufism. The social and spiritual supremacy of Sufism had been firmly established.[21]

DEVIANT INDIVIDUALISM

Antisocial dervish piety had its historical roots primarily in the ascetic tradition as domesticated within Sufism. In addition to asceticism, however, dervish renouncers drew upon another mode of piety also available within Sufism: uncompromising and often fiercely unconventional individualism.

In Weberian terms, "inner-worldly mysticism" is closely connected with its typological counterpart, "contemplative flight from the world." Sufism, which demonstrated its this-worldly credentials by appropriating and naturalizing asceticism, was still subject to the antisocial pull of the option of other-worldly contemplation. The domestication of this trend was an extremely difficult, almost impossible proposition. Individualist gnosis was inherent at the very core of Sufism. Insofar as the highest levels of Sufi experience, passing away from the self (*fanā' ʿan al-nafs*) and passing away in God (*fanā' fī allāh*), meant the annihilation of the self as a social entity, the temptation to slip into unbridled antisocial individualism was very real. This tendency was kept at bay largely through sober emphasis on *baqāʾ*, the idea that the "reconstituted self" of the mystic should "subsist" in society.[22] Nevertheless, the fault line along the axis that separated Sufi this-worldly tendencies from other-worldly ones remained forever active. Sufis felt obliged to acknowledge the superiority of divine attraction (*jadhbah*) over active self-exertion, "striding along the path" (*sulūk*). It is true that a qualified spiritual guide had to have experience of both divine attraction and striding, since neither one alone could produce a well-rounded master.[23] Yet Sufis consistently ranked *jadhbah* the highest on the level of private mystical experience.[24] Contemplative flight from the world continued to inform Sufism.

The history of the other-worldly individualist strain within Sufism, at once complex and obscure, cannot be given here. Such a history would have, on one hand, to deal extensively with concepts like *ibāḥah* (antinomianism), *ḥulūl* (incarnation), and *ittiḥād* (union) and, on the other hand, to display sensitivity to social consequences of central Sufi beliefs and practices.[25] However, one particular manifestation of uncompromising individualism that is pertinent to dervish piety demands attention here: the mode of religiosity that was denoted by terms deriving from the word *qalandar* even before the appearance of the Qalandars as a distinct group of renouncing dervishes under the formative influence of Jamāl al-Dīn Sāvī.[26]

There is considerable evidence that Qalandarīyah was in existence as a religious attitude well before the seventh/thirteenth century. Such evidence can be grouped into two separate categories, one that deals with the Qalandar-topos in Persian literature and another that focuses on the Qalandarī trend as reflected in Sufi theoretical treatises.

Qalandars in Persian Literature

The early history of the Qalandar as a type in Persian literature is unclear.[27] If the attribution of a quatrain in which the word *qalandar* is used to Bābā Ṭāhir-i ʿUryān (d. first half of the fifth/eleventh century) is well grounded (though this remains to be established), then it might be possible to argue that the literary Qalandar had already appeared in Persian literature by the end of the fourth/tenth century.[28] Two quatrains said to have been uttered by Abū Saʿīd-i Abū al-Khayr (357–440/967–1049) would seem to complement these verses of Bābā Ṭāhir; the attribution, however, is no less problematic in this case.[29]

Somewhat later is the short *Risālah-i Qalandar'nāmah* of ʿAbd Allāh Ansārī (d. 481/1088–89). This treatise, again of uncertain attribution, records a conversation of the young Ansārī with a Qalandarī master. Its central theme is the necessity of abandoning the world, preferably through mendicancy, constant traveling, and frequenting graveyards. All of these ideals are relevant to Qalandarīyah; particularly striking in this connection is Jamāl al-Dīn's predilection for graveyards.[30]

For the following century, however, literary evidence is at once more extensive and of a more determinate nature. Aḥmad Ghazālī (d. 520/1126), ʿAyn al-Quz̤āt Hamadānī (d. 525/1130–31), Sanāʾī (d. 545/1150–51), and Khāqānī (d. 595/1198–99) all wrote what were later classified as *Qalandarīyāt* in some manuscripts, that is, poems on wine-drinking, gambling, profane love, and rejection of religion. The Qalandar type, whose characteristics in this early stage of Persian Sufi poetry remain to be determined, is almost fully developed in the works of these sixth/twelfth-century poets and writers; the word *qalandar* itself occurs on many an occasion in their works.[31] Nevertheless, it was during a later phase of Persian Sufi poetry, beginning with ʿAṭṭār (d. after 618/1221–22) continuing through ʿIrāqī (d. 688/1289) and Saʿdī (d. 691/1291–92), and culminating with Ḥāfiẓ (d. 792/1389–90), that the Qalandar type developed into a true literary topos. As a complex of tightly knit images, this topos is interwoven with other themes in individual poems, normally *ghazal*s, though one also comes across independent verse compositions devoted solely to the Qalandar image, as in the short *Qalandar'nāmah* in fifty-six couplets by Amīr Ḥusaynī (d. 718/1318–19).[32]

The main feature of the literary Qalandar was deliberate and open disregard for social convention in the cause of "true" religious love. This social anarchism was expressed in the imagery of the Qalandar-topos: visiting the *kharābāt* (tavern, gambling house, brothel), wine-drinking, gambling, and irreligion. Further elaboration of the topos clearly requires a thorough internal analysis of the relevant texts.[33] In any event, the literary evidence does not reflect any phenomenon that could be called a Qalandarī movement. There is no clear mention of wandering groups of Qalandars in our texts; the Qalandar in poetry at this stage, inasmuch as the word denotes persons rather than attitudes, is normally an isolated, lonely individual.[34] There is, however, some external evidence that makes it possible to correlate this literary Qalandar with his actual counterparts.

Qalandars in Sufi Theoretical Literature

Since the intellectual roots of the Qalandar tradition in Persian poetry are buried in darkness, it has become customary to turn to Sufi theoretical literature in search of the real meaning of the Qalandarī attitude. The most significant reference point in this respect is the following account by Abū Ḥafṣ ʿUmar al-Suhrawardī (d. 632/1234) from the ninth chapter of his *ʿAwārif al-maʿārif,* where Qalandars are discussed alongside other groups which do not belong to Ṣūfīyah but are only affiliated with it:

> The term Qalandarīyah denotes people who are governed by the intoxication [engendered by] the tranquillity of their hearts to the point of destroying customs and throwing off the bonds of social intercourse, traveling [as they are] in the fields of the tranquillity of their hearts. They observe the ritual prayer and fasting only insofar as these are obligatory and do not hesitate to indulge in those pleasures of the world that are permitted by the Law; nay, they content themselves with keeping within the bounds of what is permissible and do not go in search of the truths of legal obligation. All the same, they persist in rejecting hoarding and accumulation [of wealth] and the desire to have more. They do not observe the rites of the ascetic, the abstemious, and the devout and confine themselves to, and are content with, the tranquillity of their hearts with God. Nor do they have an eye for any desire to increase what they already possess of this tranquillity of the heart. The difference between the Malāmatī and the Qalandar is that the former strives to conceal his acts of devotion while the latter strives to destroy custom. . . . The Qalandar is not bound by external appearance and is not concerned with what others may or may not know of his state. He is attached to nothing but the tranquillity of his heart, which is his sole property.[35]

Al-Suhrawardī's account is significant for a number of reasons. First, it is very noticeable that there is in this report, reproduced almost word for word by many later writers such as al-Maqrīzī and Jāmī,[36] nothing that would suggest a familiarity with the more or less institutionalized Qalandarīyah that was already taking shape under the leadership of Jamāl al-Dīn Sāvī in Damascus and Damietta—in al-Suhrawardī's lifetime. It is highly unlikely, for instance, that anyone who was informed about Jamāl al-Dīn's activities could make the remark that Qalandars "do not observe the rites of the ascetic, the abstemious, and the devout." Moreover, al-Suhrawardī makes no reference to *chahār ẓarb* or to characteristic Qalandarī apparel. It appears, therefore, that when he finished writing the *ʿAwārif al-maʿārif* (the *terminus ad quem* for the composition of this work is 624/1227), al-Suhrawardī knew nothing of the nascent Qalandarī movement in Damascus.[37]

Second, it is clear that during al-Suhrawardī's lifetime it was possible to talk of a distinct religious attitude identified as Qalandarīyah.[38] Indeed, al-Suhrawardī's description of this attitude is strongly reminiscent of the Qalandar-topos in Persian poetry. Particularly striking in this regard is the deliberate anticonventionalism of both the literary Qalandar and al-Suhrawardī's "real" Qalandars. In addition, al-Suhrawardī's insistence on the Qalandarī fascination with the tranquillity of the heart and, perhaps more significantly, his observation that the Qalandars have a minimalist understanding of the religious law increase the likelihood of this convergence. The passage in the *ʿAwārif al-maʿārif* on the Qalandarīyah suggests therefore that the Qalandar-topos in pre-thirteenth-century Persian poetry was not just a poetic convention but also reflected a religious attitude that was represented in society by real Qalandars.

Third, it is significant that al-Suhrawardī makes a distinction between Qalandarīyah and Ṣūfīyah. The validity of this distinction is rather dubious. The basis of al-Suhrawardī's argument seems to have been that since the Qalandar did not have any goal other than asserting his state of inner contentment at all costs, he did not strictly speaking partake in any mystical quest. Such a definition, however, can equally be used to describe many Sufis, especially of the passive *majdhūb* type. It is likely al-Suhrawardī was disturbed by the fact that the Qalandar did not hesitate to transgress the boundaries of what was socially permissible and, worse, had only minimal respect for the law. It is, therefore, possible to see in al-Suhrawardī's distinction between Qalandarīyah and Ṣūfīyah the somewhat tendentious attempt of a socially conscious, highly this-worldly Sufi master to dissociate the former, a clearly antisocial current within Sufism, from the latter, an overwhelmingly "inner-worldly," socially respectable mode of piety.

As a fourth and final point, it is remarkable that al-Suhrawardī discusses the Qalandars along with the Malāmatīyah, possibly an originally non-Sufi religious movement. He argues that the Qalandar clearly differed from the Malāmatī in certain respects. The Malāmatī's main concern was to hide his inner state from others for fear that an ostentatious display of piety would lead to overindulgence in the self and ultimately to self-complacency, thus distancing the believer from God. It was because of his painstaking endeavor to conceal the true nature of his religiosity that he sought to incur public blame by deliberately transgressing the limits of social and legal acceptability. There were, however, limits to such transgression, since the overwhelming concern of the Malāmatī was to blend into society in an effort to construct a veil of anonymity around himself. Most significant in this regard was the Malāmatī refusal to adopt distinctive attire, paraphernalia, and rites and practices. Similarly, the Malāmatī took care to earn his own livelihood and looked with contempt on those Sufis who survived only on alms and charity. Thus, while he could be, in extreme cases, as socially deviant as the Qalandar, the Malāmatī functioned within a "performance paradigm," where the nature and meaning of religious belief and practice as performed by individual believers were conditioned by other believers' perception of them. The Qalandar, however, claimed to have transcended this paradigm altogether. He too was concerned exclusively with his own inner state, yet he rejected the basic premise of the Malāmatī in his refusal to acknowledge the importance of any audience other than God, the auditor par excellence. From this standpoint, the social and legal transgression of the Qalandar was only an incidental outcome of his primary endeavor, the attainment and preservation of the tranquillity of his heart with respect to God. Insofar as it distracted the Qalandar from achieving this goal, social attachment of all kinds was perceived as an obstacle and simply discarded.

The Qalandarīyah and Dervish Piety before Jamāl Al-Dīn

What was the historical relation between the pre-thirteenth-century Qalandar and the new renunciation of the Later Middle Period? The most obvious connection is, of course, the use of the name Qalandar to designate the followers of Jamāl al-Dīn. It is not known how or exactly when the name came to be given to these dervishes. Certainly, they referred to themselves as Qalandars by the time Khaṭīb Fārisī wrote his sacred biography of the master in the mid-eighth/fourteenth century, but it is impossible to tell if this practice dates back to the lifetime of Jamāl al-Dīn or if it was a later accretion. Whatever the truth about its timing, the application of the name Qalandar to the Jawlaqs is significant in that it indicates the existence of more than nominal continuity between the Qalandarī trend before Jamāl al-Dīn and the later Qalandarīyah. Even if the first generation of Jamāl al-Dīn type Qalandars did not deliberately attempt to realize the older Qalandarī ideal in practice, there can be little doubt that in the long run this ideal came to inform the activity of the later Qalandarīyah. Otherwise, it would be rather difficult to account for the appearance of the somewhat this-worldly Qalandars described by Sir Paul Rycaut, the mid-eleventh/seventeenth-century observer of Ottoman society:

> [The Qalandars] consume their time in eating and drinking; and to maintain this gluttony they will sell the stones of their girdles, their Ear-rings and Bracelets. When they come to the house of any rich man or person of Quality, they accommodate themselves to their humor, giving all the Family pleasant words, and chearful expressions to perswade them to a liberal and free entertainment. The tavern by them is accounted holy as the Mosch, and they believe they serve God as much with debauchery, or liberal use of his Creatures (as they call it) as others with severity and Mortification.[39]

The degree to which such observations by both external and internal observers of Islamic societies reflected reality is naturally open to question. Such reservations notwithstanding, it is clear that the anarchist individualism of the Qalandarī trend before Jamāl al-Dīn was perpetuated in the activities of anarchist dervish groups, especially through their emphasis on flagrant social deviance.

Renunciatory modes of piety had deep and firm roots in the historical development of Islamic religion. Powerful currents of other-worldly asceticism as an alternative way of life were present during the first three centuries of Islam in the Fertile Crescent and throughout the third/ninth, fourth/tenth, and fifth/eleventh centuries in and around Iran. Such trends were eventually absorbed and domesticated, though not completely nullified, by "inner-worldly" Sufism. As a mystic mode of piety, however, Sufism also contained within itself strong tendencies toward contemplative flight from the world. As a result, it was the source of continual outbursts of anarchist individualism. The most prominent, and for our purposes the most pertinent, of such manifestations of individualism was the Qalandarī trend that developed primarily within the Persian cultural sphere. It was as a powerful revitalization and combination of this trend with the powerful currents of other-worldly asceticism that dervish piety developed in the Fertile Crescent and Iran toward the end of the Early Middle Period and surfaced at the beginning of the seventh/thirteenth century.

CHAPTER FOUR

Ascetic Virtuosi

The emergence of new renunciation is most clearly visible in the careers of individual ascetics who played key roles in the formation of movements of socially deviant renunciation. The exemplary piety of ascetic virtuosi everywhere served as a catalyst for the construction of social collectivities that translated the ideals forged by the master renouncers into salvational social action on a large scale. It is therefore appropriate to open this reconstruction of the history of the new renunciation with a series of biographical portrayals of the most prominent dervish masters.

JAMĀL AL-DĪN SĀVĪ: THE MASTER OF THE QALANDARS

The Qalandars emerged as a new and distinct group of dervishes in Damascus and Damietta during the early decades of the seventh/thirteenth century. The formation of the Qalandarī path was concomitant with and centered around the activity of its master, Jamāl al-Dīn Sāvī (Sāvajī in some sources). His personal example played a decisive role in the emergence of the Qalandars, who preserved their separate identity through adherence to practices advocated by Jamāl al-Dīn or by his immediate circle of followers. The most characteristic of these practices, shaving the hair, beard, moustache, and eyebrows (sometimes eyelashes as well), which came to be known later as "four blows" (*chahār ẕarb*), certainly originated with Jamāl al-Dīn himself. Fortunately, it is possible to reconstruct the contours of his life and personality.

In 748/1347–48, Khaṭīb Fārisī (born 697/1297–98) of Shīrāz, a fifty-one-year old disciple of the Qalandarī master Muḥammad Bukhārāʾī in Damascus, completed a biography of Jamāl al-Dīn in Persian verse.[1] Written about a century after the death of the grand master, his hagiography reflects, at the very least, the message of Jamāl al-Dīn as it was understood by a particular group of Qalandars in that city in the mid-eighth/fourteenth century.

The central concern of Khaṭīb Fārisī is Jamāl al-Dīn's conversion from the Sufi to the Qalandarī path. At the beginning of the work, Jamāl al-Dīn is carefully presented as a very well-respected, though young, Sufi master. The author renders Jamāl al-Dīn a contemporary and a cherished companion of Bāyazīd Basṭāmī and contends that ʿUthmān Rūmī, unanimously depicted in other sources as the early Sufi master of Jamāl al-Dīn, was in fact his disciple.[2] Entrusted to Jamāl al-Dīn's care by Bāyazīd Basṭāmī, ʿUthmān Rūmī finds him delivering sermons on the Qurʾān and *ḥadīth*, from a gold pulpit richly studded with jewels, to a large group of followers in a *khānqāh* in Iraq. His views on *taṣawwuf* appear to have been mainstream. In a lengthy section that reproduces material from Najam al-Dīn Rāzī Dāyah's (d. 654/1256) *Mirṣād al-ʿibād min al-mabdaʾ ilā al-maʿād,* for instance, Jamāl al-Dīn elaborates on the real meanings of the terms "macrocosmos" and "microcosmos" in a totally predictable, conservative manner.[3] In the limited information that his biographer provides on this phase of Jamāl al-Dīn's career, it is possible to detect a special emphasis on the concept of detachment in his outlook.

Soon after ʿUthmān Rūmī joins him, Jamāl al-Dīn delivers an extended speech on the merits of traveling and, practicing what he has preached, begins to roam the land in the company of forty of his dervishes, including ʿUthmān Rūmī. These journeys, which last until the moment when he spots Jalāl Darguzīnī in the mausoleum of Zaynab (the daughter of the fifth Shīʿī leader Zayn al-ʿĀbidīn) in the Bāb al-Ṣaghīr cemetery of Damascus, prepare him for his conversion to the Qalandarī path. Darguzīnī, who is completely naked except for a few leaves covering his private parts, eats nothing but weeds, and remains silent and motionless in one place, makes a deep impression on Jamāl al-Dīn. He prays to God that he may be relieved of both worlds and that all the obstacles on his path may be cleared away. By divine intervention, all the hair on his head and body falls off. This is a sign that Jamāl al-Dīn's prayer is accepted and that he is now "dead before his death." Thenceforth, Jamāl al-Dīn becomes a Qalandar, with the same outward appearance and habits as Jalāl Darguzīnī, whose bodily hair also disappears at Jamāl al-Dīn's intervention. Jamāl al-Dīn later verbalizes and justifies this experience with the *ḥadīth* "die before you die" (*mūtū qabla an tamūtū*): a Qalandar is one who frees himself from the two worlds through self-imposed death (*mawt-i irādī*) with the purpose of attaining continuous proximity to the Divine.[4] The peculiarly Qalandarī habits of going naked with only leaves to cover the loins, removing all bodily hair, and sitting motionless and speechless on graves without any sleep or food except wild weeds are all viewed as direct consequences of this "premortem" death.[5] The Qalandar looks and, so to speak, acts like a dead person. Thus, the Qalandarī practice of uttering four *takbīrs*, a deliberate reference to the funeral prayer, functions as a constant reminder of the Qalandar's real state: "dead to both worlds." In brief, the Qalandar rejects society altogether and severs himself from both the rights and duties of social life. He spurns all kinds of social intercourse like gainful employment, marriage, and even friendship and devotes himself solely to God in complete seclusion.

Khaṭīb Fārisī portrays the rest of Jamāl al-Dīn's career as a struggle to remain a recluse. Curiously, perhaps the most serious challenge to Jamāl al-Dīn in this respect is the emergence of a community of Qalandars around him based on his personal example. Initially consisting of Jamāl al-Dīn and three disciples (Jalāl Darguzīnī, Muḥammad Balkhī, and Abū Bakr Iṣfahānī, but not ʿUthmān Rūmī, who nonetheless acknowledges Jamāl al-Dīn's greatness), the core group is soon surrounded by a much larger circle of converts to the way of Qalandars. Recruitment of new members is not sought actively. The credit, or more properly blame, for propagating the example of Jamāl al-Dīn falls not on the master himself, but on his core disciples, especially Abū Bakr Iṣfahānī.[6] At first, Jamāl al-Dīn reluctantly acknowledges the necessity of leadership and to a certain extent even adapts his extreme eremiticism to collective life. For instance, he allows his disciples to eat food offerings brought by pious believers, though he himself refrains from touching the food of others. His institution of donning uncomfortable, heavy woolen garments (*jawlaq*) also appears to have been a concession in the direction of accepting increased contact with human society. In the long term, however, Jamāl al-Dīn's firm commitment to remain detached from the two worlds weighs heavier than his sense of responsibility toward his followers as their master. Delegating his authority to his foremost disciple, he leaves Damascus in order to remain faithful to his erstwhile solitary mission and travels to Damietta, Egypt. In Damietta, he proves his holiness through a beard-producing miracle and spends six peaceful years there, refusing to accept any followers, including the magistrate of the town.[7] Upon his death, he is buried in the same town.

Khaṭīb Fārisī's account indicates clearly that the Qalandars of Damascus cherished Jamāl al-Dīn's world-rejecting eremiticism as a vibrant ideal roughly three generations after his activity in that city. The disciple/biographer recasts this ideal in the form of a spirited defense of "poverty" (*faqr*). The narrative proper itself starts with a section entitled "On the Merits of Poverty" (*dar ṣifat-i faẕīlat-i faqr*), and the same theme punctuates the whole text. The central messages delivered in this context are that the Prophet Muḥammad, the best of all creatures and the master of the two worlds, himself chose absolute poverty and that Jamāl al-Dīn is the king of poverty.[8] Although Khaṭīb Fārisī does not give specific information on the Qalandarī movement of his own time, all the signs indicate that his fellow dervishes not only upheld but also honored this ideal of poverty ascribed to Jamāl al-Dīn.

It is possible to reconstitute the historical core of Jamāl al-Dīn's life on the basis of numerous accounts in Arabic, Persian, and Turkish sources. Jamāl al-Dīn was born toward the end of the sixth/twelfth century, probably in the Iranian town of Sāvah, situated just southwest of present-day Tehran. Although next to nothing is known of his youth, there is some evidence that he may have studied to become a religious scholar. According to an oral tradition kept alive in the Chishtī circles of Delhi during the eighth/fourteenth century, for instance, Jamāl al-Dīn was known as the "walking library," since he issued legal opinions without consulting any books.[9] Since this tradition was transmitted by a compiler who was himself a Qalandar with scholarly pretensions, its reliability is questionable.[10] It may nevertheless contain a kernel of truth since Jamāl al-Dīn is reported in Mamlūk sources to have studied the Qur'ān as well as religious sciences and to have written at least a partial Qur'ānic exegesis.[11] As a young man, he traveled to Damascus to continue his studies, where he became affiliated with the hospice of ʿUthmān Rūmī located at the foot of the Qāsiyūn mountain to the northwest of the city.[12] ʿUthmān Rūmī was almost certainly the father of Sharaf al-Dīn Muḥammad Rūmī, the director of the Rūmīyah hospice at Qāsiyūn, who died in 684/1285. We know next to nothing about the father, who, according to one contemporary source, was celebrated for his strict conformity to the *sunnah*.[13] The son is described in his brief obituary notice as "incredibly generous and modest, much given to *samāʿ*."[14]

Jamāl al-Dīn's involvement with respectable Sufism as evidenced by his allegiance to ʿUthmān Rūmī led to a dramatic conversion to extreme asceticism through his encounter with the remarkable young ascetic Jalāl Darguzīnī.[15] Darguzīnī, an epitome of detachment and solitude, wrought a deep transformation in Jamāl al-Dīn's religiosity. Overcome by an ascetic mood, Jamāl al-Dīn shaved his face and head and began to spend his time sitting motionless on graves with his face turned in the direction of Mecca, the *qiblah*, speechless and with grass as his only food.[16] Another tradition of reports would have it that Jamāl al-Dīn's turn to ascetic practices was facilitated by his scrupulous endeavor, in a way reminiscent of one part of the Qurʾānic story of Yūsuf (the Qurʿān, 12:21–35), to preserve his chastity. According to this tradition, which provides an alternative explanation for Jamāl al-Dīn's practice of shaving his beard and eyebrows, Jamāl al-Dīn was constantly harassed by a certain woman, who had fallen in love with him on account of the beauty of his face and figure. Although initially unsuccessful in her attempts to seduce Jamāl al-Dīn, the woman finally managed to trick him into entering her house. Jamāl al-Dīn had no escape and, in a final effort to save himself, shaved his beard and eyebrows with a razor that he happened to have. The woman, taken aback and disgusted, rebuked him severely and had him thrown out of her house. Having thus overcome temptation through shaving, Jamāl al-Dīn thereafter made it his habit to keep his face clean-shaven at all times.[17] Whatever its truth content, this "fantastic" explanation for the origin of Jamāl al-Dīn's practice of shaving can safely be rejected as being a generic feature of hagiography.[18]

The story of the rest of Jamāl al-Dīn's career is in conformity with information found in his sacred biography. His solitude disturbed by the growing number of followers, Jamāl al-Dīn decided to leave the group and travel to a place where he was totally unknown. Delegating his authority to his foremost disciple, Muḥammad al-Balkhī, he left Damascus and spent the last years of his life in carefully preserved social isolation in a cemetery in Damietta, where a hospice (*zāwiyah*) was later built around his tomb.[19]

Jamāl al-Dīn was first and foremost an uncompromising renouncer. He was stringent in his rejection of this world, as evidenced by his penchant for residing in cemeteries, in both Damascus and Damietta, as well as by the extreme care he took to dissociate himself from all established patterns of social life through such practices as shaving his head and all facial hair, donning woolen sacks, and refusing to work for sustenance. Presumably, he was also celibate. Though not totally averse to having disciples and not oblivious of their needs, he shunned all kinds of attention and preferred to lead the life of a complete recluse. It is not possible to determine the nature of his attitude toward the religious law. While there is no sign that he deliberately eschewed prescribed religious observances or clearly violated legal prohibitions, reports on his life leave the impression that conformity to the *sharīʿah* was not a major issue in his career. The unmistakable message of his personal example was world-rejecting eremiticism, and the power and attraction of the ascetic mode of piety this message embodied was instrumental in the formation of the Qalandarī path.

QUṬB AL-DĪN ḤAYDAR: THE MASTER OF THE ḤAYDARĪS

The Ḥaydarī dervish, with his distinct penchant for iron collars, bracelets, belts, anklets, and rings suspended from his ears and his genitals, became a familiar sight in many parts of Islamdom from the beginning of the seventh/thirteenth century onward. The eponymous master of this most peculiar group of mendicant dervishes was a certain Quṭb al-Dīn Ḥaydar. Although the historical life of this key ascetic figure is clouded in legend, his religious predilections are still evident in the reports of his miraculous feats.

Quṭb al-Dīn Ḥaydar lived in and around the town Zāvah in Khorasan, present-day Turbat-i Ḥaydarīyah in northeast Iran.[20] Unlike his followers, he was not much taken with the itinerant life and spent his life in solitude on a mountain near Zāvah.[21] His tomb still stands today in that location.[22] The long career of this figure spanned the entire sixth/twelfth century and came to an end around 617/1200, when Zāvah was destroyed by the Mongols.[23] He was apparently of royal Turkish descent and might have had a particular appeal among Turkish speakers.[24] Beyond these externalities, few facts of Quṭb al-Dīn's biography can be ascertained.[25] He probably went through a Sufi phase early in life. In some sources he is portrayed as a one-time disciple of either Shaykh Luqmān, who was active in the town of Sarakhs close to Zāvah, or the famous Turkish Sufi Aḥmed Yesevī (d. 562/1166) of Turkistan.[26] It is not possible to confirm the existence of such allegiances. His association with Aḥmed Yesevī, reported only in late sources and conspicuously absent from the Yesevī tradition itself, is doubtful, especially if one keeps in mind the *sharīʿah*-bound nature of Yesevī's mysticism, in which there would be little room for the world-denying asceticism of Quṭb al-Dīn Ḥaydar. That Quṭb al-Dīn indeed had some Sufi connections, however, is suggested by a report that he was close to Shāh-i Sanjān (d. 597/1200–1201 or 599/1202–3), a disciple of Quṭb al-Dīn Mawdūd-i Chishtī (d. 527/1132–33), who may have composed a quatrain (*rubāʿī*) for Quṭb al-Dīn.[27] In this same vein, some claim that Ibrāhīm Isḥāq ʿAṭṭār Kadkanī, the father of the celebrated poet Farīd al-Dīn ʿAṭṭār, was a follower of Quṭb al-Dīn and that Farīd al-Dīn ʿAṭṭār himself, who had received the blessing of Quṭb al-Dīn Ḥaydar as a child, dedicated one of his first works, *Ḥaydarnāmah,* to the ascetic master. While the celebrated poet was indeed born in Kadkan, a town not far from Zāvah, it is not possible to confirm the details of this claim, especially since such a *Ḥaydarnāmah* is not extant.[28]

The religious profile of the Ḥaydarī master can be drawn in broad strokes. It is clear that he abandoned civilized life in favor of a solitary existence in the wilderness. An account of his conversion to asceticism is found in the *Khayr al-majālis* (comp. after 754/1353), where the compiler Ḥamīd Qalandar records a story about Ḥaydar that he heard from Shaykh Naṣīr al-Dīn Maḥmūd Chirāgh-i Dihlī (d. 757/1356). While still a young boy, Ḥaydar ascended a mountain in a trance and failed to return. After many years, he was finally spotted one day by a traveler, clothed in a dress made of leaves and busy milking a female gazelle. Informed of his son's survival by the traveler, Ḥaydar's father searched for him on the mountain without success. In despair, he asked Shaykh Luqmān for his help. Indeed, when Luqmān himself came to the foot of the mountain, Ḥaydar appeared of his own accord to see the shaykh. When the shaykh advised him to go to the city and spend his time inviting people to the path of God, Ḥaydar declared that it was no longer possible for him to abandon the wilderness, but he agreed to see his parents every day if they came and settled at the foot of the mountain. The place where Ḥaydar's parents settled later grew into the village of Zāvah.[29]

Quṭb al-Dīn Ḥaydar's merger with nature was then remarkably complete. He apparently used only leaves to cover his body and relied solely on nature for his sustenance. It is, therefore, not strange to see his name associated with the discovery of the intoxicating effects of cannabis leaves.[30] Even more than his uncompromising withdrawal from human culture and his discovery of hashish, however, Quṭb al-Dīn's fame and influence on others rested on his dramatic attempts to control his animal soul (*nafs*). The miraculous feats most celebrated by posterity were his immersion in ice water during winter and entering fire in the summer.[31] He was also well known for handling molten iron "like mere wax" in order to fashion collars and bracelets.[32] Combined with the well-attested Ḥaydarī habit of wearing iron rings around the genitals, which in all likelihood derived from Quṭb al-Dīn's own example, these miracle stories suggest that a significant portion of Quṭb al-Dīn's extreme asceticism was occasioned by his attempt to tame his sexuality. Continence in particular and austere self-denial in general, conspicuously represented by heavy iron equipment, was the special legacy of Quṭb al-Dīn Ḥaydar to his followers.

OTMAN BABA: THE MASTER OF THE ABDĀLS OF RŪM

Unlike Jamāl al-Dīn Sāvī and Quṭb al-Dīn Ḥaydar, the founding fathers of the Qalandars and the Ḥaydarīs, Otman Baba cannot be considered the founder of the Abdāls of Rūm. This group had a checkered history that can be traced back to the seventh/thirteenth century. It was only during the second half of the ninth/fifteenth century, however, that the Abdāls of Rūm emerged as a distinct dervish band with peculiar beliefs and practices. Otman Baba was without doubt the key player in the Abdāl drama of this period.

Otman Baba is known basically through his hagiography, which was written by one of his followers called Küçük Abdāl in 888/1483, five years after his master's death.[33] According to this work, Otman Baba's real name was Ḥüsām Şāh. He apparently came to Asia Minor from Khorasan during or soon after Temür's (r. 771–807/1370–1405) campaign into that peninsula, although even his close disciples did not know his true origins. A complete ascetic and ecstatic practicing the *chahār ẕarb*, he mostly wandered about the mountains and high plateaus of northwest Asia Minor and the Balkans, accompanied by a few hundred dervishes. The date of his death is given as 883/1478–79; as he is said to have been born in 780/1378–79, he must have lived to be a centenarian.[34]

Otman Baba's religious views were most intriguing. In keeping with a well-attested Sufi tradition, he believed that sainthood (*walāyah*) was simultaneously the inner dimension and the guarantor of prophecy (*nubūwah*).[35] As Otman Baba expressed it, sainthood was the "shepherd" of prophecy. Since sainthood served to perpetuate and confirm the validity of prophecy, its denial amounted to a declaration of unbelief.[36] Otman Baba apparently rested these views on a peculiar interpretation of the famous Qurʾānic verse of the primordial covenant (7:172). God extracted the future humanity from the loins of Adam and asked them, "Am I not your Lord?" Those who answered in the affirmative, Otman Baba asserted, were the believers and the true unitarians, those who answered negatively were the unbelievers, and those who did not respond at all were the saints, presumably because they were so secure in their relationship to God that they had no need of a covenant.[37]

After the termination of the cycle of prophecy in the figure of Muḥammad, the cycle of sainthood was initiated by his son-in-law and cousin ʿAlī ibn Abī Ṭālib. The saintly institution was thereafter preserved by a network of saints. Otman Baba divided saints into the two broad categories of "insane" (*dīvānah*) and "licit" (*mashrūʿ*), according to whether the elements dominant in their nature were fire and air or water and earth. While both of these two kinds were acceptable, the "insane" saints were clearly superior to those bound by the *sharīʿah*. The excesses of the former, the divinely attracted (*majdhūb*) saints, were legally permitted to them.[38]

Otman Baba also insisted that the true saints were hidden from humanity and cited the reputed extra-Qurʾānic divine saying "My friends are under My tents [or My cloak]; no one knows them except Me" as confirmation of this view.[39] Consequently, he was extremely critical of all Sufi masters who claimed exclusive rights to the instruction and guidance of novices. He alleged that the hidden agenda of the "people of hospices," as he called the Sufi masters, was nothing more than the accumulation of worldly goods. He himself was completely averse to owning property and consistently rejected gifts of any kind, especially money, which he likened to feces. Absolute poverty was the only social condition conducive to religious salvation.[40]

Otman Baba's own religious agenda seems to have been twofold. On one hand, much of his saintly activity was directed toward open and radical criticism of "people of hospices." In general, he did not venerate any saint of his time or of the past, with the exception of Sulṭān Şücāʿ and Ḥācī Bektāş.[41] It is ironic, therefore, that Bektāşīs in particular were treated with contempt by Otman Baba. Long sections of Otman Baba's sacred biography are devoted to vehement criticism of a certain Müʾmin Derviş and the latter's master Bāyezīd Baba, both "hospice saints" who apparently were Bektāşīs or at least held Ḥācī Bektāş in high esteem. More specifically, on one occasion in İstanbul, Otman Baba intimidated the Bektāşī master Maḥmūd Çelebi to such an extent that the latter ended up seeking refuge from him in a nearby Edhemī hospice.[42]

On the other hand, Otman Baba put into practice in his own career a vision of the doctrine of the unity of being whereby he thought God to be manifest in everything and particularly in every human being. In keeping with this view, he claimed to be in reality identical with Muḥammad, ʿĪsā, and Mūsā (at times also Ādam) or even with the Deity himself. In the same vein, he drank used bath water and declared that there were no impure objects, since all things equally reflected God.[43] Presumably, this immanentist view formed the basis of his own claim to sainthood, though it is not clear if he actually considered himself to be one of the hidden saints or, indeed, the "Pole" of the universe.

Otman Baba cultivated a special relationship with the Ottoman sultan Meḥmed II (2d r. 855–86/1451–81). He predicted Meḥmed II's rise to power while the latter was still a prince and later warned the sultan against his unsuccessful campaign to capture Belgrade. His aim in his dealings with the sultan was the demonstration of his superiority, and, still according to his biographer Küçük Abdāl, Meḥmed II actually admitted that the "real" sultan was Otman Baba.[44]

The most prominent feature of Otman Baba's renunciation was its social activism. In contradistinction to Jamāl al-Dīn Sāvī, who targeted the religious consciences of Muslim individuals as his audience by confining himself to cemeteries, and in even greater contrast to Quṭb al-Dīn Ḥaydar, who attempted to avoid human audiences altogether by disappearing into the wilderness, Otman Baba aimed his rejectionist agenda against institutions, primarily Sufi operations, but also those of the political and non-Sufi religious elites.

1. Qalandar. From Nicolas de Nicolay Daulphinoys, *The Nauigations, Peregrinations, and Voyages, Made into Turkie by Nicholas Nicholay Daulphinois*, trans. T. Washington the Younger, 105 verso.

2. Abdāl-i Rūm. From Nicolas de Nicolay Daulphinoys, *The Nauigations, Peregrinations, and Voyages, Made into Turkie by Nicholas Nicholay Daulphinois*, trans. T. Washington the Younger, 103 recto.

3. Ḥaydarī. From Nicolas de Nicolay Daulphinoys, *The Nauigations, Peregrinations, and Voyages, Made into Turkie by Nicholas Nicholay Daulphinois,* trans. T. Washington the Younger, 101 verso.

4. Jāmī. From Nicolas de Nicolay Daulphinoys, *The Nauigations, Peregrinations, and Voyages, Made into Turkie by Nicholas Nicholay Daulphinois*, trans. T. Washington the Younger, 100 verso.

5. Fakhr al-Dīn ʿIrāqī and the Qalandars on the way to India. From a manuscript of the *Majālis al-ʿushshāq,* dated 959/1552. By permission of the Bodleian Library, Oxford (Ms. Ouseley Add. 24, fol. 79b).

6. Portrait of a Qalandar, Tīmūrid, late 9th/15th century. By permission of the Metropolitan Museum of Art, New York (Cora Timken Burnett Collection, 57.51.30).

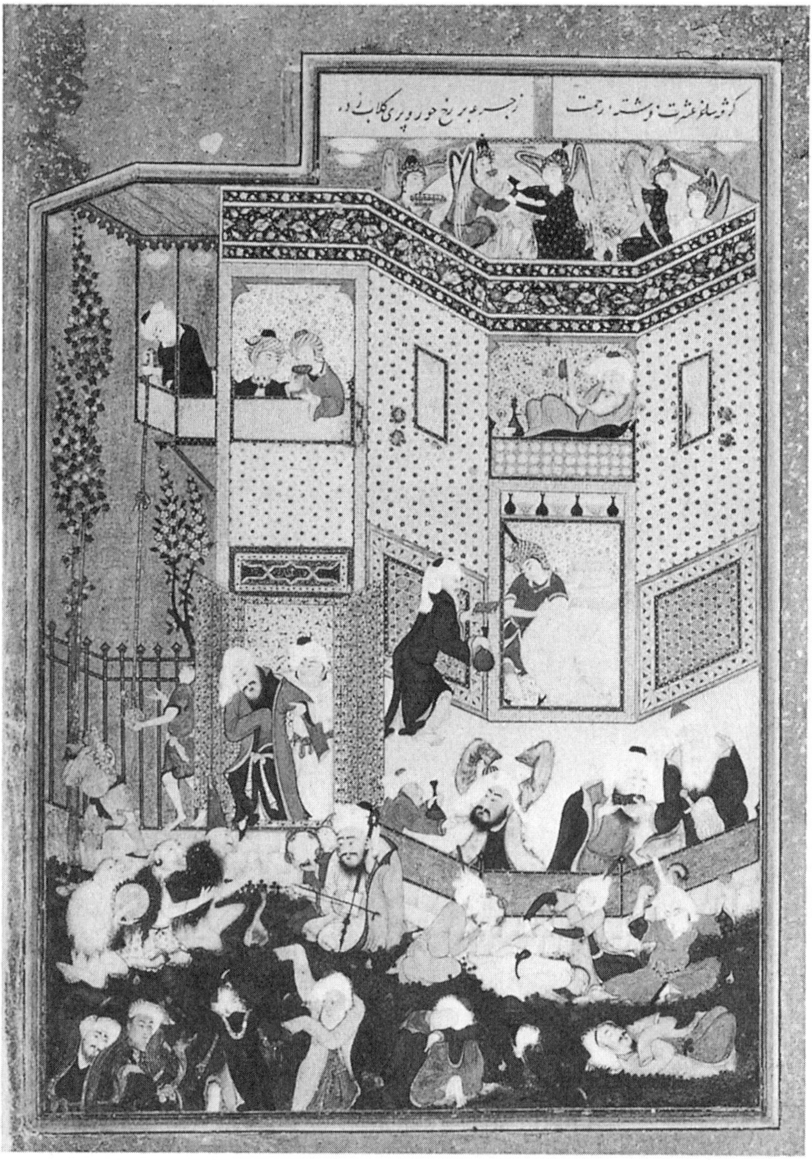

7. Three merry Qalandars, by Sulṭān Muḥammad, Ṣafavid, early 10th/16th century. By permission of the Fogg Art Museum, Harvard University, Cambridge, Mass. (the collected works of Ḥāfiẓ, fol. 135r).

CHAPTER FIVE

Dervish Groups in Full Bloom, 1200–1500

The exemplary piety of the ascetic virtuosi was perpetuated and spread throughout Islamdom through the activities of socially deviant dervish groups that transformed the renunciatory ideals of the masters into principles of religiously meaningful social action on a mass scale. Qalandars, Ḥaydarīs, and Abdāls of Rūm attempted to preserve and reproduce the peculiar modes of religiosity developed by or best represented in the lives of Jamāl al-Dīn Sāvī, Quṭb al-Dīn Ḥaydar, and Otman Baba, respectively. The study of the history of these movements of renunciation is fraught with difficulties. The relevant historical evidence is widely scattered in various sources, somewhat thin, and at times imprecise. This should not be surprising. On one hand, the dervishes themselves were not likely to "document" their way of life in writing, since rejection of this-worldly learning was a logical item on their agenda. This did not prevent them from producing written testimonies of deviant renunciation, especially in the form of hagiographies of the ascetic masters. These accounts were apparently targeted for internal consumption within the dervish groups and did not have wider circulation. On the other hand, the fact that the dervishes negated society through flagrant social deviation ensured that they normally attracted the attention only of their detractors, who had reason to misrepresent the message of deviant renunciation. The dervishes were ignored by the rest of the cultural elite, except insofar as their actions fleetingly came within the ambit of scholarly and literary agendas of historians, biographers, religious reformers, and litterateurs.

Thus, while only short accounts on key figures of renunciation were incorporated into biographical literature and dervish groups were mentioned only in passing in historical chronicles and large literary compositions, self-appointed critics of deviant asceticism, such as Muḥammad al-Khaṭīb and Vāḥidī, provided longer and independent treatments of the subject. When combined with the internal accounts of the deviant dervishes themselves, all this material, fragmented and biased as it may be, allows us to reconstruct the contours of the movements of deviant renunciation in the Later Middle Period.

THE ARAB MIDDLE EAST

Damascus, the most prominent city of Syria, was the earliest center of new asceticism in Islamdom. After Jamāl al-Dīn Sāvī left the city to travel to Damietta, the leadership of the nascent community of Qalandars was assumed first by Jalāl al-Dīn al-Darguzīnī, then by Muḥammad al-Balkhī, the two foremost disciples of the master. The group was exiled from the city by al-Malik al-Kāmil of Egypt when he captured Damascus and became its ruler in 635/1238. This was apparently a short-lived exile for the Qalandars. They must have returned to the city soon thereafter, since al-Malik al-Ẓāhir (r. 658–76/1260–77) is known to have revered Muḥammad al-Balkhī, the leader of the Qalandars in Damascus during his reign. Muḥammad al-Balkhī stipulated the wearing of heavy *jawlaqs* for the Qalandars and, presumably during the rule of al-Ẓāhir, built a hospice for his dervishes at the expense of the public treasury. During a visit to Damascus, al-Ẓāhir bestowed a gift of one thousand silver coins (*dirhams*) and several rugs to the Qalandars, who hosted the sultan in their hospice. In spite of al-Balkhī's refusal to accept al-Ẓāhir's invitation to Egypt, al-Ẓāhir also arranged for the delivery of a yearly stipend of thirty sacks of wheat and a daily allowance of ten *dirhams* to the Qalandars.[1]

The Qalandars were not the only deviant dervishes in Damascus during al-Balkhī's time. The Ḥaydarīs entered the city in 655/1257. They wore loose robes open in the front (*farajīyah*), and tall hats (*ṭarṭūr*); they shaved their beards while they let their moustaches grow. This practice was reportedly after the example of their shaykh Ḥaydar, whose beard was shaven by his captors when he was a prisoner in the hands of the Ismāʿīlīs. A hospice was constructed for them in the ʿAwnīyah quarter.[2]

In the same decade as the arrival of Ḥaydarīs in Damascus, a group of Qalandars were sighted in Ḥarrān, northeast of Aleppo. They presented themselves in 658/1259–60 to the Mongol Hülegü, who was accompanied by the renowned scholar Naṣīr al-Dīn Ṭūsī (d. 672/1274). Hülegü wanted to know who these people were. Naṣīr al-Dīn's concise and unequivocal answer, "[They are] the excess of this world," was sufficient for the Qalandars to be executed at Hülegü's orders.[3]

Ḥasan al-Jawālaqī al-Qalandarī, who earlier founded a hospice for Qalandars in Cairo, traveled to Damascus with Sultan Kitbughā (r. 694–96/1295–97) in 695/1295–96. Kitbughā there visited the Qalandars in the mountain of al-Mizzah, while Ḥasan organized a very large gathering (*waqt*) of dervishes in the hospice of al-Ḥarīrī, thanks to a gift of one thousand gold coins (*dīnār*) that he received from Kitbughā.[4] Ḥasan did not return to Egypt, but stayed in Damascus, where he died in 722/1322.[5] During the time of Khaṭīb Fārisī (ca. 740–50/1340–50), there was still a sizable group of Qalandars in Damascus headed by Muḥammad Bukhārāʾī. The original hospice of the Qalandars continued to function and was in existence during the early sixteenth century.[6]

The Qalandars spread to other cities in the Arab Near East soon after their emergence in Damascus. In the Egyptian town of Damietta, there was a band of Qalandars in the hospice of Jamāl al-Dīn, headed by a certain al-Shaykh Fatḥ al-Takrūrī at the time of Ibn Baṭṭūṭah's visit to that town in 725/1325.[7] Another Qalandarī hospice in Egypt was in Cairo. The founder of this institution was Ḥasan al-Jawālaqī al-Qalandarī. Ḥasan learned the ways of Qalandars from Iranian shaykhs (*fuqarāʾ al-ʿajam*) and settled in Cairo shortly before or during the reign of Kitbughā. He soon became a celebrity, grew rich, and founded a *zāwiyah* outside Bāb al-Manṣūr in the direction of "tombs and graveyards." This hospice became a center for Qalandars in Cairo, where there were always large numbers of Qalandars under the guidance of a master. Almost half a century later, in 761/1359–60, al-Malik al-Nāṣir al-Ḥasan (2d r. 755–62/1354–61) issued a decree in which he forbade the Qalandars to shave and to dress in the manner of Iranians and magi (*al-majūs wa-al-aʿājim*). It was delivered in person to the master of the Qalandars in Cairo, whose blessings, however, the sultan did not neglect to solicit.[8]

In Jerusalem, an old church known as Dayr al-Akhmar in the middle of the Māmilā cemetery was converted into a Qalandarī hospice toward the end of the eighth/fourteenth century by a Shaykh Ibrāhīm al-Qalandarī. Ibrāhīm won the admiration of a woman named Tonṣuq bint ʿAbd Allāh al-Muẓaffarīyah, who had a mausoleum (*qubbah*) built for him next to the hospice in 794/1391–92. The hospice was inhabited by a group of Qalandars. It collapsed in 893/1487–88 and was still in ruins during the early tenth/sixteenth century.[9]

Evidence of a different kind pointing to the prominence of Qalandars in the Fertile Crescent during the first half of the seventh/thirteenth century is provided by ʿAbd al-Raḥmān al-Jawbarī, who attributes the origin of the "reprehensible innovation" (*bidʿah*) of shaving off the beard to them and informs his readers that these dervishes neither fast nor pray.[10] Al-Jawbarī also reports on Ḥaydarīs. These dervishes shaved their beards and were accustomed to handling red-hot iron. They pierced their genitals in order to suspend iron rings on them. They were, as al-Jawbarī would have it, mere impostors, and not one of them could live a single day without consuming hashish.[11] The puritan Ibn Taymīyah (d. 728/1328) also found occasion to condemn the Qalandars. He denounced them as unbelievers who shaved their beards, neglected to pray and fast, and violated Qurʾānic prohibitions. They believed that the Prophet Muḥammad had given some grapes to their master "Qalandar," who spoke in Persian.[12] In addition, Taqī al-Dīn ibn al-Maghribī of Baghdad (d. 684/1285–86) composed a short Qalandarī poem.[13] The image of the Qalandar in this composition is that of a dissolute hedonist who secures a living through fraudulent practices. His head is shaven, and, if not simply naked, he wears either a felt cloak (*dalq/dalaq*) or a shirt of lamb's wool.[14] He consumes marijuana juice (*bang*) and does not touch wine because of its cost. He begs in Persian. A disciple of Quṭb al-Dīn Ḥaydar is reported to have visited the *khānqāh* of Abū Ḥafṣ ʿUmar al-Suhrawardī (d. 632/1234) in Baghdad.[15] Qalandars also appear in the *Thousand and One Nights* in the form of three one-eyed dervishes with shaven heads, which is a clear sign of their reputation in the Arab lands.[16]

The formation of the Qalandarīyah occurred, then, in the predominantly Arab regions of the Fertile Crescent and in Egypt during the first half of the seventh/thirteenth century. Ethnically, however, the leaders—and one suspects the rank and file—of the movement at this stage were not Arabs but mostly Iranians. The overwhelmingly Iranian nature of the group is demonstrated in the first instance by the names of the Qalandars attested in the sources. Jamāl al-Dīn and his first "disciple" Jalāl were themselves Iranians, from Sāvah and Darguzīn, respectively. His other major disciples were also from Iran and Asia Minor, though different names are given for them in our sources (Muḥammad Balkhī, Muḥammad Kurdī, Shams Kurdī, Abū Bakr Iṣfahānī, Abū Bakr Niksārī). In the Syrian and Egyptian cultural spheres, the Qalandarīyah appears to have continued throughout the seventh–eighth/thirteenth–fourteenth centuries mostly as an Iranian group. Ḥasan al-Jawālaqī, possibly an Arab recruit, is reported to have learned the ways of Qalandars from Iranian masters. Later, the Qalandars were forbidden to shave and dress in the manner of Iranians. Further evidence supplied by the poet Taqī al-Dīn ibn al-Maghribī and Ibn Taymīyah suggests that the Qalandars normally spoke Persian. Indeed, Jamāl al-Dīn's biography was written in Persian by the Shīrāzī Khaṭīb Fārisī under the direction of the Iranian leader of the Damascus Qalandars, Muḥammad Bukhārāʾī. It is likely, therefore, that among Arabic speakers the Qalandarīyah and possibly also the Ḥaydarīyah, on which we have fewer details, were viewed as foreign, predominantly Iranian, phenomena.

Significantly, there were in the Arab Near East indigenous dervish movements that approximated socially deviant renunciation. The most prominent of these in Syria, Iraq, and Egypt was the Rifāʿīyah. Inspired by the activity of their eponymous master Aḥmad al-Rifāʿī (d. 578/1183), the Rifāʿī dervishes challenged established modes of piety through practices such as walking on fire, eating snakes, and piercing the body with swords or long and sharp iron rods. The cultivation of thaumaturgical practices was clearly a productive move that led to the rapid spread of Rifāʿīyah throughout the region and beyond in a short time and produced related localized versions like the Ḥarīrīyah, the path of Abū al-Ḥasan ʿAlī al-Ḥarīrī (d. 645/1247–48), in Damascus and the Badawīyah, the path of Aḥmad al-Badawī (d. 675/1276), in Tanta, Egypt.[17] The spread of this complex movement in the region was concomitant with the development of renunciatory dervish piety in the same area, and to judge by a number of common practices (Ḥaydarīs, like Rifāʿīs, danced on fire and Rifāʿīs, like Ḥaydarīs, wore iron collars), there was a certain degree of interaction among these different dervish groups. Although the early history of the Rifāʿīyah and its presumed offshoots has not been studied in detail, it is clear that in the long run these movements distinguished themselves through emphasis on thaumaturgy rather than antinomian rejection of society. Unlike deviant renouncers, the Rifāʿīs seem to have deviated from social convention only during miracle-working seances; at other times they were "normal" members of society who functioned within the web of everyday social relations. This impressionistic view, however, obviously needs to be tested through close scrutiny of the historical evidence.[18]

IRAN

Both Qalandars and Ḥaydarīs were active in Iran from the beginning of the seventh/thirteenth century, though the relevant evidence is rather scanty, possibly due to the paucity of source materials on Iran for this period.[19]

The anonymous biography of the Persian poet Fakhr al-Dīn ʿIrāqī (d. 688/1289) includes some information on the Qalandars. When ʿIrāqī was about seventeen years of age (ca. 627/1229–30, about a decade after the destruction of his hometown Hamadān by Mongols in 618/1221), a group of Qalandars appeared in Hamadān. ʿIrāqī soon became enamored of a youth who belonged to this group. Unable to separate from his beloved, he followed the Qalandars to Iṣfahān, where he shaved his beard and became one of them on their wanderings. Together they traveled as far as Delhi and Multān in India and visited, presumably among other shaykhs, Bahāʾ al-Dīn Zakarīyāʾ, who is said to have welcomed them. After some further adventures during which ʿIrāqī lost track of all but one of his companions because of a storm, the young poet decided to become a disciple of Bahāʾ al-Dīn and settled in Multān.[20]

On a different note, Shams Tabrīzī, one of the many famous contemporaries of ʿIrāqī, is said to have brought about the death of a reckless Qalandar who refused to make room for him during *samāʿ* in a gathering that took place in ʿIrāq-i ʿAjam.[21] Abū al-Faḍl al-Ḥasan al-ʿUqbarī heard a story about the origins of hashish from a

Qalandarī shaykh called Ja'far ibn Muḥammad al-Shīrāzī while he was in Tustar in 658/1260.[22]

Somewhat later, we hear that a group of Qalandars gathered around Bābī Ya'qūbiyān, the master of Ḥasan (or Īshān) Mengli who exercised some influence on the Ilkhānid ruler Aḥmad Tegüder (680–83/1282–84).[23] Evidently, at around the same time, there were Qalandars in Shīrvān and Gīlān. Shaykh Ibrāhīm Gīlānī (d. 700/1301), the master of the more famous Ṣafī al-Dīn Ardabīlī (d. 735/1334), warned his followers against them. More concretely, certain Qalandars attempted to kill Zāhid Gīlānī while he was in Shīrvān. Indeed, the would-be assassins were later punished at the orders of the Turkish governor of the region; the ears and noses of many were chopped off, while one was summarily executed.[24]

The presence of Qalandars is recorded in the southwest Iranian town of Shar-i Zūr, situated halfway between Mawṣil and Hamadān, before the end of the seventh/thirteenth century. Shaykh Qāẕī Ẓāhir al-Dīn Muḥammad, a disciple of the well-known Sufi Awḥad al-Dīn Kirmānī (d. 635/1237–38), retired to a mosque in a village close to Shar-i Zūr in order to spend the night. After nightfall, about ten Jawlaqs came into the mosque and locked the door behind them. Thinking that they were alone—Ẓāhir al-Dīn held his breath and carefully hid—they first had something to eat, then prepared and consumed a hemp-drink and performed a *samā'*. Following this, they engaged in other activities that Ẓāhir al-Dīn did not deem fit to describe. The fearful Qāẕī fled as soon as the Jawlaqs fell asleep.[25]

During the seventh/thirteenth century, the Ḥaydarīs were also active in Iran. It is most likely that there was a nascent community of dervishes around Quṭb al-Dīn Ḥaydar during his lifetime. The names of two direct disciples of Quṭb al-Dīn Ḥaydar, Abū Khālid and Ḥājjī Mubārak, are recorded in the sources.[26] The reports of al-Qazwīnī, Ibn Baṭṭūṭah, and Amīr Ḥasan Sijzī establish that there was a group of followers in Zāvah within about half a century of Quṭb al-Dīn's death, and the sources of the early seventh/thirteenth century are already familiar with the sight of a typical Ḥaydarī dervish, wearing iron collars, rings, and bracelets. Ibn Baṭṭūṭah, who visited Zāvah sometime between 732/1331–32 and 734/1333–34, comments that the Ḥaydarī dervishes who wear iron rings on both their ears and genitals as well as collars and bracelets are the followers of Quṭb al-Dīn Ḥaydar.[27] The presence of Ḥaydarīs in the area around Zāvah is attested by the appearance of a Ḥaydarī dervish in a short work that the Persian poet Pūr-i Bahā (d. 685/1286–87) composed in 667/1269. This dervish lived in a village of the district of Khvāf immediately southeast of Zāvah. He had a shaven chin, wore a ring on his penis, and had in his company a young, beardless boy.[28] The ethnic origins of these early followers are obscure, though Quṭb al-Dīn's possible Turkishness seems to have had its effect on Ḥaydarī recruitment, if al-Qazwīnī's observations reflect a more general trend. Quṭb al-Dīn's popularity does not seem to have been restricted to a particular social group, since he is said to have been cherished equally by slaves and by rulers.[29]

Although it is more difficult to trace Qalandars and Ḥaydarīs in Iran throughout the following two centuries when the region was politically divided among Muẓaffarids, Jalāyirids, Tīmūrids, Ḳaraḳoyunlus, and Aḳḳoyunlus, this does not indicate their total disappearance from Iran. The *zāwiyah* of Quṭb al-Dīn Ḥaydar apparently continued to be an active Ḥaydarī center. A certain Bābā Resūl is reported to have joined the "order" and spent months and years at this *zāwiyah* during Temür's time (r. 771–807/1370–1405).[30] Other evidence points to the existence of Ḥaydarīs in Tabrīz during the time of Ḳaraḳoyunlu Ḳara Yūsuf (r. 791–823/1389–1420, with a long interregnum due to the Tīmūrid invasion) and his son İskender (r. 823–41/1420–38). Ibn al-Karbalāʾī and Nūr Allāh Shushtarī, the principal sources on the subject, do not give any description of these Ḥaydarīs. There is the tantalizing possibility that these reports might be on an altogether new Ḥaydarī movement under the leadership of a certain Quṭb al-Dīn Ḥaydar Tūnī, quite distinct from any preceding Ḥaydarī groups.[31] The same ambiguity, though to a lesser extent, also persists in a letter that Aḳḳoyunlu Uzun Ḥasan (r. 857–82/1453–78) wrote to Şehzāde Bāyezīd (who acceded to the Ottoman throne in 886/1481 as Bāyezīd II) after his victory of 872/1467 over Ḳaraḳoyunlu Cihānşāh and his subsequent capture of Tabrīz. Uzun Ḥasan's statement that he suppressed heretic groups such as Qalandarīs and Ḥaydarīs is devoid of detail and leaves one in doubt as to the identity of these Ḥaydarīs.[32]

The Qalandars too continued to exist in this period. A certain Zangī-i ʿAjam-i Qalandarī (d. 806/1403–4), for example, possessed a lodge in Kirmān and may have had a group of followers in this city.[33] In the Tīmūrid domains in eastern Iran, a single Qalandar with his beard shaven and dressed in a single piece of felt without a shirt or underwear is reported in the ninth/fifteenth century.[34] At the end of the same century, Sulṭān Ḥusayn Bayḳara (r. 875–912/1470–1506) wrote a letter to the magistrate of Khvāf and Bākharz, ordering him to put an end to the innovation (*bidʿah*) of the fourfold shave (*chahār ẕarb*) that had become popular among some young people and the Qalandars.[35] In addition, Jāmī (817–98/1414–92) includes a discussion of Qalandars in his *Nafaḥāt al-uns*.[36] There are continued reports on Qalandars in Iran well into the Ṣafavid period.[37]

INDIA

In comparison with Iran, attestations of Qalandars and Ḥaydarīs in Muslim India of the seventh–eighth/thirteenth–fourteenth centuries are at once more numerous and more informative. The appearance of Qalandars in India is associated with the figures of Shaykh ʿUs̱mān Marandī (better known as Laʿl Shāhbāz Qalandar), Shāh Khiẕr Rūmī, and Bū ʿAlī Qalandar of Pānipat. ʿUs̱mān Marandī (d. 673/1274) was a prominent disciple of Bahāʾ al-Dīn Zakarīyāʾ who came to be known as "Ruby" (Laʿl) because of his habit of dressing in red, while the additional title "Royal Falcon" (Shāhbāz) was conferred upon him by his shaykh. Several poetic compositions are attributed to him. Upon his death, he was buried in his native Sihvan in Sind, where his tomb grew to be a famous pilgrimage center.[38] Of Shāh Khiẕr Rūmī, it is only possible to assert that he was in Delhi during the lifetime of the Chistī master Quṭb al-Dīn Bakhtiyār Kākī (d. 633/1235) and had some affiliation with this shaykh. He apparently met his death in his native Asia Minor.[39] Bū ʿAlī of Pānipat probably lived somewhat later than either Laʿl Shāhbāz or Shāh Khiẕr, if one accepts as genuine the report of the date of his death as 724/1324. He is alleged to have been in contact with shaykhs Quṭb al-Dīn Bakhtiyār and Niẓām al-Dīn Awliyāʾ (d. 726/1325), though these should be viewed as later legends built around Bū ʿAlī, since Quṭb al-Dīn lived much earlier than Bū ʿAlī, and the Chistī sources of the period about Niẓām al-Dīn do not contain any references to the shaykh of Pānipat. He established a *khānqāh* in his native Pānipat, which later became a pilgrimage center for Qalandars and related groups.[40]

Other than these well-known figures, the presence of anonymous Qalandars in Muslim India of the seventh/thirteenth century is attested by several anecdotes found in Sufi literature as well as in historical chronicles. The *khānqāhs* of the Suhrawardī Bahā' al-Dīn Zakarīyā' (d. 666/1267–68) in Multān and of the Chishtī Farīd al-Dīn Ganj-i Shakar (d. 664/1265) in Ajodhan were at times visited by Qalandars who, traveling alone or in groups, did not refrain from engaging in provocative, if not outright hostile, behavior toward settled Sufis.[41] Somewhat later, a certain Qalandar known as Sulṭān Darvīsh and his companions seem to have enjoyed the patronage of Ṭughril, the rebel governor of Bengal, who gave the Qalandars three *mans* of gold from which to fashion their distinctive metal paraphernalia. These Qalandars were executed along with other followers of Ṭughril by Sulṭān Balban (r. 664–86/1266–87) upon his suppression of the revolt in 677–78/1279.[42] Around the turn of the seventh/thirteenth century and in the following decades, Qalandars frequented the *khānqāhs* of the Chishtī masters Niẓām al-Dīn Awliyā' and Naṣīr al-Dīn Chirāgh-i Dihlī in Delhi.[43] Groups of Qalandars wandering in the countryside as well as in cities continued to be a familiar sight in eighth/fourteenth-century Muslim India, to judge, for instance, by frequent warnings of Shaykh Muḥammad Gīsū'darāz against association with Qalandars.[44]

The spread of Ḥaydarīs into India is also well attested. During the reign of Jalāl al-Dīn Fīrūz 'Shāh (689–95/1290–96), there was a prominent Ḥaydarī shaykh by the name of Abū Bakr Ṭūsī Ḥaydarī in Delhi. One of his dervishes called Baḥrī was involved in the murder of Sīdī Muwallih in the presence of the sultan. Abū Bakr had a *khānqāh* on the bank of the Jamnah river and is said to have enjoyed the company of many established Sufi shaykhs as well as respected scholars.[45] Ibn Baṭṭūṭah came across Ḥaydarīs in India on two occasions. The first was in the vicinity of Amroha in northern India, where Ibn Baṭṭūṭah and his company spent a night with a group of Ḥaydarī dervishes headed by a black shaykh. Having built a fire with some wood that the company of Ibn Baṭṭūṭah procured for them, the Ḥaydarīs danced on the burning wood until the fire died out. The famous traveler was amazed to see that a shirt that he had given to their leader before he started to dance on the fire was returned to him intact; the fire had left no traces on the fabric. Ibn Baṭṭūṭah met another group of Ḥaydarīs at Ghogah in Malabar, also headed by a shaykh.[46]

It appears that the example of the Qalandars and the Ḥaydarīs was instrumental in the formation of at least two separate indigenous deviant dervish groups in India during the ninth/fifteenth century: Madārīs and Jalālīs. The Madārī movement crystallized around the activities of Badīʿ al-Dīn Quṭb al-Madār (d. ca. 844/1440), one of the most celebrated saintly figures of Muslim India. His dervishes were mendicants who refused all clothing and rubbed their naked bodies with ashes. They had long matted hair, wound iron chains around their heads and necks, wore black turbans, and carried black banners. They were notorious for their open rejection of religious observances as well as for their excessive consumption of hemp. The Madārīs spread to all regions of northern India from Sind to Bengal, as well as to Kashmir and Nepal.[47] The Jalālīs, for their part, professed allegiance to the renowned saint of Uch in Sind, Jalāl al-Dīn Ḥusayn al-Bukhārī, known as Makhdūm-i Jahāniyān Jahāngasht (707–85/1308–84). They closely resembled the Madārīs in appearance, but distinguished themselves by practicing the *chahār ẓarb* (shaving the head, beard, moustache, and eyebrows). In spite of the documented Sunnism of Makhdūm-i Jahāniyān, this particular group of his followers were fervent Shīʿīs, who also adopted strange practices such as eating snakes and scorpions.[48] The history of the particularly Indian movements of the Madārīs and the Jalālīs is obscure, and the nature of the interaction among all the socially deviant renouncers of Muslim India, not to say anything about their Hindu counterparts, is extremely difficult to establish. It is clear, however, that by the end of the ninth/fifteenth century, rejection of society through blatant social deviance had become a prominent religious option in Indian societies.

ASIA MINOR

As in other regions of the Islamic world, the Qalandars and the Ḥaydarīs found their way into Asia Minor within decades of their emergence around the beginning of the seventh/thirteenth century. There may have been Qalandars in Antalya and even Constantinople already during Jamāl al-Dīn's lifetime.[49] More definite is the presence of a disciple of Jamāl al-Dīn by the name of Abū Bakr Niksārī in Konya a few decades later. Niksārī was alive and well known in that city at the time of the death of Jalāl al-Dīn Rūmī (672/1273). One of the seven bulls in the funerary procession of Rūmī was later sent to the hospice (*langar*) of "the divine gnostic Shaykh Abū Bakr Jawlaqī Niksārī" as a present.[50] Rūmī himself was familiar with the Qalandars and on one occasion told his barber that he was envious of them because they had no beard at all.[51] The famous Sufi poet also knew and conversed with Ḥājjī Mubārak Ḥaydarī, a direct disciple of Quṭb al-Dīn Ḥaydar, who lived in Konya and greatly venerated Rūmī.[52]

Outside Konya, the Qalandars were probably present in many other spots in Asia Minor. The famous Ḥācī Bektāş (possibly d. 669/1270–71), for instance, is said to have welcomed a group of Qalandars from Khorasan to his dwelling in Sulucakarahöyük, Kırşehir.[53] The *Fusṭāṭ al-ʿadālah fī qavāʿid al-salṭanah* of Muḥammad ibn Muḥammad al-Khaṭīb, a work of heresiography that contains the earliest known account of the emergence of the Qalandars, was written in 683/1284–85 for a local audience in Kastamonu, which suggests general familiarity with the Qalandars in that area.

As in Iran, there is little sign of Qalandar and Ḥaydarī presence in the peninsula during the eighth–ninth/fourteenth–fifteenth centuries. It is quite clear, however, that the path of deviant renunciation left its imprint on the development of Sufi modes of piety in the Turkish cultural sphere. The key players in this process all felt the attraction of dervish piety, and many completely succumbed to its pull. Some prominent representatives of this latter option were Baraḳ Baba, Ḳayġusuz Abdāl, and Sulṭān Şücāʿ.

Baraḳ Baba was a native of Tokat in central Anatolia. His father was a military commander and his paternal uncle a famous clerk. He became a devoted disciple of the warrior saint Sarı Ṣaltuḳ, who gave him the name Baraḳ, "hairy dog," when the disciple eagerly swallowed a morsel Sarı Ṣaltuḳ had expectorated.[54] Toward the end of the seventh/thirteenth century, Baraḳ Baba traveled to Iran, where he gained the trust of the Ilkhānid Ghāzān Khān and of his successor, Muḥammad Khudābandah Öljeytü. In 706/1306 he and his dervishes traveled to Syria and Egypt, apparently on some mission on behalf of Öljeytü. After a colorful entry into Damascus, Baraḳ Baba moved to Jerusalem but failed to enter Egypt. On his return to Iran, he was killed on an expedition to Gīlān in 707/1307–8. His bones were carried to Sulṭānīyah, where a hospice was constructed for his followers by the Mongol ruler. When the Mevlevī master Ulu ʿĀrif Çelebi visited the hospice in 716/1316, a certain Ḥayrān Emīrci was the master of the Baraḳī dervishes.[55]

Barak Baba was an ecstatic figure, with a most peculiar appearance.[56] He had a predilection for dancing, singing, and uttering enigmatic sayings. Some of his ecstatic expressions are preserved in a learned Persian commentary written by a certain Quṭb al-ʿAlavī in 756/1355.[57] While these utterances are practically opaque for present-day readers, the mere existence of al-ʿAlavī's ingenious and sophisticated work suggests that Baraḳ Baba's influence on posterity was not inconsiderable. Also significant in this connection is the chain of initiation that runs from Baraḳ Baba through Ṭaptuḳ Emre to the famous Turkish Sufi poet Yūnus Emre (possibly d. 720/1320–21).[58]

Ḳayġusuz Abdāl lived in the second half of the eighth/fourteenth and the first quarter of the following century. He was a disciple of Abdāl Mūsā, himself a rather merry figure with a clear liking for food, who carried a club and addressed his dervishes as Abdāls. Abdāl Mūsā's followers donned animal hides, were equipped with dervish bowls, and practiced blood-shedding during Muḥarram.[59] Ḳayġusuz Abdāl himself normally wore a felt cloak without sleeves or collar (kepenek), practiced the fourfold shave (*chahār ẕarb*), and carried a horn. He consumed hashish freely and, like his master, had a predilection for food.[60] His writings are colorful elaborations upon a twofold central theme: each human individual forms a microcosmos and, conversely, the cosmos is the meganthropos.[61]

Sulṭān Şücāʿ was a contemporary of Ḳayġusuz Abdāl. Already a master Abdāl during the reign of the Ottoman Bāyezīd I (r. 791–805/1389–1403), he continued to be active throughout the first half of the ninth/fiteenth century and had dealings with celebrated Sufis such as Ḥācī Bayram (d. 833/1429–30) and Ümmī Kemāl as well as the Ḥurūfī poet Nesīmī (d. ca. 820/1417–18). He reportedly met Temür (Tamerlane) during the latter's Anatolian campaign (804–5/1402) and refused to accept any gifts from him.[62] Sulṭān Şücāʿ shaved his hair, eyebrows, eyelashes, and beard, wore no garments, and traveled in the company of two to three hundred Abdāls in the summertime, while he spent the winters in a cave. He apparently caught the eye of the Ottoman Murād II (r. 824–55/1421–51), who is known to have built a mosque in Şücāʿ's name in Edirne.[63]

The movements of deviant renunciation that crystallized around the figures of Baraḳ Baba, Ḳayġusuz Abdāl, and Sulṭān Şücāʿ formed the basic stock from which the more readily identifiable and distinct Abdāls of Rūm at the turn of the sixteenth century came into being under the formative influence of their master, Otman Baba.

CHAPTER SIX

Dervish Groups in the Ottoman Empire 1450–1550

The general survey of the spread and proliferation of movements of socially deviant renunciation in the Arab Middle East, Iran, India, and Asia Minor presented in the preceding chapter makes it possible to narrow the field of investigation by concentrating on dervish groups active in a specific cultural zone during a more limited period. The Ottoman cultural sphere of the late ninth/fifteenth and early tenth/sixteenth centuries is well suited for this purpose. An exceptionally high number of dervish groups were in operation in Asia Minor and the Balkans during this time. Apart from the ubiquitous Qalandars and Ḥaydarīs, more specifically Ottoman bands such as the Abdāls of Rūm, Bektāşīs, Jāmīs, and Shams-i Tabrīzīs roamed the empire. More significantly, these groups are clearly, though not always extensively, documented in the sources. Consequently, it is possible to construct a panoramic view of the movements of deviant renunciation in Ottoman Southeast Europe and Anatolia during the "classical age" of this colossal empire.[1]

QALANDARS

The earliest genuinely descriptive account of the Qalandars in the Ottoman empire was supplied by the Cantacuzene Theodoros Spandounes (Spandugino in Italian), the first European to describe the dervish groups in the Ottoman Empire. In his Turkish history composed between 1510 and 1519, there is the following passage on

Qalandars, whom Spandugino called the "torlacchi" (*ṭorlaḳ,* "beardless, handsome youth"):

> the torlacchi . . . are of the greatest numbers. The founder [of this religion] was one who confessed that Jesus Christ was divine in nature and was burned alive. The torlacchi are naked and wear the hide of either sheep or some other [animal] on their shoulders. In addition, the great majority of them wear felt [cloaks] without any kind of garment and are thus afflicted with horrible colds in excessively cold weather. For this reason, they cauterize their temples. They shave their beards and moustaches and are men of a most evil nature. They are not to be found in convents like monks, but are thieves, rascals, and assassins. . . . They carry on their heads a felt cap that has wings and they demand alms with great importunity from Christians, Jews, and Turks. Each of them carries a mirror with a long handle that he holds toward all people and says, "Look in and consider how before long you will be different from what you are now; so become modest and pious, think the better of [your] soul." Having spoken in this manner, he gives [the listener] an apple or an orange, which obliges one to give him one asper as alms in return. They ride donkeys during the day while they beg in the name of God, and at night they couple with these [same donkeys] like women.[2]

Menavino (the first Italian print of his work dates back to 1548) also referred to Qalandars as *ṭorlaḳ*s. He confirmed Spandugino's description of the dervishes' appearance and repeated the accusation of reprehensible sexual practices. In addition, he noted that the Qalandars appealed especially to women and claimed that these dervishes devised crafty tricks to extract alms from the populace.[3]

The details found in the descriptions of Spandugino and Menavino are matched on the Ottoman side by an exceptional source from the early tenth/sixteenth century, Vāḥidī's *Menāḳıb-i Ḫvoca-i Cihān ve Netīce-i Cān* (comp. 929/1522). According to Vāḥidī, Qalandars had clean-shaven faces. They were naked except for loose woolen golden or black mantles. They wore conical caps made of hair. Carrying drums, tambourines, and banners, they chanted prayers and sang melodious tunes with joy and fervor. They asserted that they had attained the state of *baqā*ʾ in the world of *fanā*ʾ. In fact, they believed themselves to be the "cream of God's creation": the whole of creation existed only for their sake. Contentment and complete resignation, they argued, were the chief attributes of a Qalandar, who was thus free from the need to earn a livelihood and lived solely on charity. The Qalandar could come face to face with the Divine Truth without the need of veils or curtains, a fact symbolized by the clean-shaven face. On account of his frequent encounters with the Divine, the Qalandar often found himself inspired to ecstatic dance. Similarly, his unwillingness to settle in one place was the manifestation of his realization, imparted to him through his contact with the Divine, that one should not get attached to this evanescent world. Instead, one should constantly be on the move in search of one's origins, a quest common to all created beings. Vāḥidī designated Hamadān as the place of origin of Qalandars.[4]

The revelatory accounts of Spandugino, Menavino, and Vāḥidī are enriched by supplementary information gathered from Ottoman sources. There was a *zāwiyah* known as Ḳalenderḫāne ("the house of Qalandars") in Istanbul during the reign of Meḥmed II.[5] Several decades later, a tax-register (*taḥrīr*) dated 929/1522–23 records another *ḳalenderḫāne* in Lārende, in the province of Karaman.[6] These reports, when coupled with other less certain notices of *ḳalenderḫānes* in Birgi, Bursa, Erzincan, and Konya, suggest that such hospices were not uncommon.[7] The presence of the Qalandars themselves is noted in Ottoman literary sources. They were definitely present in Istanbul and elsewhere in the empire soon after the conquest of the city, since Mevlānā Eşrefzāde Muḥyiddīn Meḥmed, a very prominent religious scholar, gave up scholarship in order to join a group of Qalandars; the Mevlānā apparently ended his days traveling around the empire with the group.[8] In a similar vein, an anecdote concerning the Ḫalvetī Şeyḫ Sünbül Efendi (d. 936/1529–30) includes the story of a young man who confesses to having desired to run away with some Qalandars in his search for knowledge and wisdom.[9] The Qalandars were present in Edirne in 949/1542, when they joined the crowds who welcomed Sulṭān Süleymān to the city.[10]

ḤAYDARĪS

As in the case of the Qalandars, Spandugino and Menavino gave detailed descriptions of the Ḥaydarīs. Spandugino described a group of dervishes whom he called Calendieri, though it is clear that he really had Ḥaydarīs in mind. These dervishes had long beards and long hair. They covered themselves with sacks, coarse felt, or sheepskins. Bearing iron rings on their ears, necks, wrists, and genitals, they were, according to Spandugino, more virtuous and worthy of respect than others of their kind.[11] Menavino, who also called Ḥaydarīs Calenders, supplied greater detail. According to him, the members of this group were for the most part celibates who had their own little churches called *tekkes*. On the doors of these *tekkes* appeared the phrase *caedanormac dilresin cuscuince alchachecciur,* which Menavino translated as "he who wants to enter our religion should live as we do and preserve his chastity."[12] Dressed in short sleeveless coats made of wool and horse-hair and ordinarily with shaven heads, these dervishes wore felt hats like those of Greek priests, around which they hung strings of horse-hair about one hand in length. They wore large iron earrings, collars, and bracelets as well as iron and silver rings of unequal size and weight on their genitals in order to keep themselves from engaging in sexual intercourse. They wandered around reciting poems of "Nerzimi" (Nesīmī), whom they took to be the first hero of their religion. The poems were pleasantly rhymed; in the opinion of Menavino, who claimed to have read some of them, they reflected Christian influences.[13]

More extensive than the accounts of Spandugino and Menavino is Vāḥidī's detailed description.[14] As described by Vāḥidī, the Ḥaydarīs kept their faces clean-shaven, except for moustaches that drooped down like leeches over the chin, only to turn back upward to the ears; the parts of the moustaches above the lips were twisted inward like prawns. Single locks of twisted hair covered their foreheads (the hair was presumably shaven). They wore iron rings around the neck, waist, wrists, ankles, and genitals as well as tin earrings. Iron bells were suspended on their sides. They were clothed in felt cloaks, with twelve-gored conical caps on their heads. Carrying drums of various sizes, tambourines, and banners, they chanted prayers and praises to God.

According to Vāḥidī, the Ḥaydarīs believed that the human face was a mirror that reflected the Prophetic Spirit. The face of a Ḥaydarī in particular, they argued, was like the sun that illuminated the universe and should, therefore, be kept free of dust; hence the shaving of the beard. By contrast, they did not touch the moustache at all, after the example of ʿAlī, who, according to the Ḥaydarīs, never shaved or trimmed his moustache. Locks of twisted hair symbolized resistance to the animal soul. Similarly, rings in general signified repression of the animal soul. In particular, earrings symbolized ignoring unworthy speech; collars, total subjugation to ʿAlī; girdles, freedom from debasement; bracelets, refraining from touching that which is illicit; and anklets, avoiding sinful paths. Iron bells served to keep the group together and also to convey secret messages to those who were capable of receiving them. Legally prescribed ritual practices were superfluous for the Ḥaydarīs, since they were blessed with God's grace and guaranteed enry to Paradise. Therefore, they threw aside not only religious observances (for they neither prayed nor fasted) but also rules of social conduct: they did not earn their living themselves, traveled constantly, and openly sought the company of young boys.

It is remarkable that the descriptive accounts of Spandugino, Menavino, and Vāḥidī are in almost complete agreement on points of detail. There is some uncertainty only concerning the Ḥaydarī headgear. Could they really have been wearing conical hats with twelve gores just like the nomadic Turkish supporters of the Shīʿī Ṣafavid rulers known as "Red Heads" (*ḳızılbaş*), as Vāḥidī has it? The fact that the crimson caps of the *ḳızılbaş* are said to have been first fashioned for them by Shaykh Ḥaydar (864–93/1460–88) and are therefore known as the "cap of Ḥaydar "(*tāj-i Ḥaydarī*) does not make it any easier to answer this question.[15] Although there is evidence that the Ḥaydarīs used to wear some kind of tall cap even before the time of Shaykh Ḥaydar (see the account of al-Nuʿaymī above in chapter 5), Menavino said that the Ḥaydarīs wore a different headgear altogether. In the absence of more information, one can only speculate that the Ḥaydarīs exchanged their former twelve-gored conical caps for hats of the type depicted by Menavino some time after Vāḥidī composed his work, most likely because they were eager to distance themselves from the *ḳızılbaş*, who were persecuted in the Ottoman Empire.[16]

The descriptions given above are complemented by evidence of a different kind on the presence of Ḥaydarīs in the Ottoman domains during the tenth/sixteenth century. Menavino, as noted, referred to Ḥaydarī hospices; indeed, it is certain that at least three Ḥaydarī hospices existed in the Ottoman Empire in this period. One of these is recorded in the tax-register (*taḥrīr*) of Karaman dated 929/1522–23, and another in a list of pious foundations of Erzincan dated 937/1530.[17] The other lodge in Istanbul is attested by an imperial edict to the judge of Istanbul dated 992/1584, in which the judge was requested to inspect the Ḥaydarī hospice in order to determine if its inhabitants maintained practices that were in violation of the religious law. From the contents of this document, it appears that the Ḥaydarī *zāwiyah,* reportedly founded for Ḥaydarī dervishes by Meḥmed II, was earlier ordered closed by imperial decree in accordance with the complaints of some citizens who denounced its inhabitants as heretics in contact with Ṣafavid Iran. The dervishes in turn registered a petition in which they dismissed the accusations as fabrications of a few individuals who wanted to take over the *zāwiyah* in order to construct a new building on its site and substantiated their charge with testimonies of the co-inhabitants of their quarter. It was this confusing affair that the sultan asked the judge of Istanbul to investigate in his order of 992/1584.[18]

There are other traces of Ḥaydarī activity in the Ottoman Empire. The dervish who attempted to assassinate Bāyezīd II on the road to Manastır in 897/1492 is described as a Ḥaydarī in the contemporary chronicle of Oruç ibn ʿĀdil.[19] Faḳīrī's *Taʿrīfāt* (comp. 941/1534–35), though less informative in this case than it usually is, does include three verses on the Ḥaydarīs.[20] In addition, at least one passage in the chronicle of Küçük Nişāncı (d. 979/1571) no doubt refers to the Ḥaydarīs.[21] More informative and colorful is a passage in the *Meşāʿir-üş-şuʿarā* of ʿĀşıḳ Çelebi (d. 979/1572) contained in the chapter on Ḫayālī Beg. From ʿĀşıḳ Çelebi's description, it is clear that Ḫayālī Beg's master Bābā ʿĀlī Mest was a Ḥaydarī. He wore earrings, a collar around his neck, chains on his body as well as a "dragon-headed" hook under his belt, and a sack (*cavlaḳ*) for clothing.[22] Ḫayālī Bey himself did not remain a Ḥaydarī for very long, though some lesser-known poets seem to have spent their lives as wandering Ḥaydarīs, as suggested by the examples of Ḥayderī and Meşrebī.[23]

ABDĀLS OF RŪM

Extensive descriptive accounts provided by Vāḥidī, Menavino, and Nicolas de Nicolay leave no doubt that in the Ottoman Empire of the early and mid-tenth/sixteenth century there was a particular group of dervishes distinguished from other similar groups by their distinctive apparel and paraphernalia (hatchet, club, leather pouch, spoon with ankle-bone), peculiar customs (self-cauterization, tattoos), and special allegiance to the hospice of Seyyid Baṭṭāl Ġāzī in Eskişehir, commonly called Abdāls or Işıḳs.[24]

The physical appearance of the Abdāls as described by Vāḥidī is quite striking.[25] They were completely naked except for a felt garment (*tennūre*), secured with a woolen belt. Their heads and faces were shaven and their feet bare. They carried "Ebū Müslimī" hatchets on one shoulder and "Şücāʿī" clubs on the other.[26] Each Abdāl possessed two leather pouches (*curʿadāns*), presumably attached to the belt, one filled with flint and the other with hashish. They carried large yellow spoons, ankle-bones, and dervish bowls. Their bodies and their temples featured burned spots. A picture of ʿAlī's sword was drawn or his name was written on their chests; also prominent were pictures of snakes on their upper arms. They carried lamps and played tambourines, drums, and horns, at the same time screaming. They were normally intoxicated on hashish (*ḳan ḥayrān*).

According to Vāḥidī, Abdāls maintained that the Prophet Adam was their model for many of their practices. When he was expelled from Paradise, Abdāls explained, Adam was completely naked except for a fig-leaf that he used to cover his private parts and had to survive on "green leaves" only. Similarly, Abdāls wandered around naked except for a *tennūre* symbolizing Adam's fig-leaf and consumed hashish ("green leaves") in considerable quantities. Their nudity was a symbol of "tearing the garment of the body" and the nothingness of this world. Hashish was a means to find respite from the unreal phenomena of time and space and to attain the hidden treasure of reality. Abdāls held that the hair, the beard, and the moustache were contingent things that should be shaven in order to render brilliant the "mirror of the face." They were very fond of food (a long list of dishes is provided). The meals were followed by hashish-taking and musical sessions (*samāʿ*). They normally slept on the ground and were awakened with the sound of a horn, a symbol of the trumpet of the archangel Isrāfīl: thus every morning awakening was likened to resurrection. Abdāls were free from all prescribed religious observances since they were not really in this world at all. Their true guide was ʿAlī and, as indicated by the Ebū Müslimī hatchet, they were the enemies of ʿAlī's enemies. They also highly cherished Ḥasan,

Ḥüseyn, and the twelve *imāms*. Their *kaʿbe,* however, was the hospice of Seyyid Ġāzī, as represented by the distinctive lamps they carried.

Menavino's long account of the Abdāls, reproduced here in its entirety, is equally detailed and informative:

> The Dervisi are men of good humor. They have as clothing sheepskins dried in the sun which they suspend from their shoulders [in such a way as to] cover their private parts, one in the front and one in the back. The rest of their bodies are totally naked and devoid of all bodily hair. They have in their hands clubs, no less big than long, thick and full of nodes. On their heads are white conical hats, one hand in height. Their ears are pierced, where they wear earrings of precious stones and jasper. They live in various places in Turkey where travelers are fed and accommodated. In summertime they do not eat in their dwellings but live on alms that they ask for with the words *sciaimer daneschine* [*şāh-i merdān ʿaşḳına*], that is, demanding alms for the love of that brave man called ʿAlī, the son-in-law of Muḥammad. . . . In Anatolia they have the tomb of another called Scidibattal [Seyyid Baṭṭāl/Seydī Baṭṭāl] who they say was responsible for the greatest part of the conquest of Turkey. There they have a house wherein live more than five hundred of them and where, once a year, they hold in joy and exultation a general meeting that lasts seven days, in which more than eight thousand participate. Their chief is called Assambaba [Aʿẓam Baba?], which means the father of fathers. Among them are found many learned youths who wear white garments reaching down to their knees. When they arrive [at the *tekke* of Seydī Baṭṭāl], one of their numbers narrates a story that contains [an account of] miraculous things seen during the course of travels through [different] regions, which they then write down along with the name of the author and present it to the chief. On Fridays, which is their Sunday, they prepare a good meal and eat it on the grass in an open field that is not far from their dwelling. Assambaba . . . sits among them, surrounded by the learned ones dressed in white. After the meal, the chief rises to his feet and the rest do likewise. They say a prayer to God and then all cry out in a loud voice *Alacabu Eilege* [*Allāh ḳabūl eyleye*], that is, may God accept this our prayer. Also among them are certain youths called *cuccegler* [*köçekler*], who carry in certain hand-trays a pulverized herb called

> *asseral* [*esrār*], which, when eaten, makes one merry just as if one had drunk wine. First the chief then all the others in order take this into their hands and eat, and this done, read of the book of the new story. They then move to a place closer to their dwelling where they prepare a great fire of more than one hundred loads of wood. Taking each other's hands, they turn round [the fire], singing praises of their order, in the same way as our peasants are accustomed to by their festivities, men and women in a round dance. When the dance ends, they take out knives and with the sharp point draw pictures of branches, leaves, flowers, and wounded hearts on the arms, breasts, or thighs, just as if they were engraving on wood. They engrave these in the name of those with whom they are enamored. Afterward, they approach the fire and place hot embers on the wounds, which they then cover with old cotton [rags] wetted with urine that they have prepared; the wounds heal by the time the cotton [rags] fall off on their own. In the evening, having received the permission of their chief, they form a squadron, like soldiers in arms, and return to their dwelling with banners and tambourines [in hand], asking for alms on their way. In Constantinople they are not viewed with much tolerance since one of them once attempted to kill the Great Turk with a sword that he carried under [his cloak]. All the same, they give them alms since these latter care for travelers in their own dwelling.[27]

Nicolas de Nicolay, although he largely paraphrased Menavino, also made some additions and alterations. According to him, the Abdāls, whom he called *deruis,* were bare-headed and carried small hatchets instead of clubs under their girdles. Nicolas noted that the herb that they ate was called *matslach* (*maṣlıḳ*) and the wounds that they inflicted upon themselves were cured by means of a certain herb. He mistakenly identified the sultan upon whose life an attempt was made by a dervish as Meḥmed II and, in addition, accused the Abdāls of robbery, sodomy, and other similar vices.[28]

The combined testimony of Vāḥidī and Menavino allows us to identify as Abdāls the "derwissler" described in some detail in the much earlier account of Konstantin Mihailović, who served as a Janissary from 1455 to 1463 C.E.:

> [The derwissler] have such a custom among them: they go about naked and barefoot, and they wear only deerskins, or the skins of

> some other beasts. Some also have skirts made of felt according to their custom. And they gird themselves with chains in criss-cross fashion. They go about bare-headed. And they sheathe their *instrumentum,* alias penis, in iron. They burn themselves on the arms with fire and cut themselves with razors. In what they walk about, so do they sleep. They do not drink wine, nor do they have any *kvas*. They beg for dinner. And what is left after dinner they give back to distribute to the poor as charity. They do likewise at supper. They never have anything of their own, but walk about the cities like lunatics. . . . And also at vespers they dance, going around [in a circle]. Having placed a hand on each other's shoulder, nodding their heads and hopping with their feet they cry in a great voice, *Lay lacha ylla lach* which means in our language "God by God and God of Gods." So vehemently do they dance and cry out that they are to be heard from afar just as if dogs were barking—one low and the other high. This dance of theirs is called the *samach,* and they hold it to be some sort of sacred thing and great piety. And they whirl about so violently that water flows from them, and they froth at the mouth like mad dogs. They overexert themselves so much that one falls here and another there. Then having recovered from this insane overexertion, each goes to his den.[29]

Evidence on the Ottoman side is by no means restricted to Vāḥidī's *Menāḳıb*. References scattered in the works of such Ottoman writers as ʿĀşıḳpaşazāde (d. after 889/1484), Faḳīrī, Küçük Nişāncı, and Muṣṭafā ʿĀlī (d. 1008/1600) suggest that the Abdāls of Rūm were a well-known and distinct dervish type.[30] More significantly, there were quite a few poets in the tenth/sixteenth century who were Abdāls, if only for a certain period of their lives, or at least Abdāls in character (*Abdāl-meşreb*). Ḥasan Rūmī, Seḥer Abdāl, Şırī, Muḥyiddīn Abdāl and Feyżī Ḥasan Baba, all minor poets who survive only in name with at most a few poems to their credit, were probably Abdāls.[31] ʿAskerī of Edirne, Kelāmī, Yetīmī, Yemīnī, and Şemsī of Seferihisar, better-known poets, were definitely Abdāls. ʿAskerī, for instance, lived as an Abdāl, frequenting the hospice of Seyyid Ġāzī as well as the tomb of the tenth Ithnā ʿAsharī *imām* al-ʿAskarī (d. 254/868 in Sāmarrāʾ)—hence his pen name—until he became the owner of considerable properties through a brief marriage.[32] Kelāmī appears to have been the follower of a certain Ḥüseyn Dede of the Abdāls' hospice in Karbalāʾ, this being the only evidence for the existence of such a center of Abdāl activity in that place.[33] Yetīmī of Germiyān is expressly said to have lived at the Seyyid Ġāzī hospice itself.[34] Yemīnī, who composed in 925/1519 a long work in verse on the life and miracles of ʿAlī ibn Abī Ṭālib entitled "The Book of the Virtues of ʿAlī, the Leader of the Faithful" (*Fażīletnāme-i emīrü'l-müʾminīn ʿAlī*), was a disciple of the Abdāl master Aḳyazılı Sulṭān, the preeminent disciple of Otman Baba.[35] Şemsī of Seferihisar, the author of the work entitled "Ten Birds" (*Deh murġ*), which brought him to the notice of Sulṭān Selīm I (r. 918–26/1512–20), also seems to have been an Abdāl and indeed was known as Işıḳ Şemsī. The chapter of the *Deh murġ* devoted to the speech of the vulture (the "Abdāl of the birds" in the poem) contains an accurate description of a typical Abdāl that is in remarkable agreement with the reports of Vāḥidī and Menavino.[36]

Perhaps the most significant poet of all is the famous Ḥayretī (d. 941/1535) of Vardar Yenicesi, who not only referred to the Abdāls of Asia Minor on numerous occasions in his poetry but also described and praised them in separate poems composed for this purpose.[37] Although these poems do not really add to our knowledge of the Abdāls, they do serve to confirm it in many respects, especially since they were composed, for once, by a poet who openly declares his admiration for this much-criticized group of dervishes. Thus, Ḥayretī's testimony establishes beyond doubt that the Abdāls were fervent Twelver Shīʿīs, that they did indeed inflict wounds upon their bodies, and that they were very fond of consuming hashish and wine.[38] They did claim to have completely subdued the animal soul and to have attained the state of "death before death."[39]

On a different note is the testimony of a certain ʿAbdülvehhāb known as Vehhāb-i Ümmī, said to have been a disciple of the Ḫalvetī Yigitçibaşı Aḥmed (d. 910/1504). In two poems which he composed in denunciation of the Abdāls, Vehhāb-i Ümmī provides us with an image that, apart from its negative tone, is very similar to that of Ḥayretī.[40]

More detailed information on the Abdāls of Seyyid Ġāzī Ocağı itself, however, is to be found in the entry on ʿİşretī (d. 974/1566–67), himself not an Abdāl, in the biographical dictionary of ʿĀşıḳ Çelebi. Upon being appointed the judge of Eskişehir through the influence of his benefactor, Şehzāde Bāyezīd (d. 969/1562), shortly after the Ottoman campaign to Iran of 960–62/1553–55, ʿİşretī went on an inspection tour to the Seyyid Ġāzī hospice and reported his observations to Sulṭān Süleymān himself.[41] ʿİşretī's report was presumably similar in content to ʿĀşıḳ Çelebi's own description of the Abdāls, colorful as usual:

> The *tekke* of Seydī Ġāzī in the province of Anatolia supported vice and immorality. [It was full of] vagabonds who had broken ties with their parents [and] run-aways who had become Işıḳs in search of a place in a hospice, singing in harmony like musical instruments, with faces that are free from the adornment of belief which is the beard, and their dark destinies [written on their foreheads] concealed by the clean-shaving of their eyebrows. Saying that their prayers had already been performed and their shrouds already sewn and fastened, they only uttered four *tekbīr*s at the times of the five daily prayers and did not take ablutions or await the prayer-call or heed the prayer-leader. They were a few gluttonous asses who survived on the alms-giving of sultans and charity of good people. Hoisting a different flag than that of Sulṭānöñü, they would raid the surrounding areas and would sound the horn of ridicule whenever they saw regiments of military commanders with banners and drumbeat. If the people of villages and cities were to heed the precedents [that the Abdāls set], they would, like Deccāl, follow their backs [that is, do everything in inverse order], would strip the maidens that they run into and would have them dress in their own manner. The student who fell out with his teacher, the provincial cavalry member [*sipāhī*] who broke with his master [*aġa*], and the beardless [youth] who got angry at his father would [all] cry out "Where is the Seyyid Ġāzī hospice?"; go there, take off their clothes, [be put in charge of] boiling cauldrons; and the Işıḳs would make them dance to their tunes, pretending that this is [what is intended by] mystical musical audition [*semāʿ*] and pleasure. For years on end, they remained the enemies of the religion and the religious and the haters of knowledge and the learned. According to their beliefs, they would not be true to the Truth if they did not show hostility to the people of the Law and would not be worthy of becoming a *müfred*[42] if they did not humiliate the judges.[43]

Additional information about the tomb and hospice (*tekke*) of Seyyid Ġāzī itself in the tenth/sixteenth century is provided by archival documentation and, much later in mid-eleventh/seventeenth century, the travel accounts of Evliyā Çelebi.[44] Significantly, it appears that the *tekke,* in its organization and social-economic activities, was no different from institutions of larger, well-established orders such as the Mevlevīye and Ḫalvetīye. Mosque, hostel, hospice, refectory, and center of pilgrimage in one, the *tekke,* which housed around two hundred servants and dervishes according to a document dated 935/1528–29, apparently never ceased to receive financial support from the central government.[45] The disciplinary measures adopted in various efforts to curb heretic practices never seem to have led to the total disruption of the activities of the *tekke*. Süleymān's response to the above-mentioned report of ʿİşretī, for example, was to order the expulsion of recalcitrant heretics and the foundation of a *madrasah* on *tekke* grounds.[46] All the same, the establishment continued to function, if on a diminished scale, throughout the tenth/sixteenth and the first half of the following century.[47] The most significant development by this latter date, other than the decline of the *tekke* in economic terms, which was most likely connected more with downward trends in the overall agricultural economy than with disciplinary measures of the government against the foundation,[48] was the transformation of the longtime center of Abdāl activity into a Bektāşī center. When Evliyā Çelebi visited the foundation around 1058/1648, he was entertained in a thoroughly Bektāşī institution. In the absence of sufficient evidence, it is not possible to trace the different stages of this curious transformation, which, however, adequately reflects the final fate of the Abdāls: gradual submersion in the growing and stronger network of the officially accepted Bektāşīye.[49]

Although they are difficult to trace, it would appear that the same fate befell other Abdāl centers as well. Other than the *tekke* in Karbalāʾ, mention should be made, in the first instance, of two *tekkes* situated very near to Seyyid Ġāzī: that of ʿUryān Baba in the village of Yazıdere and that of Sulṭān Şücāʿ in the village of Aslanbey. Very little is known about the former, a modest construction consisting of a single room attached to ʿUryān Baba's tomb that appears to have been constructed at around the same time as the *tekke*s of Seyyid Ġāzī and Sulṭān Şücāʿ at the beginning of the tenth/sixteenth century.[50] Significantly, the name of the "master of the [present] master" of the Abdāls in Vāḥidī's *Menāḳıb* is given as ʿUryān Baba.[51] The other *tekke* in question was built in 921/1515–16 in the name of Sulṭān Şücāʿ.[52]

Although the activity of Abdāls was concentrated around their main center in Seyyid Ġāzī, it was by no means restricted to midwestern Asia Minor. Indeed, Otman Baba, the patron saint of the group, whose historical personality is reasonably clear, appears to have spent the greater part of his life in the Balkans. His *zāwiyah*, which can be traced back to the time of Süleymān (r. 926–74/1520–66) though probably built earlier, still stands today close to Uzuncaova between Haskovo and Harmanlı in Bulgaria.[53]

Otman Baba had a number of disciples, at least some of whom seem to have followed his advice toward the end of his life that his dervishes should found *tekke*s and begin to lead settled lives. The most famous of such disciples was Aḳyazılı Sulṭān, who, according to the testimony of his own follower Yemīnī (the above-mentioned poet), became the leader of Abdāls in the year 901/1495–96 and still held that post when Yemīnī wrote his *Fażīletnāme* in 925/1519.[54] The *tekke* of Aḳyazılı Sulṭān, still partially standing today north of Varna in Bulgaria, was evidently an impressive building. In or even before the eleventh/seventeenth century, it became one of the largest Bektāşī centers in the Balkans.[55] Another disciple of Otman Baba was Ḳoyun Baba, who apparently established a *zāwiyah* in Osmancık, Amasya. He is mentioned in the hagiography of Otman Baba as Arıḳ Çobān and is thought to have died in 873/1468–69.[56] It is certain that close scrutiny of the sources will unearth many more members of the group.[57]

Abdāls of Rūm, Qalandars, and Ḥaydarīs were not the only groups of deviant renouncers in Ottoman lands at the turn of the tenth/sixteenth century. There were several others, of which the Jāmī group is the easiest to trace in the sources.

JĀMĪS

The earliest report on Jāmīs is found in the work of Spandugino, who said that the Jāmīs ("Diuami") had the same outward appearance as Ḥaydarīs, except that they did not wear iron rings on their genitals. They asked for alms from anyone and chanted psalms.[58] Compared to this nondescript account, Vāḥidī's description is much more colorful. Jāmīs had very long hair reaching down to the knees, matted and twisted like snakes. Their beards were clean-shaven, while their moustaches were left untouched. They were dressed in felt and wore earrings of Damascene iron on their right ears, iron rings on their wrists, and belts studded with bells on their waists. They wandered about barefoot. Vāḥidī assures his readers that Jāmīs were very proficient in music. Endowed with very pleasant and moving voices, they chanted prayers and eulogies to God to the accompaniment of tambourines and drums. They also consumed large quantities of wine.

Jāmīs maintained, still following Vāḥidī's testimony, that long, matted hair symbolized the unbroken Jāmī tradition that enabled the dervishes to attain to the presence of (their eponymous leader) Aḥmad of Jām in the hereafter. At the same time, long hair was also a sign of their spiritual descent from ʿAlī. Alternatively, if twisted locks of hair were taken to stand for wicks, the heart for an oil-container, and the body for a lamp, then the heads of the Jāmīs could be said to be afire with flames of love. Indeed, Jāmīs believed that they, especially their faces burning with the fire of love, were the source of light for the whole of creation. For this reason, they argued that the beard, which was like a cloud that stained the sun, should be shaved. The moustache, however, had to be grown, since the people of Paradise wear moustaches. Their earrings reminded Jāmīs not to listen to the words of anyone but ʿAlī. Iron bracelets demonstrated that Jāmīs do not have anything to do with the devil. Iron belts served as the anchor of the ship of existence (that is, the body), while bells were for musical harmony. They were indeed highly skilled in the art of music; their David-like voices were God-given gifts. Finally, Jāmīs had no worries concerning their livelihood, as God provided them their sustenance at all times.[59]

Equally detailed and informative is Menavino's account on Jāmīs, reproduced here in full:

> The religion of Giomailer [Jāmīs] is not far removed from this world. Mostly men of imposing stature, they generally love to travel through different lands like Barbary, Persia, India, and Turkey in order to see and understand the ways of the world. The majority of them are excellent artisans. They can give accounts of [the customs of] all the places that they have traveled to and are able to give answers about everything; they also keep written accounts of their travels. They are for the most part sons of noblemen, not less rich in goods than in nobility and are all

perfectly literate, since they begin their studies at an early age. Their dresses, devoid of stitches and more often brown and purple in color, are worn wrapped around the shoulders. They wear belts of no mean beauty, entirely embroidered in gold and silk, at the ends of which are suspended bells of silver mixed with other metals that give out a very pleasant sound from far and near alike; each of them carries five or six of these bells, not only on their belts but also on their knees. Over their shoulders are hides, of some animal like lion, leopard, tiger, or panther, the legs of which are tied in the front. They have silver earrings on their ears and long hair reaching down onto the shoulders, like our women, and in order to make it longer, they have various tricks, using turpentine and varnish to attach another kind of hair (of which camlet is made) to their own, so that from a distance their hair appears to be of marvelous beauty and length. They spend more time for this than for their own vocation. They generally carry a book in their hands, written in Persian and containing amorous songs and sonnets composed in rhyme according to their custom. They do not wear anything on their heads, and on their feet are shoes made of ropes. When there is a group of them, the bells produce very pleasant sounds that give the listener great pleasure. If by chance they run into a youth in the street, they give him such a beautiful concert, taking him into their midst, that people gather round to listen, and while they sing, one in tenor and others in other voices, one of them sounds a bell in unison, and at the end all of them sound the bells of their girdles and knees altogether. They visit all artisans alike, and these latter give them one asper each. It is they who frequently incite a passionate love for themselves in women and young men. They wander about anywhere they please. The Mohammedans call them "men of the religion of love" and regard them as nonobservants, which is true.[60]

In comparison to the lively accounts of Vāḥidī and Menavino, the latter repeated with few changes by Nicolas de Nicolay, the reports in other sources fade in importance.[61] Cumulatively, however, the relevant evidence is certainly sufficient to demonstrate that the Jāmīs were well known to the Ottoman populace of the first half of the tenth/sixteenth century as a distinct religious group. While the profile of the Jāmī movement during this period is thus clearly established, its historical origins remain obscure. The life and religious personality of the person whom the Jāmīs claimed as their spiritual leader, Shihāb al-Dīn Abū Naṣr Aḥmad ibn Abī al-Ḥasan al-Nāmaqī al-Jāmī, known as Zhandah'Pīl (441–536/1049–1141) has been studied in some detail.[62] From his prose works of certain attribution, it appears that Aḥmad of Jām was a devout Sunnī, eager to base Sufism, much like al-Kalābādhī (d. 380/990 or 384/994) and al-Qushayrī (d. 465/1072), firmly on the Qur'ān, the *sunnah,* and the *sharīʿah.* A collection of Persian poems that circulates under his name, however, would make him out to be an ecstatic Sufi who harbored almost pantheistic views and is, therefore, of doubtful attribution.[63] Aḥmad had a group of followers during his lifetime, though their fate after the death of the master is obscure. Aḥmad's descendants, however, continued to be revered as eminent religious personalities through the end of the ninth/fifteenth century.[64] It is thus quite difficult to explain when and how the later Jāmī dervishes in the Ottoman Empire have come into existence. One could only speculate that the same tendencies that led to the attribution of highly ecstatic poetry to Aḥmad were also at work in the emergence of a group of distinctly antinomian dervishes who adopted him as their spiritual leader.

SHAMS-I TABRĪZĪS

Vāḥidī, the incomparable observer of the Ottoman dervish scene at the beginning of the tenth/sixteenth century, included in his *Menāḳıb* a brief description of the Shams-i Tabrīzīs, a group of dervishes otherwise unattested under this name.[65] The heads and faces of Shams-i Tabrīzīs were clean-shaven. They wore felt caps with flat tops, dressed in black and white felt cloaks, and were barefoot. They would frequently become intoxicated on wine, play drums and tambourines, and dance and chant prayers to God. They claimed to have achieved union with the Beloved and stated that the "sword of attainment" had shaved their hair. Itinerants and mendicants, they believed that they functioned as mirrors in which everyone could see his/her true self. They thus illuminated the world like the sun.

Shams of Tabrīz (d. 645/1247), who was the spiritual mentor of Jalāl al-Dīn Rūmī (d. 672/1273), is not known to have started a spiritual path in his own name. He was, however, particularly revered by certain dervishes of the Mevlevīye, the Sufi order that evolved around Rūmī's exemplary religious activity and took its name from Rūmī's sobriquet "Mawlānā" ("our master"). The Mevlevīye is commonly thought to have been inextricably associated with Ottoman high culture and thus *sharīʿah*-bound, presumably because of the existence of good relations between the Ottoman court and major Mevlevī masters in late Ottoman history. In reality, the order harbored, from its inception, two conflicting modes of spirituality. The first was a socially conformist approach that tried to direct Rūmī's ecstatic piety into legally acceptable channels. The conformists were known collectively as the "arm of Veled" after Rūmī's son, Sulṭān Veled (d. 712/1312), who was rightly seen as the originator of this mode of piety. The second approach, however, took shape around the refusal to exercise any kind of control over ecstatic spiritual experience and was associated with the name of Shams of Tabrīz. The social deviants were therefore known as "the arm of Shams." The Shams-i Tabrīzīs of Vāḥidī were none other than the followers of Shams within the Mevlevīye.

The arm of Shams had been in evidence since the early phases of the Mevlevī order. Ulu ʿĀrif Çelebi (d. 720/1320), the grandson of Rūmī and master of the path, openly consumed wine, eschewed social and religious convention, and maintained good relations with socially deviant dervishes, among them the followers of Barak̦ Baba. The overvaluation of uncontrolled ecstasy seems to have peaked during the first half of the tenth/sixteenth century (when Vāḥidī wrote his account of Shams-i Tabrīzīs) around the figures of Yūsuf Sīneçāk (d. 953/1546), Dīvāne Meḥmed Çelebi (died second half of the century), and the latter's disciple Şāhidī (d. 957/1550). These "Shamsians," especially Dīvāne Meḥmed, were notorious for their open violation of and disregard for the *sharīʿah*. They shaved their heads and faces, donned special caps with flat tops, consumed wine, and were generally noted for their flagrant unconventional social behavior. The chasm between them and the socially respectable Mevlevīs must have been quite deep, since Vāḥidī treated them as two distinct groups, including separate descriptions of the Shams-i Tabrīzīs and Mevlevīs, whom he praised for their compliance with the *sharīʿah* and the *sunnah*.[66] The spiritual duality remained a characteristic of the order beyond the tenth/sixteenth century, and the Mevlevīye continued to harbor the "Shamsian" trend until modern times.[67]

BEKTĀŞĪS

The Bektāşīs are well known to students of Ottoman history as a major Sufi order in Ottoman lands. The order took shape during the tenth/sixteenth century and exerted tremendous influence on all levels of Ottoman life during the next two centuries.[68] It is not generally known, however, that at the beginning of the tenth/sixteenth century, when Vāḥidī wrote his *Menāḳıb* (completed in 929/1522), the Bektāşīs, far from being a Sufi order, were but one, and not even the largest, of the many distinct groups of socially deviant dervishes operating within Ottoman borders.

Vāḥidī's account on the Bektāşīs is the earliest attestation of this group.[69] According to his description, the heads and faces of Bektāşīs were clean-shaven. They wore twelve-gored conical caps of white felt, two hands wide and two hands high. These caps were split in the front and in the back and ornamented with a button made of "Seyyid Ġāzī stone" (meerschaum?) at the top, with long woolen tassels reaching down to their shoulders. On four sides of the fold of the cap were written (1) "There is no God but God," (2) "Muḥammad is His messenger," (3) "ʿAlī Mürteżā," and (4) "Ḥasan and Ḥüseyn." The dervishes were dressed in short, simple felt cloaks and tunics. They carried drums and tambourines as well as banners and chanted hymns and prayers. Bektāşīs, as reported by Vāḥidī, kept their faces and heads clean-shaven after the example of Ḥācī Bektāş, their spiritual leader, who, they believed, had lost all the hair on his head and face as a result of forty years of ascetic exercises on top of a tree. They also wore their caps as symbols of their submission to Ḥācī Bektāş. In a similar vein, the writings on the caps were intended as means of glorifying the Prophet, ʿAlī, Ḥasan, and Ḥüseyn. The button on the cap stood for the human head, since the Bektāşīs are in reality "beheaded dead people" (*ser-bürīde mürde*): they had died before death. Indeed, Bektāşīs claimed to be none other than the hidden saints themselves.

Later Bektāşī dervishes of the end of the tenth/sixteenth century and beyond were substantially different in both belief and practice from the Bektāşīs of the early tenth/sixteenth century as described by Vāḥidī.[70] These differences came about through a complicated process. During the tenth/sixteenth century, the Ottoman state, for various reasons, exerted increasing pressure upon socially deviant dervish groups. As a result, the Qalandars, Ḥaydarīs, Abdāls of Rūm, Jāmīs, and Shams-i Tabrīzīs lost vigor and ceased to exist as independent social collectivities, while the Bektāşī dervish group was transformed into a full-fledged Sufi order that continued to uphold the legacy of deviant renunciation. The reason for the success of the Bektāşīs was their firm connection with the Ottoman military system: the Janissaries, by long-standing tradition, paid allegiance to Ḥācī Bektāş, the patron saint of the Bektāşī group.[71] Armed with this advantage, the Bektāşī allegiance became the privileged ideological discourse of renunciation and was actively adopted during the course of the tenth/sixteenth century by the other dervish groups, with the exception of the "Shamsians" who had a safe refuge in their parent organization, the Mevlevīye. The "classical" Bektāşī order of the later Ottoman periods thus arose as a fusion of the beliefs and practices of the earlier Qalandars, Ḥaydarīs, and Abdāls of Rūm as well as the original Bektāşīs described by Vāḥidī.[72]

CHAPTER SEVEN

Renunciation in the Later Middle Period

Movements of deviant renunciation took shape under particular social and cultural circumstances. The Qalandarīyah and the Ḥaydarīyah first flourished in the Arab Middle East and Iran in the seventh–eighth/thirteenth–fourteenth centuries, simultaneously spreading to Muslim India in the east and Anatolia in the west. The Abdāls of Rūm, by contrast, attained their apogee in the second half of the ninth/fifteenth and the first half of the tenth/sixteenth centuries. They were, moreover, on the whole restricted to Ottoman lands in Anatolia and the Balkans. Significantly, the rise to prominence of this particularly Ottoman group was accompanied by a revivification of the older movements of the Qalandarīyah and the Ḥaydarīyah in the same period and same geographical area.

The Qalandars, Ḥaydarīs, and Abdāls of Rūm were, however, only the most prominent in spread and duration, so far as this is reflected in historical sources, of the ascetic dervish groups of the Later Middle Period. There were many others. The followers of Baraḳ Baba emerged as a separate dervish band in Asia Minor and western Iran shortly after the formation of the Qalandarīyah and the Ḥaydarīyah during the seventh/thirteenth century. Later, while the Abdāls of Rūm were active in Ottoman lands, other dervish groups—the Jāmīs, Shams-i Tabrīzīs, and early Bektāşīs and the Jalālīs and Madārīs—made their presence felt in Asia Minor and in India, respectively.

What the Arab Middle East and Muslim India in the seventh–eighth/thirteenth–fourteenth century had in common with Ottoman Anatolia in the late ninth/fifteenth century was the presence of societal conditions that allowed the firm and decisive incorporation of institutional Sufism into the social fabric of everyday life. In the Fertile Crescent, the spread of institutional Sufism, already set in motion by the Selçuḳids, was clearly associated with the devoted patronage of the ruling Ayyūbid elite, who were responsible for the construction of numerous hospices as well as the establishment of pious endowments of all sizes for the Sufis. The policies of the Ayyūbids, continued by their successors the Baḥrī Mamlūks, were paralleled by those of the ruling classes of the Sultanate of Delhi in India, where the Chishtī, Suhrawardī, and Qādirī orders rapidly became ineradicably implanted in Indian Muslim culture. However, in Asia Minor, and to a certain extent in Iran, the spread of the Sufi orders (*ṭarīqahs*) was delayed considerably owing to a social upheaval of the first order—the Mongol invasions, which were followed by unprecedented social and cultural instability as well as political fragmentation. When, after the first quarter of the ninth/fifteenth century, a remarkable degree of political and cultural unity was achieved under the Tīmūrids in Khorasan and Transoxania as well as the Ottomans in Anatolia and the Balkans, the *ṭarīqah*s rapidly asserted themselves in the form of the Naqshbandīyah in the case of the Tīmūrids and initially the looser Bayrāmīye and later the Ḫalvetīye and Zeynīye in that of the Ottomans, to mention only the most important.

The antinomian rejection of society represented by deviant dervish groups developed concomitantly with, and primarily in reaction to, the organized Sufism of the socially respectable *ṭarīqah*s. The former trod in the footsteps of the latter and inevitably surfaced in places where institutional Sufism had taken root. Before reviewing the complicated relationship between organized Sufism and socially deviant renunciation, however, a typological account of the institutionalization of Sufism will be useful.

INSTITUTIONAL SUFISM

Sufism, as noted earlier, developed primarily in Iraq as a brilliant synthesis of world-affirming and world-denying tendencies within Islam during the third–fourth/ninth–tenth centuries. It quickly and successfully domesticated the powerful renunciative movement active in that region by absorbing asceticism and transforming it into a step in a larger process of spiritual purification. Partly on account of this success and partly owing to the attractive power of its socially tame individualism, Sufi piety began to appeal to ever greater numbers of the "people of the community," in particular the religious scholars. At first tenuous, this nascent alliance between Sufism and the thoroughly populist piety of the religious scholars (*ʿulamāʾ*) demonstrated its social efficacy when it completely absorbed or neutralized Malāmatī and Karrāmī trends in Khorasan, culturally the second most developed region of Islamdom after Iraq during the fourth–fifth/tenth–eleventh centuries.

During late High Caliphal times and the first century of the Early Middle Period (fourth–fifth/tenth–eleventh centuries), Sufism was thus poised to become a major building block of the new international Islamic social order that was taking shape after the collapse of the ʿAbbāsid Empire.[1] The inner-worldly mystical outlook of Sufism, with its distinctive conceptual framework now largely in place, was about to step into the social arena to transform society along channels that conformed to this new worldview. The social mission of Sufism, which was, in broad terms, to infuse all levels of social life with Sufi ideas and practices, was accomplished through the progressive unfolding of two closely related processes, the rise of the *ṭarīqah* and the development of popular cults around the friends of God, the *awliyāʾ*.

During the course of the Early Middle Period, Sufi ideas and practices were subjected to a far-reaching process of organization and regularization that led, at the end of the period, to the emergence and spread of a new social institution, the *ṭarīqah*. The evolution of this socially most significant phase of Sufism, hitherto studied only in its barest outlines, followed different timetables in different regions of Islamdom, which consisted of many distinct political and cultural components.[2] The contours of the *ṭarīqah* were the same everywhere, however, and can be described along diachronic and synchronic axes.

The central feature of the *ṭarīqah* on the diachronic level was the establishment of a *silsilah,* the temporal propagation of a master's teaching in the form of a continuous chain of authorities. The *silsilah* is best visualized as a spiritual chain of intermediaries. It served simultaneously to perpetuate the example of a particular Sufi master and to create a single spiritual family of adherents around his "path." When they were later extended backward in time from the founding masters to the Prophet Muḥammad through members of his family or the first caliph, Abū Bakr (d. 13/634), *silsilah*s also provided religious legitimacy to the Sufi paths by linking them directly to the *sunnah*.[3]

The elevation of the religious example of a historical figure to the seat of transgenerational authority was by no means peculiar to Sufism. The rise of a class of intermediaries between God and the community in the form of a set of pious forefathers was a feature shared by all areas of religious learning in the Early Middle Period. This mediationist mode of religiosity, always kept alive by the Shīʿī tradition, was behind not only the development and consolidation of the four Sunnī legal schools but also the concomitant phenomenon of imitation (*taqlīd*) of pious forefathers, which crystallized at the end of this period in the form of clearly articulated intellectual positions. It was a sign of the increasingly communal nature of the mission of Sufism that it too participated vigorously in the creation of the mediating *religiosi*. The Sufi masters now stepped out of their restricted social enclaves to embrace the Muslim community at large, and their spiritual and physical presence became evident in the form of great numbers of tomb-complexes that punctuated the landscape of Islamdom with ever increasing frequency.

The creation of mediating hierarchies on the diachronic level was accompanied by the construction of mediating structures on the synchronic level, reflected in the gradual replacement of the looser teacher-pupil relationship of "classical" Sufism by one of director and disciple. The process involved four elements.

1. Physical concentration of directors and disciples within the confines of a single residential quarter, the Sufi lodge or hospice (*khānqāh, zāwiyah, tekke, dargāh*).

2. Careful delineation of a group identity through the development of distinct rites and practices for the core members of the *ṭarīqah*. The most significant of these included (a) the initiation ceremony, which marked entry into the group through specific rites such as investiture with the woolen habit and cutting of the hair; (b) the stipulation of distinct spiritual disciplines and techniques such as the mystical prayer (*dhikr*), mystical audition sometimes accompanied by ritual dance (*samāʿ*), and regulated seclusion (*khalwah*); (c) the specification of special apparel and paraphernalia; and (d) the adoption

of a series of injunctions that regulated all other aspects of disciples' lives such as moral etiquette and economic behavior.

3. Articulation of a distinct spiritual path to be traversed by all disciples and to be enforced on them by the master.

4. Propagation of the master's teaching from the center toward the community in the form of rippling group identities. When fully realized, this hierarchy of groups included the grades of director (*shaykh, pīr, murshid*), subordinate leader (*khalīfah, muqaddam*), disciple (*murīd*), associate or lay affiliate, and sympathizer. The core of the *ṭarīqah* was thus surrounded by social factions on several levels.[4]

The formation of institutional Sufism was not completed with the full-fledged development of the ṭarīqah. Sufism grew deeper institutional roots in society with the evolution of popular cults around the *awliyāʾ* or friends of God. Although the cult of the *awliyāʾ*, defined as "an ideological and ritual complex," should analytically be distinguished from the *ṭarīqah* as "a form of religious association," the ideational and practical overlap between the two phenomena is remarkable.[5] From the perspective of the present study, the significant point is that the cult of the *awliyāʾ* proved to be fertile ground for the propagation, admittedly in transmuted fashion, of Sufi ideas and practices. The entire ideological component of the *awliyāʾ* cult—sainthood (*walāyah*) and many of its ritual aspects such as the communal *dhikr* and/or *samāʿ*—was adapted from Sufism. Other constituent elements, most notably the *ziyārah* (visitation of tombs and related holy sites), have their origins outside Sufism proper.

The complicated history of the *awliyāʾ* cult remains to be written.[6] It is clear, however, that its widespread dissemination occurred concomitantly with the formation of the Sufi orders during the sixth–seventh/twelfth–thirteenth centuries. Whatever the exact nature of the relationship between these two processes, there is no doubt hat they were closely intertwined. Sufism supplied the theoretical underpinning of the *awliyāʾ* cult, while the cult ensured the entrenchment of the orders in all social strata. The *ṭarīqah* and the saint cult came to function as two sides of the same coin.

Although the evolution of the Sufi orders and of the popular saint cults around them took place along different routes in different regions of Islamdom, the major characteristics of this process remained the same everywhere. The legal institution of the charitable endowment (*waqf*) was the most prominent instrument in the creation of Sufi social agencies. The wealthy upper classes, especially the political elites, endowed numerous facilities for the use of Sufis. In Syria, Iraq, and Egypt, the Ayyūbids and the Baḥrī Mamlūks were committed to the idea of the "royal hospice" (*khānqāh*), grandiose establishments totally controlled by the state that were normally used to house foreign Sufis, though these were counterbalanced from the beginning, and superseded from the end of the ninth/fifteenth century, by modest personal lodges (*zāwiyas*) of the *ṭarīqah* Sufis.[7] In India, the political elites successfully extended their patronage to the Suhrawardīyah and, over time, even to the Chishtīyah, an order in which any form of contact with the state was strongly discouraged.[8] In Asia Minor, the Ottomans, ever respectful of the Sufis, began to support the older Mevlevīye and the nascent Ḫalvetīye and Zeynīye extensively during the late ninth/fifteenth and early tenth/sixteenth centuries.[9] Patronage by political elites was, however, only the most prominent sign of the spread of Sufi piety throughout Islamic societies of the Early Middle Period. Sufism gradually became a respectable, and even desirable, vocation among the cultural elites as a whole and emerged as an integral, perhaps the key, component of Islamic high culture. Having secured more than a firm foothold in upper urban society and its culture, it rapidly permeated all social and cultural strata, adapting to lower urban and rural culture with remarkable ease. Sufi piety thus emerged as a "mainstay of the international social order."[10]

DEVIANT RENUNCIATION AS A PROTEST AGAINST INSTITUTIONAL SUFISM

The growth of institutional Sufism produced a strong reaction from within its own ranks to the increasing this-worldliness of the *ṭarīqah* and the saint cult, which exhibited a considerable degree of accommodation with the ruling political and cultural elites. Growing institutionalization entailed the establishment and preservation of close ties with the wealthy and power-holding classes of society. Such worldly connections intensified the communal tendency within Sufism at the expense of its individualist core and increased the tension between its world-embracing and world-denying aspects. Ascetic renunciation, absorbed and domesticated by Sufism, now resurfaced along the fault line created by this tension as a radical critique of co-opted Sufi religiosity. In this process, it joined forces with anarchist individualism, a latent but potent current within Sufism.

World-renouncing dervish groups were radical protest movements directed against medieval Islamic society at large but, more specifically, against the kindred but socially respectable institution of the *ṭarīqah*.[11] The tension between the dervish group and the Sufi *ṭarīqah* is well documented in the sources. The founder of the Qalandarīyah himself, Jamāl al-Dīn Sāvī, was reacting against his own erstwhile Sufi training, which he apparently had received under his mainstream master ʿUthmān Rūmī, when he broke away to embark on a distinctively ascetic saintly career. The story of his conversion to the path of renunciation leaves no doubt that he decisively rejected not only his Sufi past but, by all indications, a successful future as a Sufi master. And, as some reports suggest, he may have been denounced in the process by ʿUthmān Rūmī. The same may have been true of Quṭb al-Dīn Ḥaydar's relationship with the Sufi master Luqmān-i Parandah. The hostile and aggressive behavior of some later Qalandars against reputed shaykhs of established Sufi *ṭarīqah*s such as the Suhrawardī Bahāʾ al-Dīn Zakarīyā and the Chishtī Farīd al-Dīn Ganj-i Shakar; their assassination attempts against the latter, Naṣīr al-Dīn Chirāgh-i Dihlī, and Ibrāhīm Gīlānī; and the openly contemptuous attitude of the Abdāl Otman Baba against all Sufi shaykhs demonstrate the explosive nature of the tension between ascetic renunciation and institutional Sufism. The reverse side of the coin was, of course, the summary and often angry dismissal of renouncers by many mainstream Sufis such as ʿUthmān Rūmī, Ibrāhīm Gīlānī, and Muḥammad Gīsū'darāz, not to mention the Ottoman Vāḥidī, who produced a book-length denunciation of deviant dervishes.

It is not enough to characterize the conflict between Sufi piety and dervish religiosity as simple mutual hostility, however. It would be more accurate to compare this relationship to the complex bond between "socially conformist" parents and their "rebellious" offspring. Thus, although the dervishes vociferously rejected the main features of institutional Sufism, in the final analysis they could not help but retain essentially Sufi beliefs and practices. The *ṭarīqah* determined the general pattern and shape of its shadow counterpart, the dervish group. The latter was a mirror image, in its negation, of the former.

Thus, the general structure of the loose dervish group, complete with eponymous master, actual leader, distinctive apparel, and paraphernalia as well as peculiar practices, reflected the structure of the *ṭarīqah*. Just as members of Sufi orders traced their spiritual lineage back to founding masters, the dervishes too harkened back to exemplary figures like Jamāl al-Dīn, Quṭb al-Dīn, and Otman Baba. As in the case of Ḥaydarīs, Jāmīs, Shams-i Tabrīzīs, and Jalālīs, they were at times even known by the name of their founding fathers. Similarly, all major dervish groups were headed by elders experienced in the path of renunciation, so that the director-disciple relationship that was so central to the orders was reproduced in some fashion in dervish communities. Nor were the dervishes averse to constructing a socially visible group identity for themselves by means of distinctive clothing as well as the adoption of peculiar accoutrements. They even utilized, though naturally only after radical remodeling, time-honored Sufi options like the woolen habit, the dervish headgear (*tāj*), and the staff. Here their penchant to cultivate and preserve separate group affiliations clearly paralleled Sufi predilection for paying allegiance to distinct orders. Finally, although we are not well informed on dervish rites and rituals, it is likely that here too their practices mirrored, if only by contrast, those of the *ṭarīqah*s.

In the realm of ideas, the parentage of Sufism is equally obvious. The dervishes appropriated Sufi conceptual complexes like *faqr* (poverty), *fanāʾ* (passing away of the self), and *walāyah* (sainthood), but applied extremist and radical interpretations to them. Indeed, the essential traits of dervish piety, asceticism, rejection of society, and uncompromising individualism can all be traced back, in theory if not always in practice, to such radical reinterpretations. The early Qalandars and probably the Ḥaydarīs, for instance, apparently worked the concept of poverty to its logical conclusions. The later Abdāls, for their part, were engrossed in their own understanding of *walāyah,* which in their eyes gave them license to reject the claims of Sufis to be the friends of God. Like many Sufis, most dervishes seem to have possessed the certainty of being infused with God's grace and provided typically Sufi explanations for this privilege.

The parent-offspring analogy can be pressed even further if we turn our attention to the question of recruitment to the path of renunciation. Close scrutiny of the biographies of prominent dervishes reveals a typical pattern: a male adult member of the cultural elite (the same social stratum from which Sufism normally recruited), with a bright future in front of him if still young or a fairly distinguished career behind him if middle-aged or elderly, rejects his cultural status and becomes a dervish. A clear case in point is that of Jamāl al-Dīn Sāvī. The degree of learning that he displayed as a young man prior to his conversion, heavily emphasized in his sacred biography, is also attested by the fact that he was called "the walking library" as well as by his recorded attempt to compose at least a partial exegesis of the Qur'ān. The cases of the celebrated Persian poet Fakhr al-Dīn ʿIrāqī, who joined the Qalandars as an impeccably educated young man of about seventeen years of age; the writer and poet Ḥamīd Qalandar (d. after 754/1353), who became a Qalandar in adolescence; the Ottoman Mevlānā Eşrefzāde Muḥyiddīn Meḥmed (fl. during the reign of Meḥmed II), who gave up a life of religious scholarship in order to join a group of Qalandars; and the Ottoman poet Ḫayālī Beg (fl. first half of the tenth/sixteenth century) all conform to this pattern. Further instances of such, especially youthful, conversion from the elite to the dervish way of life are found in the biographies of the proto-Abdāls Baraḳ Baba, whose father was a military commander and uncle a famous clerk; Ḳayġusuz Abdāl (d. the first quarter of the ninth/fifteenth century), who was the son of a local ruler; Quṭb al-Dīn Ḥaydar, said to be the son of a Turkish sultan; the Qalandar Khaṭīb Fārisī (d. after 748/1347–48), who converted to the Qalandarī path as a young man in search of wisdom and spiritual enlightenment; and the poet Ḥayretī, who chose the Abdāl path in his youth.

Our evidence suggests, therefore, that the architects and key personalities of dervish piety were mostly young dissenters from the elite. To judge by the examples enumerated, the precondition for becoming a dervish would appear to have been access, or guaranteed entry, to high culture. The direct connection between high culture and dervish piety is demonstrated both by the elite social background of prominent dervishes and by the presence of proficient poets and writers among them. In a similar vein, the veneration extended to dervishes by many a political ruler should be seen as further proof of the close ties between ascetic renunciation and elite culture. The examples of the Mamlūks al-Malik al-Ẓāhir and Kitbughā, who highly revered the Qalandarī leaders Muḥammad al-Balkhī and Ḥasan al-Jawālaqī, respectively; the Khaljī Fīrūz'Shāh II in India, who freely associated with Abū Bakr Ṭūsī Ḥaydarī, and Ṭughril, the rebel governor of Bengal, who extended gifts to an anonymous Qalandar and his companions; and the Ottoman Murād II, who had a mosque built in Anatolia in the name of Sulṭān Şücāᶜ, demonstrate that deviant dervishes exercised a degree of influence, probably owing to shared cultural origin, on power-holding classes. Deviant renunciation, it appears, took shape through the formative activities of dissenters from the cultural and political elite. In a very real sense, the dervishes were the offspring of socially respectable Sufis.[12]

At this point, it should no longer be surprising that youths seem to have been exceptionally responsive to the dervish calling or that the dervishes themselves apparently took a special interest in adolescents and young men. The story of Jamāl al-Dīn's conversion as a young man under the influence of a most peculiar boy called Jalāl al-Dīn Darguzīnī sets the tone in this regard. Thereafter, the Qalandars were frequently accused of attempting to entice children into adopting their own way of life, as attested, for instance, by the invective of the Chishtī Muḥammad Gīsū'darāz against them. Practically all of the examples of conversion to the dervish path enumerated above provide testimony to the validity of this claim. The irresistible pull of renunciation over young males is also recorded in the verses of Saᶜdī:

> Where there's a son who sits among the Qalandars
> Tell the father he may wash his hands of any good for him;
> Grieve not for his destruction, ruin:
> Better that one disowned should die before his father![13]

Much later, in Ottoman Anatolia, there were considerable numbers of learned youths as well as adolescents who specialized in serving hashish among the Abdāls, while the Jāmīs, themselves mostly young men of distinguished descent, paid special attention to men of the same age.

The new renunciation was, therefore, the offspring, in all senses of the word, of institutional Sufism. The two modes of piety were too intimately related to exist in continuous mutual antagonism. If the this-worldly orders were at times ready, out of not only political expediency but genuine attraction and sympathy, to accommodate their disturbingly antisocial counterparts within their own ranks, the deviant dervishes for their part, having manifested a considerable degree of institutionalization from their very first days, were not always reluctant to be invested with a certain degree of social recognition. It may have been a combination of these two factors that lay behind the emergence of not only suborders such as the Chishtīyah-Qalandarīyah in India but also antinomian orders such as the Bektāşīye in the Ottoman Empire. The accommodation of dervish piety by institutional Sufism was already signaled by the tolerant attitude of prominent orders' shaykhs such as Bahāʾ al-Dīn Zakarīyāʾ, Farīd al-Dīn Ganj-i Shakar, and Naṣīr al-Dīn Chirāgh-i Dihlī toward the Qalandars, including even those who were downright hostile to them. In this connection, the fascination of celebrated Sufi poets with Qalandarī themes, as attested by the numerous examples of *Qalandarīyāt* in Arabic, Persian, and Turkish Sufi poetry, adequately demonstrates the attractive power that deviant rejection of society exercised on the hearts and minds of the Sufis. In spite of the verses of Saʿdī, Sufi parents could not totally disown their offspring. For their part, the latter could hardly resist the inexorable pull of institutionalization that operated within Sufism in particular and within Islamic societies in general. There were strong social pressures to conform to the formidable demand coming from political powers anxious to provide religious legitimacy to their sovereignty by safeguarding the *sharīʿah*. This was definitely the case in the Ottoman Empire, where the dervish groups must have felt the necessity to acquire sufficient respectability to avoid severe persecution by the state. Presumably, this problem was particularly acute for the Abdāls, who openly professed Shīʿī beliefs, probably as a result of their attempt to negate the dominant Sufi-Sunnī alliance within the empire. It is plausible, therefore, that they should, whether deliberately or in the course of time, have joined the ranks of the Bektāşīs, who were given official approval owing to their unbreachable connections with the backbone of the Ottoman army, the Janissaries. Other dervish groups, notably the Qalandars and Ḥaydarīs, followed suit. The definitive establishment of the great regional empires of the Ottomans, Ṣafavids, Üzbeks, and Mughals during the tenth/sixteenth century led, therefore, to the return of the rebellious, if not prodigal, son to the household.

The Later Middle Period witnessed the spread and entrenchment of the new Islamic social institutions of the *ṭarīqah* and the *madrasah*. These institutions themselves were the products of momentous social transformations that occurred in Islamdom in the Early Middle Period. From the perspective of this study, the most significant overall feature of this latter phase of Islamic history was the decisive triumph of this-worldly religiosity in the form of a powerful Sunnī-Sufi alliance. The decisive triumph of the communal tendency within Sufism as manifested in the establishment of the *ṭarīqahs* signaled the attenuation of its other-worldly dimensions. This forceful turn toward this-worldly piety generated a strong other-worldly reaction within Sufism by reactivating its latent renunciatory potentials. The ascetic and anarchist individualist trends gained renewed vigor and broke into the open as socially distinct movements of deviant renunciation. The institutional Sufism of the *ṭarīqahs* thus directly engendered and in the long run determined the nature and shape of the dervish group. The latter mirrored, in its very negation and if only in mockery, practically all aspects of the former. The relationship between the *ṭarīqah* and the dervish group was, nevertheless, not exclusively one of mutual antagonism. The institutionalization of Sufism did not mean the complete devaluation of the Sufi respect and admiration for the option of contemplative flight from the world, and many prominent Sufis looked upon the dervishes with sympathy and fascination. For their part, the dervishes could never completely sever the umbilical cord that connected them to Sufism. The volatile bond between the two related modes of piety thus remained operative in spite of the confrontational nature of the relationship between them.

CHAPTER EIGHT

Conclusion

Intriguing in dress, behavior, and mode of piety, yet socially and legally marginal, the mendicant dervishes of Islamdom in the Later Middle Period have remained enigmatic figures for modern students of Islamic history. Little scholarly interest has been directed to them; by and large scholars have fallen victim to the temptation to view them through the distorting prism of "popular religion," an all-inclusive and ill-defined concept used to explain away religious phenomena resistant to the smooth application of simplistic models of Islamic religiosity. As a result of such neglect and carelessness, dervish piety has been obsured beyond recognition and generally ignored in favor of research into "mainstream" religious phenomena.

The history of the new renunciation as reconstructed here demonstrates clearly that what may from a distance appear to have been a confused and amorphous dervish movement in fact consisted of a set of clearly differentiated religious collectivities that maintained their distinct identities over time and space. In spite of a considerable degree of fluidity in appellation, the Qalandars, Ḥaydarīs, Abdāls of Rūm, and others were essentially separate dervish groups. The uncontrolled ecstasy of the Abdāls of Rūm diverged considerably from the learned gaiety of the Jāmīs, while both of these groups stood quite apart from the fierce asceticism of the Ḥaydarīs and the early Qalandars. The acknowledgment of the existence of noticeably demarcated currents of dervish piety does not, of course, imply that the lines of differentiation among different groups remained unchanged throughout the Later Middle Period and over a vast geographical area of extreme cultural diversity. The suggestion is not that there was an unbridgeable separation among the groups that prevented interaction, interpenetration, or merger. In fact, it is highly likely, though impossible to document, that dervish bands heavily influenced each other. Rather, the argument is that there were, in any given temporally and spatially specific cultural sphere, several socially and ideally distinct types of dervish piety. Outsiders to dervish piety, Muslim and non-Muslim, frequently confused these types, yet the same cannot be said for the dervishes themselves, who appear to have been highly conscious of their own distinctive group identities.

The defining characteristic of dervish piety was socially deviant renunciation. Briefly, the adoption of the radically ascetic practices of poverty, mendicancy, itinerancy, celibacy, and self-inflicted pain can be understood properly only in the context of the dervishes' rejection of society, the basic institutions of which they regarded as unsuitable and unconducive to other-worldly salvation. Thus salvation lay in active and socially conspicuous renunciation of society through uncompromisingly antisocial practices.

Renunciation was not particular to the Islamic Later Middle Period. High Caliphal times, usually and rightly portrayed as an intensely this-worldly phase of Islamic history, also generated powerful movements of other-worldly renunciation, which remained active through the Early Middle Period. The early ascetic movement of the first two Islamic centuries in the Fertile Crescent was followed by Karrāmīyah that spread chiefly in eastern Iran. In the long run, both of these movements were neutralized by the Sufi mode of piety, mainly because of its successful synthesis of other-worldly and this-worldly tendencies. Neutralization, however, did not entail destruction, and the legacy of asceticism remained potent within Sufism. In addition, Sufism itself carried the seeds of another, if related, kind of renunciation—anarchist individualism. The temptation for Sufis to cross the threshold between inner-worldly mystical activity and contemplative flight always remained close to the surface.

During the Early Middle Period, Sufism and Sunnism, now in close if not untroubled alliance, became the major constituents of the new Islamic social order that emerged after the disintegration of the universalist ʿAbbāsid dispensation. The this-worldly potential of Sufism was actualized in full force and speed with the emergence of the Sufi *ṭarīqah* and the Sufi-colored institution of the cult of *awliyāʾ*

throughout Islamdom. The entrenchment of Sufism in society in the form of ubiquitous social institutions refranchised the dormant other-worldly trends of renunciation and anarchist individualism within Sufism. While anarchist individualism surfaced early in the form of the literary and idealized Qalandar-topos, other-worldly trends soon won the day by harnessing anarchism and asceticism to the cause of renunciation. Deviant renunciation thus reclaimed its place on the agenda of Islamic religiosity as the active negation of institutional Sufism.

The relationship between institutional Sufism and dervish movements was a familial one. The latter emerged from the bosom of the former as rebel progeny who reflected, if negatively, the parent *ṭarīqah*s. The dervish groups closely resembled the Sufi orders in ideology and organization, if only in conscious mockery. The bond that held the two broad social collectivities together was, so to speak, organic so that their respective historical trajectories remained permanently intertwined. Where and whenever the *ṭarīqah*s entrenched themselves in the fabric of Islamic society, the other-worldly dervishes inevitably followed suit. Moreover, the relationship between Sufi and dervish piety was multidimensional. On both sides, antagonism was accompanied by respect, at times even admiration. In particular, the Sufis, in true this-worldly fashion, proved themselves to be sufficiently resilient to accommodate their rebellious brothers in their midst even beyond the ninth/fifteenth century during the period of the great regional empires.

Perhaps the most specific question that has arisen in the course of this study is one that can be dubbed the "ethnic connection." Thus, it is noteworthy that the movements of new renunciation arose primarily in the Iranian, Turkish, and Indian cultural spheres and that, conversely, there were no "indigenous" major dervish movements within predominantly Arab regions. Even the Qalandarīyah, although it took shape in the Fertile Crescent, remained a non-Arab, chiefly Iranian mode of piety, at least throughout the seventh–eighth/thirteenth–fourteenth centuries, and much the same can be said of the Ḥaydarīyah during that period. Later, similar groups were active among non-Arab populations of the Ottoman Empire and northern India. It appears, therefore, that the new renunciation did not resonate with prevalent modes of religiosity in the Arab cultural spheres of Islamdom. In spite of similarities on the surface, the popular

Arab Sufi movements of the Rifāʿīyah, the Badawīyah, and, in the Maghrib, the ʿĪsāwah did not uphold the basic principles of deviant renunciation. These appear, rather, to have been regular *ṭarīqahs* that did not practice asceticism and antinomianism on a permanent basis and were not radical protest movements directed against Islamic society at large. The reasons behind such divergent development of piety within different cultural spheres must remain unexplored in this study. It is possible, of course, that closer scrutiny of the Arab scene in the Later Middle Period will modify and refine the picture drawn here.

A second question is whether the same forces that generated the movements of deviant renunciation from within institutional Sufism were not also at work in other aspects of Islamic religiosity during the same period. More specifically, it seems legitimate to inquire if the ascendancy of the *madrasah,* like that of the *ṭarīqah,* did not produce a reaction among the *ʿulamāʾ* against the increasing, or at the very least potential, this-worldliness of *madrasah*-piety. From this vantage-point, it is tempting to see just such a reaction in the lifelong religious activity of Ibn Taymīyah (d. 728/1328) and much later in the religious legacy of his Ottoman counterpart, Meḥmed Birgivī (d. 981/1573). Both figures clashed all too frequently with socially respected and politically well-placed *ʿulamāʾ* precisely over issues that can be seen as measures of the degree of *ʿulamāʾ*-co-optation with society (namely, popular religion, especially the cult of *awliyāʾ*) and *ʿulamāʾ* willingness to exercise "extreme" flexibility on politically and socially sensitive issues.[1] The suggestion here is that there may be a connection between puritanical reformism as an intellectual current on the one hand and the thorough dominance of this-worldly piety among religious scholars on the other hand. This point clearly needs to be developed further and tested independently. In this connection, the idea of searching for critical reactions among the religious scholars to the entrenchment of the *madrasah* in Islamic society is certainly worthy of serious consideration.

A third and methodologically the most interesting question has to do with the social and economic factors behind the emergence and spread of the movements of new renunciation. On a general level, it is possible to associate ascetic world-rejection in premodern societies with urban as opposed to rural society. Renunciatory ideals were clearly the products of urban civilization.[2] The more meaningful question, however, is whether one can go beyond such a simple correlation to assert the existence of a close connection between social prominence of religious ideals based on the concept of poverty on the one hand and the ascendancy of commercial capital within urban economies on the other. A strong argument along these lines has been elaborated for European history for the period between 1000 and 1300.[3] Since the relative strength of merchant capital within the economies of Islamic societies especially during the High Caliphal and Early Middle Periods is a generally accepted feature of Islamic economic history, it seems possible to see the same connection between "voluntary poverty" and the "profit economy" operative throughout Islamic history as well. Once again, however, this must remain at best a tentative suggestion at this point.

Finally, the temporal correspondence between the rise of the mendicant orders, especially the Franciscans and Dominicans, in Europe and that of the dervish groups, in particular the Qalandars and Ḥaydarīs, in Islamdom makes one wonder if there was any connection between these two parallel developments. The question is highly intriguing, yet the absence of a critical mass of scholarly work on the economic history of Islamdom during the period in question makes it difficult if not impossible to answer. Recent work in world history suggests, however, that the possibility of unearthing such connections, at least on the economic level, between different cultural spheres is a real one and should be borne in mind in future research directed to this issue.[4]

Given that so many Muslim individuals actually converted to the dervish way of life during the Later Middle Period, the modern historian of religion has the responsibility to approach this phenomenon with genuine concern and respect. The temptation to explain dervish piety away as being peculiar to "less capable" members of Islamic society should be resisted. If nothing else, this study demonstrates clearly that such basic respect for the human subjects of historical study inevitably opens up new and fruitful avenues of research.

The attempt to retrace the historical trajectory of the dervish groups has led us through all major cultural spheres of Islamdom in the Later Middle Period. The true nature and significance of the Qalandars and the Ḥaydarīs as well as of the culturally more specific groups like the Abdāls of Rūm, Jāmīs, Madārīs, and Jalālīs emerged only after such a broad cross-cultural investigation. Notwithstanding the crucial role of culturally and regionally restricted case studies, it should now be obvious that there is a distinct need to adopt holistic inclusive perspectives in the study of the history of premodern Islamic religion.

In a similar vein, the results of a close scrutiny of dervish piety contain a strong warning against the scholarly tendency to avoid what are generally assumed to be "marginal" religious phenomena. This inquiry into "marginal" dervish groups leads to a new understanding of the place of renunciatory trends in the history of Islamic religion in general and within Sufism in particular. Moreover, it casts new light on Sufism itself, which can now be viewed as the successful development of a this-worldly mystical piety within Islam. Nothing, it appears, is marginal in the history of religions.

Abbreviations

Abdāl	Küçük Abdāl. *Velāyetnāme-i Sulṭān Otman Baba.* Ms. Adnan Ötüken İl Halk Kütüphanesi (Ankara), no. 495, dated 1316/1899. Copyist Ḥasan Tebrīzī.
Aflākī	Shams al-Dīn Aḥmad al-ʿĀrifī al-Aflākī. *Manāqib al-ʿārifīn.* Edited by Tahsin Yazıcı.
ʿĀşıḳ	ʿĀşıḳ Çelebi. *Meşāʿirüş-şuʿarā or Teẕkere of ʿĀşıḳ Çelebi.* Edited by G. H. Meredith-Owens.
Ayverdi	Ekrem Hakkı Ayverdi. *Osmanlı Mimārīsinin İlk Devri.*
Baranī	Ẕiyāʾ al-Dīn Baranī. *Tārīkh-i Fīrūz'Shāhī.* Edited by Saiyid Aḥmad Khān.
Baṭṭūṭah	Ibn Baṭṭūṭah. *Voyages d'Ibn Batoutah* [*Tuḥfat al-nuẓẓār fī gharāʾib al-amṣār wa ʿajāʾib al-asfār*]. Edited by C. Defrémery and B. R. Sanguinetti.
Dhahabī	Shams al-Dīn Abū ʿAbd Allāh Muḥammad ibn ʿUthmān al-Dimashqī al-Dhahabī. *Taʾrīkh al-islām,* Part 63 (years 621–30). Edited by Bashshār ʿAwār Maʿrūf, Shuʿayb al-Arnaʾūṭ, and Ṣāliḥ Mahdī ʿAbbās.
Digby	Simon Digby. "Qalandars and Related Groups: Elements of Social Deviance in the Religious Life of the Delhī Sultanate of the 13th and 14th Centuries." In *Islam in South Asia,* vol. 1, *South Asia,* edited by Yohanan Friedmann, 60–108.
Dihkhudā	ʿAlī Akbar Dihkhudā. *Lughātnāmah.*
EI	*The Encyclopaedia of Islam,* new edition.
EIR	*Encyclopaedia Iranica.*
Ergun 1	Sadeddin Nüzhet Ergun. *Bektaşi Edebiyatı Antolojisi: Bektaşi Şairleri ve Nefesleri.*
Ergun 2	Sadeddin Nüzhet Ergun. *Türk Şairleri.*
Evliyā	Evliyā Çelebi. *Evliyā Çelebi Seyāḥatnāmesi.* Edited by Aḥmed Cevdet and Necīb ʿAṣım.
Fārisī	Khaṭīb Fārisī. *Manāqib-i Jamāl al-Dīn Sāvī.* Edited by Tahsin Yazıcı. A later edition: *Qalandarnāmah-i Khaṭīb Fārisī yā Sīrat-i Jamāl al-Dīn Sāvajī.* Edited by Ḥamīd Zarrīnkūb.
Gölpınarlı	Abdülbaki Gölpınarlı. *Mevlānādan Sonra Mevlevīlik.*
Gramlich	Richard Gramlich. *Die Schiitischen Derwischorden Persiens.*
Hodgson	Marshall G. S. Hodgson. *The Venture of Islam: Conscience and History in a World Civilization.*
Jawbarī	ʿAbd al-Raḥmān al-Dimashqī al-Jawbarī. *Kitāb al-mukhtār fī kashf al-asrār wa-hatk al-astār.* Ms. Süleymaniye Kütüphanesi (Istanbul), Karaçelebizade 253, dated 717/1317–18.

Karbalāʾī	Ibn Karbalāʾī, Ḥāfiẓ Ḥusayn Karbalāʾī Tabrīzī. *Rawẓat al-jinān va jannāt al-janān*. Edited by Jaʿfar Sulṭān al-Qurrāʾī.
Khaṭīb	Muḥammad ibn Muḥammad al-Khaṭīb. *Fusṭāṭ al-ʿadālah fī qavāʿid al-salṭanah*. Edited by Osman Turan, "Selçuk Türkiyesi din tarihine dair bir kaynak: Fusṭāṭ ul-ʿadāle fī ḳavāʿid is-salṭana," 553–64 (Persian text). In *60. Doğum Yılı Münasebetiyle Fuad Köprülü Armağanı*, 531–64.
Ḳınalızāde	Ḳınalızāde Ḥasan Çelebi. *Tezkiretü'ş-şuʿarā*. Edited by İbrahim Kutluk.
Köprülü 1	Mehmed Fuad Köprülü. "Anadolu'da İslāmīyet: Türk istilāsından soñra Anadolu tārīḫ-i dīnīsine bir naẓar ve bu tārīḫiñ menbaʿları." *Dārü'l-fünūn Edebīyāt Fakültesi Mecmūʿası* 2 (1922–23): 281–311, 385–420, 457–86.
Köprülü 2	Mehmed Fuad Köprülü. *Türk Halkedebiyatı Ansiklopedisi*.
Laṭīfī	ʿAbdüllaṭīf Çelebi Laṭīfī. *Teẕkire*.
Meier	Fritz Meier. *Abū Saʿīd-i Abū l-Ḫayr (357–440/967–1049): Wirklichkeit und Legende*.
Menavino	Giovan Antonio Genovese da Vultri Menavino. *Trattato de costumi et vita de Turchi*. German translation: *Türckische Historien: von der Türcken Ankunfft, Regierung, Königen und Kaisesrn, Kriegen, Schlachten, Victorien und Sigen, wider Christen und Heiden. . . .* Translated by Heinrich Müller.
Nicolas	Nicolas de Nicolay Daulphinoys, Seigneur d'Arfeuille. *Les navigations, peregrinations et voyages, faicts en la Turquie, par Nicolas de Nicolay. . . .* English translation: *The Nauigations, Peregrinations and Voyages, Made into Turkie by Nicholas Nicholay Daulphinois. . . .* Translated by T. Washington the Younger.
Nişāncı	Ramāẓānzāde Nişāncı Meḥmed, known as Küçük Nişāncı. *Tārīḫ-i Nişāncı Meḥmed Paşa*.
Nizami	Khaliq Ahmad Nizami. *Some Aspects of Religion and Politics in India during the Thirteenth Century*.
Nuʿaymī	ʿAbd al-Qādir al-Nuʿaymī. *Al-dāris fī taʾrīkh al-madāris*. Edited by Jaʿfar al-Ḥasanī.
Ocak	Ahmet Yaşar Ocak. *Osmanlı İmparatorluğunda Marjinal Sūfilik: Kalenderīler (XIV–XVII. Yüzyıllar)*.
Pouzet	Louis Pouzet. *Damas au VIIᵉ/XIIIᵉ siècle: Vie et structures religieuses d'une métropole islamique*.
Qalandar	Ḥamīd Qalandar. *Khayr al-majālis: Malfūẓāt-i Ḥaẓrat-i Shaykh Naṣīr al-Dīn Maḥmūd, Chirāgh-i Dihlī*. Edited by Khaliq Ahmad Nizami.
Qazwīnī	Zakarīyāʾ Muḥammad al-Qazwīnī. *Āthār al-bilād wa-akhbār al-ʿibād*.
Ritter	Helmut Ritter. *Das Meer der Seele: Mensch, Welt und Gott in den Geschichten des Farīduddīn ʿAṭṭār*.
Rizvi	Saiyid Athar Abbas Rizvi. *A History of Sufism in India*. Vol. 1, *Early Sufism and Its History in India to 1600 A.D.*
Rosenthal	Franz Rosenthal. *The Herb: Hashish versus Medieval Muslim Society*.
SA	*Studia Islamica*.
Ṣafadī	Ṣalāḥ al-Dīn Khalīl ibn Aybak al-Ṣafadī. *al-Wāfī bi-al-wafayāt*. Vol. 5. Edited by Sven Dedering.

Storey	Charles Ambrose Storey. *Persian Literature: A Bio-bibliographical Survey*. Vol. 1, pt. 2, *Biography*.
Suhrawardī	Shihāb al-Dīn Abū Ḥafṣ ʿUmar al-Suhrawardī. *ʿAwārif al-maʿārif.* German translation: *Die Gaben der Entkenntnisse des ʿUmar as-Suhrawardī (ʿAwārif al-maʿārif)*. Translated by Richard Gramlich.
TA	*Türk Ansiklopedisi*.
Trimingham	J. Spencer Trimingham. *The Sufi Orders in Islam*.
Vāḥidī	Vāḥidī. *Menāḳıb-i Ḫvoca-i Cihān ve Netīce-i Cān*. In Ahmet T. Karamustafa, *Vāḥidī's Menāḳıb-i Ḫvoca-i Cihān ve Netīce-i Cān: Critical Edition and Analysis*, 88–293.
Yemīnī	Yemīnī. *Fażīletnāme-i emīrü'l-mü'minīn ʿAlī*. Edited by Aḥmed Hıżır.
Zarrīnkūb	ʿAbd al-Ḥusayn Zarrīnkūb. "Ahl-i malāmat va rāh-i Qalandar." *Majallah-i Dānishkadah-i Adabīyāt va ʿUlūm-i Insānī* (Tehran) 22 (1354sh/1975): 61–100.

Notes

1. INTRODUCTION

1. Muḥammad ibn Manṣūr Mubārak'Shāh, known as Fakhr-i Mudabbir, *Ādāb al-ḥarb va al-shajā'ah,* ed. Aḥmad Suhaylī Khvānsārī, 446–47; Meier, 511, n. 250.

2. Hamid Algar, "Barāq Bābā," in *EIR,* 3:754–55. Barak Baba is discussed in chapter 5 below.

3. Ruy Gonzales de Clavijo, *Clavijo: Embassy to Temerlane 1403–1406,* trans. Guy Le Strange, 139–40.

4. The periodization of Islamic history follows Hodgson, especially 1:96. Hodgson's scheme in C.E. dates is as follows: Late Sāsānī and Primitive Caliphal Periods, ca. (485)–692; High Caliphal Period, ca. 692–945; Earlier Middle Islamic Period, ca. 945–1258; Later Middle Islamic Period, ca. 1258–1503; Period of Gunpowder Empires, ca. 1503–1789; Modern Technical Age, ca. 1789–present.

5. This section has been adopted with extensive changes from Ahmet T. Karamustafa, "The Antinomian Dervish as Model Saint," in *Modes de transmission de la culture religieuse en Islam,* ed. Hassan Elboudrari, 241–60.

6. Notable studies on the Qalandars are Mahammad Tagi Ahmad, "Who Is a Qalandar?" *Journal of Indian History* 33 (1955): 155–70; Digby; Abdülbaki Gölpınarlı, "Kalenderiye," in *TA,* 21:157–61; Meier, 494–516; Ahmet Yaşar Ocak, "Kalenderīler ve Bektaşīlik," in *Doğumunun 100. yılında Atatürk'e Armağan,* 297–308; idem, "Quelques remarques sur le rôle des derviches kalenderis dans les mouvements populaires et les activités anarchiques aux XVe et XVIe siècles dans l'empire Ottoman," *Osmanlı Araştırmaları* 3 (1982): 69–80; Ocak; Tahsin Yazıcı, "Ḳalandar" and "Ḳalandariyya," in *EI,* 4:472–74; and Zarrīnkūb, esp. 78–92 (also on Ḥaydarīs), reprinted in idem, *Justujū dar taṣavvuf-i Īrān,* esp. 359–75. The Ḥaydarīs and Abdāls of Rūm are discussed in passing on many occasions in the larger works of Mehmed Fuad Köprülü and Abdülbaki Gölpınarlı cited later in this work and in the works of Ocak cited above (Ocak relies largely on Köprülü and Gölpınarlı).

7. Ocak is the most comprehensive existing study. Ocak prefaces his study with a long coverage of renunciatory trends (which he collectively labels "Kalenderīlik") in Islamic history up to the eighth/fourteenth century and maintains a broad definition of renunciation throughout the book. He does not, however, identify new renunciation as a distinct phase in the history of Islamic religiosity and, further, limits his focus to the Ottoman Empire. Ocak's study came to my attention after the completion of the present monograph.

8. Jawbarī, fols. 17b–18a. Al-Jawbarī's account of Qalandars and Ḥaydarīs is paraphrased in chapter 5 below.

9. See chapter 5, note 3, for full documentation.

10. Khaṭīb, 531–64 (Persian text on 553–64); praise for the Mongols is on 53b.
11. See chapter 5, notes 24 and 44, respectively.
12. Vāḥidī, fols. 52a–52b.
13. Laṭīfī, 110 (biography of the poet Temennāyī).
14. On the word *ṭorlaḳ,* "beardless, handsome youth," see Gerard Clauson, *An Etymological Dictionary of Pre-Thirteenth-Century Turkish,* 546, col. ii; and Ettore Rossi, " 'Torlak' kelimesine dair," *Türk Dili Araştırmaları Yıllığı—Belleten* (1955): 9–10.
15. Menavino, 79–82; German translation, 36b–37b. Menavino spent some years in Istanbul during the reigns of the Ottoman sultans Bāyezīd II (r. 886–918/1481–1512) and Selīm I (r. 918–26/1512–20).
16. Edward William Lane, *Manners and Customs of the Modern Egyptians,* 234. Lane resided in Cairo from 1825 to 1828 and 1833 to 1835.
17. Köprülü 1, 299–300 (the last sentence is from n. 1 on 300). Cf. English translation: *Islam in Anatolia after the Turkish Invasion (Prolegomena),* trans. and ed. Gary Leiser, 12–13 and n. 41 (70).
18. Fazlur Rahman, *Islam,* 153.
19. For a critical discussion on the "two-tiered model of religion," see Peter Brown, *The Cult of the Saints: Its Rise and Function in Latin Christianity,* 12–22. A comprehensive review of the use of the concept of popular religion in religious studies is found in Catherine Bell, "Religion and Chinese Culture: Toward an Assessment of 'Popular Religion,' " *History of Religions* 29 (1989): 35–57. Ernest Gellner, "Flux and Reflux in the Faith of Men," in *Muslim Society,* 1–85, is an interesting attempt to remedy the pychologistic bias of the two-tiered model of religion as found in the thought of David Hume through a merger with the sociological models of Ibn Khaldūn, though Gellner's own explanatory model is, curiously, also ahistorical. For a classical treatment of Islamic religiosity on the basis of the two-tiered model ("polytheistic needs within monotheism"), see Ignaz Goldziher, "Veneration of Saints in Islam," in *Muslim Studies,* ed. S. M. Stern, trans. C. R. Barber and S. M. Stern, 2:255–341. A recent reevaluation of the two-tiered model of culture in the medieval Islamic context is Boaz Shoshan, "High Culture and Popular Culture in Medieval Islam," *SA* 73 (1991): 67–107.
20. Ira M. Lapidus, *A History of Islamic Societies,* 162.
21. It is symptomatic of the thoroughly ahistorical conception of popular religion that the argument as presented here is less a summary of well-developed views on the subject in secondary literature, which are not in evidence, than a fresh construction from clues and implicit assumptions found in scholarly accounts of a general nature. See, for example, Rahman, *Islam,* 153–56.
22. On the question of survival and influence, especially in regard to Central Asian shamanism and South Asian Hindu and Buddhist asceticism, see, for instance, Mehmed Fuad Köprülü, *Influence du chamanisme turco-mongol sur les ordres mystiques musulmans;* Emel Esin, " 'Eren': Les *dervīš* hétérodoxes turcs d'Asie centrale et le peintre surnommé 'Siyāh-Ḳalam,' " *Turcica* 17 (1985): 7–41; and Digby, 66. The following description of the Śaivite Kāpālika ascetics, so similar in appearance to deviant dervishes, nicely demonstrates why the theory of survival or influence can be so tempting: "They wander about with a skull begging bowl, their bodies smeared with ashes, wearing bone or skull ornaments and loincloths of animal skin, with their hair matted in matted locks. They sometimes carry a special club . . . consisting of a skull mounted on a stick" (David N. Lorenzen, "Śaivism: Kāpālikas," in *The Encyclopedia of Religion,*

13:19). Similarity in physical appearance, however, does not entail similarity in belief and practice: a closer look at Kāpālikas reveals the difficulties of comparing them to Muslim dervishes; see David N. Lorenzen, *The Kāpālikas and Kālāmukhas: Two Lost Śaivite Sects.*

2. RENUNCIATION THROUGH SOCIAL DEVIANCE

1. Dihkhudā, s.v. "Darvīsh." Duncan Black Macdonald, "Darwīs͟h," in *EI,* 2:164–65, is devoid of interest. On the Arabic term *faqīr,* see Khaliq Ahmad Nizami, "Faḳīr," in *EI,* 2:757–78.

2. All three ascetic virtuosi mentioned here are discussed in detail with references in chapter 4 below, where information utilized in the present discussion is properly documented.

3. The sacred biography of Jamāl al-Dīn Sāvī, composed in 748/1347–48 by a Qalandar, is explicit on this point; see Fārisī; exact page references to the topic of poverty in this work are given in chapter 4, note 8.

4. Vāḥidī, fol. 43a.

5. Chapter 12 of the Qur'ān is devoted to Yūsuf. Incidentally, it is impossible to tell if Jamāl al-Dīn's continence was accompanied by misogyny, as was the case in early Christian asceticism in Egypt; see Peter Brown, *The Body and Society: Men, Women, and Sexual Renunciation in Early Christianity,* 241–58.

6. Cf. Giles Constable, *Attitudes toward Self-Inflicted Suffering in the Middle Ages,* 11.

7. The domestication of asceticism by Sufism during the High Caliphal Period (ca. 692–945 C.E.) is discussed below in chapter 3.

8. Richard Gramlich, "Madjdhūb," in *EI,* 5:1029; Michael W. Dols, Majnūn: *The Madman in Medieval Islamic Society,* ed. Diana E. Immisch, 388–410.

9. Fārisī, Yazıcı's edition, 33, line 3 (Jamāl al-Dīn and Jalāl Darguzīnī), and 71, line 17 (Muḥammad Balkhī); Zarrīnkūb's edition, verses 708 and 1389, respectively; Abdāl, several references to ritual prayer, for instance fol. 54a.

10. Algar, "Barāq Bābā," 754.

11. The Qalandarī author Khaṭīb Fārisī ends each section of the *Manāqib* with the refrain "come let us abandon this world / [and] utter a *takbīr* in the fashion of Qalandars" (*bi-yā tā dast az īn ʿālam bi-shūʾīm / qalandarvār takbīrī bi-gūʾīm*). The Abdāls, for their part, "uttered four *takbīr*s at the times of the five daily prayers and did not take ablutions or await the prayer-call or heed the prayer leader" (ʿĀşıḳ, fol. 175a). Although *takbīr* figures prominently in all Islamic rituals, the reference here is clearly to the fourfold *takbīr* of the funeral prayer that is performed standing up, with no prostrations.

12. On the dress codes endorsed by the *sunnah,* see, for instance, Muḥammad al-Bukhārī, *Ṣaḥīḥ,* Arabic-English bilingual ed. by Muḥammad Muḥsin Khān, 7:454–551 (Book 72: The Book of Dress). On Islamic costume in general, see Yedida K. Stillman, Norman A. Stillman, and T. Majda, "Libās," in *EI,* 5:732–53. Discussions on proper apparel appear in major Sufi manuals; see, for instance, ʿAlī ibn ʿUthmān al-Jullābī al-Hujwīrī, *The Kashf al-Maḥjūb: The Oldest Persian Treatise on Sufism by al-Hujwīrī,* trans. Reynold A. Nicholson, 45–57; also Suhrawardī, 318–24 (chapter 44); German translation, 306–11. On Sufi headgear, see John Brown, *The Darvisches or Oriental Spiritualism,* ed. H. A. Rose, 57–62; and Theodor Menzel, "Beiträge zur Kenntnis der Derwisch-tāğ," in *Festschrift Georg Jacob,* ed. Theodor Menzel, 174–99. For an attempt to trace the origins of

Sufi and dervish costume, see Geo Widengren, "Harlekintracht und Mönchskutte, Clownhut und Derwischmütze," *Orientalia Suecana* 2 (1953): 41–111.

13. See, for instance, al-Bukhārī, *Ṣaḥīḥ,* 7:514 and 517 (Book 72, reports 63 and 65, respectively).

14. See M. C. Lyons, "A Note on the *Maqāma* Form," *Pembroke Papers* 1 (1990): 117, for references to instances of shaving the beard as "a disgrace inflicted on drugged opponents by the man of wiles" in medieval Arabic popular literature (*Sīrat Ḥamzah, Sīrat Baybars,* and *Sīrat Dhāt al-Himmah*) as well as in the *Maqāmah* of Saymarah of Badīᶜ al-Zamān al-Hamadhānī (d. 398/1008). Cf. Widengren, "Harlekintracht," 51, n. 3.

15. On shaving in Sufism, see Gramlich, 1:88, and the references quoted there. Although the dervishes seem to have left behind a short composition of about seventy-five verses in Persian called *Tarāshnāmah,* there is no agreement among scholars on its authorship: E. E. Bertels, "Le Tarāš-nāma: Un poème didactique des dervishes Jalālī," *Comptes Rendus de l'Académie des Sciences des l'URSS* (1926): 35–38, as reported by Gramlich (bibliography), apparently attributes it to the Jalālī dervishes, while Gölpınarlı, 140, thinks that the work was composed by the Shams-i Tabrīzī poet Şāhidī (d. 957/1550). The *Tarāshnāmah,* which survives in many manuscripts (see, for instance, Süleymaniye Kütüphanesi [Istanbul], Ms. Hacı Mahmud 3843/3, fols. 7a–9b), does not reveal anything new on the practice of shaving.

16. The discovery of the "elevating" effects of cannabis leaves by Quṭb al-Dīn is reported by ᶜImād al-Dīn Abū al-Faḍl al-Ḥasan al-ᶜUqbarī (possibly d. 690/1291), *Kitāb al-sawāniḥ al-adabīyah fī al-madāʾiḥ al-qinnabīyah,* reproduced in Rosenthal, 51–53. Muḥammad ibn Bahādur al-Zarkashī, *Zahr al-ᶜarīsh fī aḥkām (or taḥrīm) al-hashīsh,* text in Rosenthal, 177, has a shorter report to the same effect, where Jamāl al-Dīn is also mentioned as Aḥmad al-Sāwajī al-Qalandarī.

17. The most explicit description of the consumption of hashish in a ritual setting by dervishes is found in Menavino's account on Abdāls of Rūm, Menavino, 76–79; see chapter 6 for a complete translation of this account into English.

18. On the legal prohibition of wine, see Arent Jan Wensinck, "Khamr, I. Juridical Aspects," in *EI,* 4:994–97. The legal and social implications of the use of hallucinogens is discussed in Rosenthal.

19. Jean-Louis Michon, "Sacred Music and Dance in Islam," in *Islamic Spirituality: Manifestations,* ed. Seyyid Hossein Nasr, 469–505; Jean During, *Musique et extase: L'Audition mystique dans la tradition soufie;* Marijan Molé, "La danse extatique en Islam," in *Les danses sacrées,* 145–280; Fritz Meier, "Der Derwischtanz: Versuch eines Überblicks," *Asiatische Studien* 1–4 (1954): 107–36.

20. On sodomy and homosexuality in Islamic history, see "Liwāṭ," in *EI,* 5:776–79 (written by the editors).

21. On *mūtū qabla an tamūtū,* see ᶜAlī Akbar Dihkhudā, *Kitāb-i amṡāl va ḥikam,* 4:1753; Badīᶜ al-Zamān Furūzānfar, *Aḥādīth-i Maṡnavī,* 116, no. 353; and Ritter, 583.

22. The biography of Jamāl al-Dīn, as reported in various sources, contains ample demonstration of this predilection for graveyards. In particular, his hagiography has one whole section on this subject, entitled "Dalīl guftan-i Sayyid dar bāb-i ānkih dar gūristān nishastan[rā] martabah chīst": see Fārisī, Yazıcı's edition, 82, line 1, to 85, line 5; Zarrīnkūb's edition, verses 1609–68. The location of later Qalandar centers in Cairo and Jerusalem within or in the vicinity of cemeteries was no doubt a legacy of Jamāl al-Dīn. Practicing retreats

in cemeteries was not, of course, particular to Qalandars: Ibn al-ʿArabī (d. 638/1240), for instance, a contemporary of Jamāl al-Dīn, is known to have followed this practice; see Michel Chodkiewicz, *Le sceau des saints: Prophétie et sainteté dans la doctrine d'Ibn Arabi,* 16.

23. On "looking at beardless boys," *naẓar ilā al-murd* in Arabic and *shāhidbāzī* in Persian, see Ritter, 459–77. A clear condemnation of the practice by a Sufi is in al-Jullābī, *Kashf al-Maḥjūb,* 416–17; for a non-Sufi counterpart, see ʿAbd al-Raḥmān ibn ʿAlī ibn al-Jawzī, *Talbīs Iblīs,* 264–78. Cf. Peter Lamborn Wilson, *Scandal: Essays in Islamic Heresy,* 93–121.

24. Alessandro Bausani, "Ḥurūfiyya," in *EI,* 3:600–601; and Abdülbaki Gölpınarlı, *Hurufilik Metinleri Kataloğu.*

25. The way of renunciation naturally remained as an option that could be adopted for reasons other than the achievement of spiritual enlightenment. As Digby observes, for instance, "the garb and personal appearance of a Qalandar might be adopted by an educated man as a matter of choice, one might almost say affectation" (Digby, 71). To the example of Malik Saʿd al-Dīn Manṭiqī that Digby adduces in this context, one might add that of Mawlanā Mīr Jamāl, a renowned logician and mathematician: the story of his entertaining confrontation with the Naqshbandī master Khvājah ʿUbayd Allāh Aḥrār (806–96/1403–90) is narrated by Fakhr al-Dīn ʿAlī ibn Ḥusayn Vāʿiẓ Kāshifī, *Rashaḥāt ʿayn al-ḥayāt,* ed. ʿAlī Aṣghar Muʿīniyān, 2:643–45.

3. RENUNCIATION, DEVIANT INDIVIDUALISM, AND SUFISM

1. The source of inspiration here is Max Weber, "Religious Rejections of the World and Their Directions," in *From Max Weber: Essays in Sociology,* trans. and ed. H. H. Gerth and C. Wright Mills, 323–59. See Said Amir Arjomand, *The Shadow of God and the Hidden Imam: Religion, Political Order, and Societal Change in Shi'ite Iran from the Beginning to 1890,* 16–18, for illuminating observations on Weber's discussion.

2. The Qurʾān, 10:7–8 and 24; 11:15–16; 13:26; 14:3; 16:107; 18:45–46; 20:131; 27:60; 29:64; 40:39; 42:34; 57:20. These verses emphasize the superiority of life in the hereafter over life in this world, which is described as temporary amusement and play.

3. The relevant verses would be too numerous to list here. A concise and clear exposition of the this-worldly nature of the Qurʾānic message appears in Fazlur Rahman, *Major Themes of the Qurʾān,* 37–64.

4. Leah Kinberg, "Compromise of Commerce: A Study of Early Traditions concerning Poverty and Wealth," *Der Islam* 66 (1989): 193–212, nicely demonstrates the pliability of the *sunnah.*

5. Emile Tyan, "Dj̲ihād," in *EI,* 2:538–40.

6. Michael Cook, *Early Muslim Dogma: A Source-Critical Study,* 43. Wilferd Madelung, "Murdj̲iʾa," in *EI,* 7:605, rightly points out, however, that political quietism was not a necessary component of the Murjiʾī movement and that many Murjiʾīs were politically active.

7. Mahmood Ibrahim, *Merchant Capital and Islam;* Maxime Rodinson, *Islam and Capitalism,* trans. Brian Pearce; Shelomo Dov Goitein, "The Rise of the Near-Eastern Bourgeoisie in Early Islamic Times," *Journal of World History* 3

(1956): 583–604. The significance of merchant capital for religious scholarship is demonstrated in Hayyim J. Cohen, "The Economic Background and the Secular Occupations of Muslim Jurisprudents and Traditionists in the Classical Period of Islam (until the Middle of the Eleventh Century)," *Journal of the Economic and Social History of the Orient* 13 (1970): 16–61. The role of commerce in the formation of Islamic cities is studied in Hughes Kennedy, "From *Polis* to *Medina:* Urban Change in Late Antique and Early Islamic Syria," *Past & Present* 106 (1985): 3–27.

8. Muhammad Hashim Kamali, *Principles of Islamic Jurisprudence,* 168–96; George F. Hourani, "The Basis of Authority of Consensus in Sunnite Islam," *SA* 16 (1962): 13–40, reprinted in *Reason and Tradition in Islamic Ethics,* 190–226; M. Bernand, "Id̲jmāʿ," in *EI,* 3:1023–26; Wael B. Hallaq, "On the Authoritativeness of Sunni Consensus," *International Journal of Middle East Studies* 18 (1986): 427–54. On authority in Sunnī Islam, also see Hamid Dabashi, *Authority in Islam: From the Rise of Muhammad to the Establishment of the Umayyads,* 71–93; and the relevant chapters in George Makdisi, Dominique Sourdel, and Janine Sourdel-Thomine, eds., *La notion d'autorité au Moyen Age: Islam, Byzance, Occident.*

9. It is possible to argue that Ḥanbalism was the epitome of the attitude that privileged the community: see George Makdisi, "Hanbalite Islam," in *Studies on Islam,* ed. Merlin L. Swartz, 216–74, esp. 251–64.

10. For detailed discussion of early Islamic asceticism, see Ignaz Goldziher, "Asceticism and Sufism," in *Introduction to Islamic Theology and Law,* trans. Andras Hamori and Ruth Hamori, 116–34; Tor Andrae, *In the Garden of Myrtles: Studies in Early Islamic Mysticism,* trans. Birgitta Sharpe, 33–71; Arthur John Arberry, *Sufism: An Account of the Mystics of Islam,* 31–44; and Leah Kinberg, "What Is Meant by *Zuhd*?" *SA* 61 (1985): 27–44.

11. On the transition to the *tawakkul* era, see Benedikt Reinert, *Die Lehre vom* tawakkul *in der klassischen Sufik.*

12. Goitein, "Rise of the Near-Eastern Bourgeoisie," 586–87.

13. Kinberg, "Compromise of Commerce," argues that "renunciation of worldly goods was always the main current in Islam, and [that] traditions [that is, *ḥadīth*] favoring property and wealth arose only as a concession to the rising economic power of the bourgeoisie" (195).

14. Goldziher, "Asceticism and Sufism," 130–31. Julian Baldick's recent survey, *Mystical Islam: An Introduction to Sufism,* demonstrates that the concern with external influences, which has a long history, continues to remain on the agenda.

15. Andras Hamori, "Ascetic Poetry (*Zuhdiyyāt*)," in *The Cambridge History of Arabic Literature: ʿAbbasid Belles-Lettres,* ed. Julia Ashtiany et al., 265–74.

16. For the expression "inner-worldly mysticism," see Weber, "Religious Rejections," 325–26.

17. Discussions on the subject of gainful employment and the relative merits of poverty and wealth appear in all major Sufi manuals under various headings. For a good example of the this-worldly trend noted here, see al-Jullābī, *Kashf al-Maḥjūb,* 19–29 and 58–61.

18. See, for instance, the discussion on seclusion in Hermann Landolt, "K̲halwa," in *EI,* 4:990–91.

19. Jacqueline Chabbi, "Khānḳāh," in *EI,* 4:1025–26.

20. On Malāmatīyah, see Hamid Algar, Frederick de Jong, and Colin Imber, "Malāmatiyya," in *EI,* 6:223–28; and Sara Sviri, "Ḥakīm Tirmidhī and the

Malāmatī Movement in Early Sufism," in *Classical Persian Sufism: From Its Origins to Rumi,* ed. Leonard Lewisohn, 583–613. On Karrāmīyah, see Clifford Edmund Bosworth, "Karrāmiyya," in *EI,* 4:667–69; and Wilferd Madelung, *Religious Trends in Early Islamic Iran,* 39–53. The most comprehensive treatment of *futuwwah,* with copious references, is Franz Taeschner, *Zünfte und Bruderschaften im Islam: Texte zur Geschichte der Futuwwa.*

21. For comparative treatment of Malāmatīyah, Karrāmīyah, and "Irāqī" Sufism, see Jacqueline Chabbi, "Remarques sur le développement historique des mouvements ascétiques et mystiques au Khurasan," *SA* 46 (1977): 5–72; and idem, "Réflexions sur le soufisme iranien primitif," *Journal Asiatique* 266 (1978): 37–55. Cf. Richard W. Bulliet, *The Patricians of Nishapur: A Study in Medieval Islamic Social History,* 41–46.

22. This is clearly a "sociological" interpretation of the concept, which, however, was not absent from Sufi understanding of *baqā*ʾ. For the standard experiential interpretations, see Gerhard Böwering, "Baqāʾ and Fanāʾ," in *EIR,* 3:722–24.

23. Suhrawardī, 84–86; German translation, 93–94 (chapter 10, 16–20).

24. "With regard to personal progress, . . . the word of the Prophet holds good: 'One single attraction by God is equivalent to the activity of men and djinn' " (Gramlich, "Madjdhūb, 5:129).

25. Carl W. Ernst, *Words of Ecstasy in Sufism,* is an admirable attempt in this direction that approaches the subject through the prism of *shaṭḥiyāt* (ecstatic expressions).

26. The origin and meaning of the word *qalandar* remains undetermined to this day. The most often cited, and indeed so far the only plausible, suggested derivation is that of the lexicographers Muḥammad Ḥusayn ibn Khalaf al-Tabrīzī and ʿAbd al-Rashīd al-Tattavī, who consider the word to be a variation of the Persian *kalandar,* "coarse stick; uncouth, uncultivated man." Al-Tabrīzī regards the transformation of the initial *kāf* into *qāf* as an arabization (*Burhān-i qāṭiʿ*, ed. Muḥammad Muʿīn, 3:1540 and 1680); al-Tattavī attributes it to the "passage of time and change of tongue" (*Farhang-i Rashīdī,* ed. Ẕūlfiqār ʿAlī and ʿAzīz al-Raḥmān, 2:164). Cf. Murtaẓā Ṣarrāf, "Āyīn-i qalandarī," *Armaghān* 52—dawrah-i sī-yu nuhum—(1349sh/1970): 705–15 and 53—dawrah-i chihilum (1350sh/1971): 15–21. In Arabic, the word *qalandar,* also found in the metathesized form *qarandal* in the seventh/thirteenth and eighth/fourteenth century sources, never seems to have meant more than "mendicant dervish," which would speak against the possibility of an Arabic origin, and an Arabic etymology is in itself quite unlikely for linguistic reasons; see Muʿīn's note in al-Tabrīzī, *Burhān-i qāṭiʿ*, 3:1540; Meier, 500–501, nn. 183–87; and Yazıcı, "Ḳalandar," 472–73. The possibility of an Indian origin cannot be altogether ruled out, however, even if a plausible Indian etymology is yet to be put forward. For a Sanskrit etymology that is not altogether intelligible to me, see Sadeddin Kocatürk, "Dar bārah-i firqah-i qalandarīyah va qalandar'nāmah-i Khaṭīb-i Fārisī, maʿnā-yi kalimah-i qalandar," *Doğu Dilleri* (Ankara Üniversitesi Dil ve Tarih-Coğrafya Fakültesi Doğu Dil ve Edebiyatları Araştırmaları Enstitüsü) 2 (1971): 89. The word survives in present-day Turkish as *kalender* and in Persian and Urdu as *qalandar,* or more often as *qalandarānah,* referring to carefree, simple, bohemian, or unconventional persons or behavior. In northern India, the word *qalandar* usually denotes a beggar or more frequently a monkey or bear player; see Digby, 65; Aziz Ahmad, *An Intellectual History of Islam in India,* 45; and Annemarie Schim-

mel, *Islam in the Indian Subcontinent,* 34–35, n. 71 (relying on Digby). In Pakistan, the word *qalandar* is largely interchangeable with *malang,* another term used to refer to antinomian dervishes (I owe this information to Jamal Elias).

27. For a general overview, see J. T. P. De Bruijn, "The *Qalandariyyāt* in Persian Mystical Poetry, from Sanaʾī Onwards," in *The Legacy of Mediaeval Persian Sufism,* ed. Leonard Lewisohn, 75–86.

28. "I am that wanderer whose name is Qalandar; / I have neither home nor goods nor kitchen. / When day comes I wander round the world; / when night falls I lay my head on a brick" (Bābā Ṭāhir ʿUryān Hamadānī, *Dīvān-i Bābā Ṭāhir ʿUryān Hamadānī,* ed. Manūchihr Ādamīyat, 8). Cf. Mujtabā Mīnuvī, "Az khāzāʾin-i Turkīyah," *Majallah-i Dānishkadah-i Adabīyāt* (Tehran) 4 (1335sh/1956): 57. The English translation is by Digby, 61.

29. Abū Saʿīd-i Abū al-Khayr, *Sukhanān-i manẓūm-i Abū Saʿīd-i Abū al-Khayr,* ed. Saʿīd Nafīsī, 41 and 58, nos. 281 and 397, respectively.

30. ʿAbd Allāh Ansārī Haravī, *Risālah-i Qalandar'nāmah,* in *Rasāʾil-i jāmiʿ-i ʿārif-i qarn-i chahārum-i hijrī Khvājah ʿAbd Allāh Ansārī,* ed. Vahīd Dastgirdī, 92–99. Cf. Meier, 495; and De Bruijn, "*Qalandariyyāt,*" 78, on the question of authorship. Also cf. characterization of the *Qalandar'nāmah* in Yazıcı, "Ḳalandariyya," 4:473: "a system of thought advocating inner contentment, the unimportance of learning, the avoidance of all display and contempt for the transient world and everything in it."

31. For a list and analysis of *Qalandarīyāt,* see Helmut Ritter, "Philologika XV: Farīduddīn ʿAṭṭār III. 7. Der Dīwān," *Oriens* 12 (1959): 1–88; Ritter, index, s.v. "*Qalandarīyāt*"; also De Bruijn, "*Qalandariyyāt*"; and Johann Christoph Bürgel, "The Pious Rogue: A Study in the Meaning of *Qalandar* and *Rend* in the Poetry of Muhammad Iqbal," *Edebiyat* 4 (1979): 43–49.

32. On Amīr Ḥusaynī, see Ẕabīh Allāh Ṣafā, *Tārīkh-i Adabīyāt dar Īrān,* 3, ii:751–63 (with ample references); and N. Māyil Haravī, *Sharḥ-i ḥāl va āṣār-i Amīr Ḥusaynī Ghūrī Haravī, mutavaffā 718.* For the text of the *Qalandar'nāmah,* see Sadeddin Kocatürk, "İran'da İslamiyetten sonraki yüzyıllarda fikir akımlarına toplu bir bakış ve 'kalenderiye ṭarikatı' ile ilgili bir risale," *Ankara Üniversitesi Dil ve Tarih-Coğrafya Fakültesi Dergisi* 28 (1970): 227–29. Both Meier and Haravī rely on fourteen verses only, as these appear in Riẓā Qulī Khān Hidāyat, *Majmaʿ al-fuṣaḥā,* 2:15. All of these fourteen couplets are to be found in the full text. Kocatürk relies on mss. in London and Tehran and reports the existence of two further copies in Ayasofya (now in Süleymaniye Kütüphanesi), Istanbul, without citing their call numbers, which are given as 1914 and 2032 by Gölpınarlı in several of his works (for instance, *100 Soruda Türkiye'de Mezhepler ve Tarikatler,* 259). A fifth copy in Paris is reported by Aḥmad Munzavī, *Fihrist-i nuskhahā-yi khaṭṭī-i Fārsī,* 4:3049, no. 32937. It could be added here that the "Shihāb-i Millah va Dīn" whom Amīr Ḥusaynī mentions in verse 54 was most likely Shihāb al-Dīn Abū Ḥafṣ ʿUmar al-Suhrawardī, to whom Ḥusaynī was connected through his own master Bahāʾ al-Dīn Zakarīyāʾ Multānī. Since Amīr Ḥusaynī's composition is the only independent long poem on the Qalandar-topos, it is useful to summarize the major themes here: indifference to both this world and the hereafter; acceptance of one's sins, and denunciation of one's acts of devotion; wandering; Qalandars as the repository of the secret of the creation and adorned with God's grace, the "cream" of creation; mirth and merrymaking, dance and ecstasy, wine-drinking, looking at beardless boys; freedom from hypocrisy, fraud, deception; dependence on love to the point of disregarding reason; the

only way to God being that of the Qalandars. It is worth noting here that the Ottoman Vāḥidī had access to Ḥusaynī's work and incorporated many of his verses in approximate Turkish translation into his *Menāḳıb,* though his debt to Ḥusaynī did not extend to a total reliance upon his text (Vāḥidī, 54, n. 40).

33. Professor J. T. P. De Bruijn is currently preparing an extensive study of the *Qalandarīyāt* in early Persian poetry (oral correspondence, May 1992).

34. Digby, 62 (n. 4) writes: "The growth and diffusion of groups of wandering Qalandars is attested by an anecdote in ʿAṭṭār's celebrated poem, the *Manṭiq al-ṭayr,* which was composed not later than 573/1177. An Arab, coming to ʿAjam (Iran and adjacent Persian-speaking areas), was amazed by the unfamiliar customs of the land. On his road he fell in with a band of shaven Qalandars, a people he had never seen before. He joined them, shaved his hair, and participated in various obscurely described but probably orgiastic experiences with them; but was maltreated, assaulted and robbed by them before he returned to his own land. The anecdote appears to indicate that groups of wandering Qalandars were a spectacle in Khurasan in the third quarter of the twelfth century; but had not then reached the Arab Middle East. They were also by that time characterized by wild and antinomian behavior similar to that found in the thirteenth-century anecdotes discussed in this paper, and had adopted the practice of shaving their eyebrows and facial hair."

In the text of Farīd al-Dīn Muḥammad ʿAṭṭār Nīshābūrī's *Manṭiq al-ṭayr* (ed. Sayyid Ṣādiq Gawharīn, 191–92), however, there is no sign that the Qalandars had shaved their heads, eyebrows, or facial hair or that the Arab for his part shaved his own hair when he joined them (the expression *ʿūr-sar,* "bareheaded," in line 3437 seems rather to refer to lack of headgear). The claim that the Arab "participated in . . . probably orgiastic experiences" with the Qalandars is equally baseless. The only possible evidence for this interpretation is the expression *gum shud mardīyash,* "he lost his manhood," in line 3435, which does, however, have other more innocuous connotations (for instance, loss of honor). The Qalandars did not maltreat, assault, and rob the Arab; instead, he lost money to one of them in straightforward gambling: *burd az-ū dar yak nadab,* "[the Qalandar] won from him in one bet." In support of the interpretation adopted here, see Ritter, 381, where the passage in question is summarized in German.

35. Suhrawardī, 66; German translation, 85 (9:23); an earlier German translation of the passage is supplied by Ritter, "Philologika XV," 14–16. English translations are found in various secondary studies (for instance, Trimingham, 267).

36. Aḥmad ibn ʿAlī al-Maqrīzī, *al-Mawāʿiẓ wa-al-iʿtibār bi-dhikr al-khiṭaṭ wa-al-āthār,* 4:301; ʿAbd al-Raḥmān ibn Aḥmad Jāmī, *Nafaḥāt al-uns min ḥaẓarāt al-quds,* ed. Mahdī Tawḥīdī'Pūr, 14–15. For other sources that quote from *ʿAwārif al-maʿārif,* see Köprülü 1, 298, n. 3.

37. For the date of *ʿAwārif al-maʿārif*'s composition, see Gramlich's introduction to his German translation of the work, 14–15. It is, of course, possible that the name Qalandar was not yet attached to members of Jamāl al-Dīn's circle at this early stage.

38. Meier, 512, thinks that al-Suhrawardī must have been describing an earlier stage of the Qalandarī movement.

39. Paul Rycaut, *The History of the Present State of the Ottoman Empire,* 260.

4. ASCETIC VIRTUOSI

1. Fārisī. In citing this work in the following discussion, page and line references refer to Yazıcı's and verse numbers to Zarrīnkūb's editions, respectively; thus 6.5/82 is page 6, line 5, in Yazıcı's text and verse 82 in Zarrīnkūb's. The title of the work is not given in the text. The author's pen-name, Khaṭīb Fārisī, appears on 6.5/82, 55.14/1068, 89.1/1746, and 90.3/1768. He gives the name of his *pīr* on 5.2/58. That he was born in 697/1297–98 can be deduced from his statement at the end of the work that he was fifty-one years of age when he completed his composition, 90.3/1768.

2. Khaṭīb Fārisī gives Jamāl al-Dīn's dates as 382/992–93 to 463/1070–71. As Bāyazīd is known to have died in the 260s/870s at the latest, more than a century before the alleged birth date of Jamāl al-Dīn, Fārisī clearly did not have a knack for historical accuracy. On Bāyazīd, see Helmut Ritter, "Abū Yazīd al-Bisṭāmī," in *EI,* 1:162–63; and Gerhard Böwering, "Besṭāmī, Bāyazīd," in *EIR,* 4:183–86.

3. Fārisī, 18.4/319–25.21/468; the parallels in the *Mirṣād* are documented by Zarrīnkūb in his notes to the text on 121–25. Naturally, it is impossible to reconstruct the origins of this use of common materials by Najm al-Dīn Rāzī and Khaṭīb Fārisī, though it is likely that the latter (or Jamāl al-Dīn himself) simply borrowed from the former.

4. See chapter 2, no. 21, for references on this *ḥadīth.*

5. All of the practices mentioned receive extended treatment in Jamāl al-Dīn's sacred biography. On dwelling in cemeteries, see especially 82–84/1609–1668, the section entitled *dalīl guftan-i Sayyid dar bāb-i ānkih dar gūristān nishastan[rā] martaba chīst* (in both Damascus and Damietta Jamāl al-Dīn resides only in cemeteries); on nakedness, 31.5–7/567–69, 32.10–14/593–97, 42.6/796; on silence, 33.2/607, 41.9/778, 42.6/796, 46.3/875, 80.2–3/1565–66, 80.16/1579, and 84 (whole page)/1646–63; on abstinence from food, 33.5–6/610–11 (eating weeds about once a week), 36.7–15/672–80 (rejection of "cooked"/other people's food), 37.20, 41.9/778, 42.5/795, 47.20–21/910–11; on keeping vigils, 41.9/778, 42.6/796; on the significance of hair, 32.5/588, especially the section called *dar ḥikmat va mawʿiẓah va taḥsīn:* 46.7/879 to 47.16/907.

6. Abū Bakr Iṣfahānī's miraculous deeds in Damascus are narrated on 47.18/908–53.15/1026.

7. The beard-producing miracle is also recorded as follows in Baṭṭūṭah, 1:61–63. Some time after Jamāl al-Dīn comes to Damietta and settles in its cemetery, he has a brief encounter with the magistrate (*qāḍī*) of the town, a certain Ibn al-ʿAmīd, who loses no time in reproving Jamāl al-Dīn for his innovation of shaving the beard. For his part, Jamāl al-Dīn declares the magistrate to be an ignoramus since, riding a mule in the cemetery, Ibn al-ʿAmīd is apparently unaware that the dead deserve as much respect as the living. When Ibn al-ʿAmīd retorts that shaving the beard is a graver offense, Jamāl al-Dīn answers, "Is this what you mean?" and, letting out a loud cry, produces a mighty black beard. At a second cry, this beard turns white and at a third disappears completely. After this miracle, Ibn al-ʿAmīd becomes a faithful follower of Jamāl al-Dīn and has a hospice (*zāwiyah*) built in his name, where Jamāl al-Dīn is buried upon his death.

8. The introductory section "On the Merits of Poverty" (*dar ṣifat-i faẓīlat-i faqr*) is on 6.7/85–8.11/126. For the emphasis on Muḥammad's choice of poverty,

see 3.2–4/17–19 and 6.12–7.11/89–105; on Jamāl al-Dīn as the king of poverty, see 10.18/172 and 11.13–15/190–92.

9. Qalandar, 130–32 (*majlis* 37). This work, which records the "oral discourses" (*malfūẓāt*) of the Chishtī master Naṣīr al-Dīn Chirāgh-i Dihlī (d. 757/1356), was composed after 754/1353; see Digby, 96, nn. 11 and 112. The anecdote that contains the epithet "walking library" may have been a stock item in Chishtī lore, since it also appears, with no mention of Jamāl al-Dīn's name, in a shorter version in the conversations of Naṣīr al-Dīn's master, Niẓām al-Dīn Awliyā᾽ (d. 725/1325); see Amīr Ḥasan Sijzī, *Favā᾽id al-fu᾽ād,* 3; English translation: *Nizam ad-Din Awliya: Morals for the Heart,* trans. Bruce B. Lawrence, 84.

10. For the story of Ḥamīd Qalandar's conversion to the path of Qalandars as a child as well as his own testimony of the value that he placed on his Qalandar allegiance, see Qalandar, 6; also Digby, 71–72. A recent discussion of the place of the *Khayr al-majālis* in Chishtī *malfūẓāt* literature appears in Carl W. Ernst, *Eternal Garden: Mysticism, History, and Politics at a South Asian Sufi Center,* 68–71, where the question of Ḥamīd's scholarship is also addressed.

11. Shams al-Dīn Muḥammad al-Jazarī recorded in his history that he saw several fascicles of a Qur᾽ānic *tafsīr* in Jamāl al-Dīn's own handwriting; see Dhahabī, 398 (al-Dhahabī died in 748/1348 or 752/1352–53); relying on al-Dhahabī, Ṣafadī, 293 (al-Ṣafadī died in 764/1363); Nuʿaymī, 2:210–12 (al-Nuʿaymī died in 927/1520–21). For Shams al-Dīn, Muḥammad al-Jazarī, see Carl Brockelmann, *Geschichte der Arabischen Litteratur,* Suppl. 2:33 and 45; cf. A. S. Bazmee Ansari, "Al-Djazarī," in *EI,* 2:522–23.

12. Dhahabī, 397; Ṣafadī, 292; Khaṭīb (written in 683/1284–85), 51b.

13. Khaṭīb, 51b.

14. The quotation is from Shams al-Dīn Abū ʿAbd Allāh Muḥammad ibn ʿUthmān al-Dimashqī al-Dhahabī, *al-ʿIbar fī khabar man ghabar,* ed. Abū Hājir Muḥammad al-Saʿīd ibn Bisyūnī Zaghlūl, 3:357. See also Ibn al-Kathīr, ʿImād al-Dīn Ismāʿīl ibn ʿUmar (ca. 700–774/1300–1373), *al-Bidāyah wa-al-nihāyah,* 13:307; Nuʿaymī, 2:197; and Ibn al-ʿImād, ʿAbd al-Ḥayy ibn Aḥmad, *Shadharāt al-dhahab fī akhbār man dhahab* (up to 1080/1670), 5:389.

15. Khaṭīb reports the young ascetic's name as Garūbad. Qalandar, 131, alone among the sources, attributes Jamāl al-Dīn's conversion to an encounter he had with a group known as "iron-wearers." Though rather weak, this piece of evidence serves to direct attention to the fact that iron-wearing Ḥaydarīs could indeed have exercised influence on Jamāl al-Dīn's turn to asceticism.

16. Fārisī, 30–34/546–629. Dhahabī, 397; Ṣafadī, 292; and Nuʿaymī, 2:210–12 also mention an ʿUthmān Kūhī al-Fārisī along with Jalāl Darguzīnī in this story.

17. Baṭṭūṭah, 1:61–63; Ebū'l-Ḥayr Rūmī, *Ṣaltuḳnāme,* ed. Fahir İz, 363b–69a; Muḥammad Qāsim Hindū'Shāh Astarābādī, known as Firishtah, *Gulshan-i Ibrāhīmī,* usually called *Tārīkh-i Firishtah,* 2:407–8; Qāsim Ghanī, *Baḥṣ dar āṣār va afkār va aḥvāl-i Ḥāfiẓ,* 2:442–43.

18. Significantly, this anecdote is not mentioned in Jamāl al-Dīn's sacred biography, *Manāqib,* written by one of his later followers. The fact that the sources do not agree on the timing and place of the anecdote is further reason to suspect its authenticity. Moreover, the same motif is found in other hagiographical material: essentially the same story, without the episode of shaving and with a different ending, is reported about a certain Shaqrān ibn ʿUbayd Allāh in one early seventh/thirteenth-century Arabic source and two early ninth/fifteenth-century ones; see Christopher Schurman Taylor, "The Cult of the Saints in Late Medieval Egypt," 158–59.

19. The presence of a hospice of Qalandars in Damietta is reported in Baṭṭūṭah, 1:61. Apart from the sources mentioned in the above discussion, there are some other, more oblique, references to Jamāl al-Dīn in the sources. If a brief note in Ḥamd Allāh Mustawfī Qazvīnī, *The Tārīkh-i Guzīdah* (730/1329–30), ed. Edward G. Browne, 1:790, indeed refers to Jamāl al-Dīn Sāvī and not to some other shaykh called Jamāl al-Dīn, then the date of his death was 4 Shawwāl 651/ 27 November 1253. In addition, in his *Zahr al-ʿarīsh fī aḥkām (or taḥrīm) al-hashīsh,* Muḥammad ibn Bahādur al-Zarkashī (d. 794/1392) mentions Aḥmad [*sic*] al-Sāwajī al-Qalandarī, along with Shaykh Ḥaydar, as the "discoverer" of hashish; see chapter 2, n. 16.

20. On the town Zāvah, see Dihkhudā, s.v. "Zāvah."

21. Only Muʿīn al-Dīn Muḥammad Zamajī Isfizārī, *Rawẓāt al-jannāt fī awṣāf madīnah Harāt* (written 897/1491–92), ed. S. M. Kāẓim Imām, 229, writes that Ḥaydar traveled from country to country; other sources are silent on this issue.

22. Ludwig Adamec, ed., *Historical Gazetteer of Iran,* vol. 2, *Meshed and Northeastern Iran,* 653–55.

23. The following sources cite 617 or 618/1220–22 as Quṭb al-Dīn's death date and also report that he was a centenarian at his death: al-ʿUqbarī (possibly d. 690/1291), *Kitāb al-sawāniḥ,* in Rosenthal, 51–53; Qazwīnī, 382–83; Ḥamd Allāh Mustawfī, *Tārīkh-i Guzīdah,* 792–93; idem, *The Geographical Part of the Nuzhat-al-Qulūb Composed by Ḥamd-Allāh Mustawfī of Qazwīn in 740 (1340),* ed. Guy Le Strange, 151–54; Giyāṣ al-Dīn ibn Humām al-Dīn Khvāndamīr, *Tārīkh-i ḥabīb al-siyar fī akhbār al-bashar,* ed. by Jalāl al-Dīn Humāʾī, 3:332; Karbalāʾī 1:444. Dawlat'Shāh ibn ʿAlāʾ al-Dawlah Bakhtī'Shāh al-Ghāzī al-Samarqandī, *Tadhkirat al-shuʿarāʾ,* ed. Edward G. Browne, 192, however, claims that Quṭb al-Dīn died in 597/1200–1201 or 602/1205–6, while Faṣīḥ al-Dīn Aḥmad ibn Muḥammad, known as Faṣīḥ al-Khvāfī, *Mujmal-i Faṣīḥī* (up to 845/1441–42), ed. Maḥmūd Farrukh, 2:288, has him die in 613/1216–17. Zāvah was burned down and its inhabitants massacred by the Mongols in 617/1220; see ʿAlāʾ al-Dīn ʿAtā Malik Juvaynī, *The History of the World-Conqueror* [*Tārīkh-i Jahān'gushā*], trans. John Andrew Boyle, 1:144.

24. Faṣīḥ al-Khvāfī, *Mujmal-i Faṣīḥī,* 2:288, cites Quṭb al-Dīn's full name as Quṭb al-Dīn ibn Tīmūr ibn Abū Bakr ibn Sulṭān'Shāh ibn Sulṭān Khān al-Sālūrī. Dawlat'Shāh, *Tadhkirat al-shuʿarāʾ,* 192, claims that Ḥaydar was a descendant of the sultans of Turkistan through his father, Shāhvar. In his extended translation into Chagatay of Jāmī's *Nafaḥāt al-uns,* ʿAlī Şīr Nevāʾī also reports that Quṭb al-Dīn Ḥaydar was the son of a sultan of Turkistan; see *Nesāyimü'l-maḥabbe min şemāyimi'l-fütüvve* (comp. 901/1495–96), ed. Kemal Eraslan, 383–84. Karbalāʾī, 1:444, repeats the report about Quṭb al-Dīn Ḥaydar's Turkish descent. Isfizārī, *Rawẓāt al-jannāt,* 216, notes that he saw the genealogy of Quṭb al-Dīn Ḥaydar recorded in the *Nasabnāmah* of Qāẓī Shams al-Dīn Muḥammad-i Zūzan; this work, however, is not extant; see the editor's note in the *Rawẓāt al-jannāt,* 217, n. 4. The possibility that Quṭb al-Dīn Ḥaydar had special appeal among Turks is raised by the testimony of the famous cosmographer and geographer Zakarīyāʾ al-Qazwīnī who saw (roughly half a century after Quṭb al-Dīn's death, presumably in Zāvah) Turkish slaves of extreme beauty, barefooted and dressed in felt; he was told that these were Ḥaydar's followers (Qazwīnī, 382–83).

25. Later sources on Quṭb al-Dīn Ḥaydar derive their information from the earlier ones cited above without in any way adding to them; see, for instance, Aḥmad Amīn Rāzī, *Haft iqlīm,* ed. Javād Fāẓil, 2:188; Zayn al-ʿAbidīn Shīrvānī,

Būstān al-siyāḥah, ed. Sayyid ʿAbd Allāh Mustawfī, 219; and Maʿṣūm ʿAlī'Shāh ibn Raḥmat ʿAlī Niʿmat Allāhī al-Shīrāzī, *Ṭarāʾiq al-ḥaqāʾiq,* ed. Muḥammad Jaʿfar Maḥjūb, 2:642. Still other sources confuse Quṭb al-Dīn Ḥaydar with a certain Sulṭān Mīr Ḥaydar Tūnī, also known as Quṭb al-Dīn, who lived in Tabrīz and died there in 830/1426–27; see, for instance, Nūr Allāh ibn Sayyid Sharīf Ḥusaynī Marʿashī Shushtarī, *Majālis al-muʾminīn,* 36 and 267; and Dihkhudā, s.v. "Quṭb al-Dīn Tūnī" and "Ḥaydar, Quṭb al-Dīn." Other sources that confuse the two Quṭb al-Dīns are noted in Ḥusayn Mīr Jaʿfarī, "Ḥaydarī va Niʿmatī," *Āyandah* 9 (1362sh/1983): 742–45 (earlier English version: "The Ḥaydarī-Niʿmatī Conflicts in Iran," *Iranian Studies* 12 [1979]: 61–142). The most reliable account on Tūnī appears to be that of Karbalāʾī, 1:467–68. The *Dīvān-i Quṭb al-Dīn Ḥaydar* reported in Ibn Yūsuf Shīrāzī, *Fihrist-i Kitābkhānah-i Madrasah-i ʿĀlī-i Sipahsālār,* entry 564, to be in the Library of Madrasah-i Sipahsālār would appear to belong to Quṭb al-Dīn Ḥaydar Tūnī; see Saʿīd Nafīsī, *Justujū dar aḥvāl va āṣār-i Farīd al-Dīn ʿAṭṭār Nīshābūrī,* mīm/dāl-mīm/ha, where, however, Nafīsī confuses the two Quṭb al-Dīns.

26. Qalandar, 174–76, makes Quṭb al-Dīn Ḥaydar a disciple of Shaykh Luqmān, while Nevāʾī, *Nesāyimü-l-maḥabbe,* 383–84; Karbalāʾī, 1:597; and *Vilāyet-nāme: Manāḳıb-i Ḥacı Bektāş-i Velī,* ed. Abdülbaki Gölpınarlı, 9–11, portray him as a follower of Aḥmed Yesevī. For references on Shaykh Luqmān, see Meier, 411–12. A concise account on Yesevī is Mehmed Fuad Köprülü, "Aḥmed Yesevī," in *İslam Ansiklopedisi,* 1:210–15. This article contains improvements over Köprülü's earlier study on Yesevī, *Türk Edebīyātında İlk Mutaṣavvıflar.* The view that Quṭb al-Dīn Ḥaydar was a disciple of Jamāl al-Dīn Sāvī (see, for instance, Trimingham, 39; and Digby, 82) is unfounded and should be rejected.

27. Khvāndamīr, *Tārīkh-i ḥabīb al-siyar,* 2:332. The *rubāʿī* in question reads as follows: "rindī dīdam nishastah bar khushk-i zamīn / nah kufr u nah islām u nah dunyā u nah dīn / nah ḥaqq nah ḥaqīqat nah ṭarīqat nah yaqīn / andar dū jahān ki rā buvad zahrah-i īn." This same *rubāʿī,* with few changes, is attributed to Fakhr al-Dīn al-Rāzī (d. 606/1209) in Karbalāʾī, 1:444; he is said to have composed it for Bābā Faraj (on whom see Dihkhudā, s.v. "Bābā Faraj"). On the same page, al-Qurrāʾī notes that the quatrain also appears in some collections attributed to Khayyām (d. 526/1131); see, for instance, ʿUmar ibn Ibrāhīm Nīshābūrī, known as Khayyām, *Tarānahā-yi Khayyām,* ed Ṣadiq Hidāyat, 102, no. 104. In this connection, it is worth noting that Shāh-i Sanjān was sufficiently close to Quṭb al-Dīn Ḥaydar both in time and in space to make the attribution of the above quatrain to him a real possibility. On Shāh-i Sanjān, see Dihkhudā, s.v., "Shāh-i Sanjān," and the list of references cited therein. To this list one should add Qalandar, 174–76, where, significantly, it is reported that both Ḥaydar-i Zāvah and Shāh-i Sanjān were among the followers of Shaykh Luqmān.

28. Dawlat'Shāh, *Tadhkirat al-shuʿarāʾ,* 192. It is not known if ʿAṭṭār really composed a *Ḥaydarnāmah* at all. Ritter, 139, writes, "Dass ʿAṭṭār ein *Ḥaidarnāma* verfasst hat, steht durch sein selbsterzeugnis im *Lisān al-ġaib* fest," yet in his later article "ʿAṭṭār," in *EI,* 1:754, he includes *Lisān al-ghayb* among a group of apocryphal works that came to be attributed to ʿAṭṭār but were certainly not composed by him. Benedikt Reinert, "ʿAṭṭār, Farīd-al-Dīn," in *EIR,* 3:25, agrees with this last judgment without touching on the *Ḥaydarnāmah*. Nafīsī, *Justujū,* 97 and 110, n. 16, merely notes that the earliest source to attribute a *Ḥaydarnāmah* to ʿAṭṭār is Dawlat'Shāh's *Tadhkirat al-shuʿarāʾ,* that Kātib Çelebi also mentions a *Ḥaydarnāmah* (see Muṣṭafā ibn ʿAbdullāh, known as Kātib Çelebi, *Kashf al-*

ẓunūn, ed. Şerefettin Yaltkaya and Kilisli Rifat Bilge, 1:694, where the name of the author is not given), and that no such *Ḥaydarnāmah* has come to light. Badīʿ al-Zamān Furūzānfar, *Sharḥ-i aḥvāl va taḥlīl-i āsār-i Shaykh Farīd al-Dīn Muḥammad ʿAṭṭār Nīshābūrī,* 31 and 76, notes that Dawlat'Shāh's entry on ʿAṭṭār is not trustworthy on the whole and rules out the possibility that ʿAṭṭār could have written a *Ḥaydarnāmah.* Ṣafā, *Tārīkh-i Adabīyāt dar Īrān,* 1:861–62, who relies only on Nafīsī, has nothing new to say on the topic. Cf. Munzavī, *Fihrist-i nuskhahā-yi khaṭṭī-i Fārsī,* 4:2777, no. 29315.

29. Qalandar, 176.

30. Al-ʿUqbarī, *Kitāb al-sawāniḥ,* as reported in Rosenthal, 51–53. It is here recorded, on the authority of a certain Shaykh Jaʿfar ibn Muḥammad al-Shīrāzī whom al-ʿUqbarī met in Tustar in 658/1260, that the use of hashish as an intoxicant was first "discovered" by Shaykh Ḥaydar while he led the life of a recluse in a small *zāwiyah* situated on a mountain between Nīshāpūr and Zāvah in Khorasan. This account of the discovery of hashish is repeated in summary in the *Zahr al-ʿarīsh fī aḥkām (or taḥrīm) al-hashīsh* of Muḥammad ibn Bahādur al-Zarkashī, 170, with the additional information that the discovery took place around the year 550/1155–56.

31. Qazwīnī, 382.

32. Sijzī, *Favāʾid al-fuʾād,* 12; English version: *Morals for the Heart,* 101–2, also 360. The Persian edition reads "Ḥaydar'zādah" instead of "Ḥaydar-i Zāvah." The same reading appears in the editions of Ḥamd Allāh Mustawfī, *Tārīkh-i Guzīdah;* and Khvāndamīr, *Tārīkh-i ḥabīb al-siyar,* 3:332, while the editor of Qalandar, 176, opts for the reading "Ḥaydar-i Zāviyah." All these are here corrected to "Ḥaydar-i Zāvah." Cf. Digby, 105, n. 76.

33. *Velāyetnāme-i Otman Baba* survives in two manuscripts: (1) Abdāl; (2) Ms. Adnan Ötüken İl Halk Kütüphanesi (Ankara), no. 495 (dated 1316/1899, copyist Ḥasan Tebrīzī). For a summary of its contents, see Ḥüseyin Fehmi, "Otman Baba ve Vilāyetnāmesi," *Türk Yurdu* 5 (1927): 239–44 (Fehmi uses ms. 1, which he incorrectly dates to 1073/1663); and Ahmet Yaşar Ocak, *Bektaşi Menākıbnāmelerinde İslam Öncesi İnanç Motifleri,* 16–17 (Ocak uses ms. 2). A selection from the work (ms. 1, fols. 10b–15a) appears in Fahir İz, *Eski Türk Edebiyatında Nesir: XIV. Yüzyıldan XIX. Yüzyıl Ortasına Kadar Yazmalardan Seçilmiş Metinler,* 330–36. The date of composition appears in Abdāl, fol. 129a.

34. Otman Baba's name is discussed in Abdāl on fol. 21b and his arrival and early activities in Anatolia on fols. 9b–11b; the dates of his birth and death are recorded on fols. 122b–123b. The date of his death also appears in Yemīnī, 83. Also see Ocak, 99–102 (relying on ms. 1).

35. On Sufi views of the relationship between sainthood and prophecy, see Hermann Landolt, "Walāyah," in *The Encyclopedia of Religion,* 15:316–23, esp. 321–22; and Bernd Radtke, "The Concept of *Wilāya* in Early Sufism," in *Classical Persian Sufism: From Its Origins to Rumi,* ed. Leonard Lewisohn, 483–96; also Chodkiewicz, *Le sceau des saints.*

36. Abdāl, fols. 5b–6b.

37. Ibid., fol. 32b. The relevant portion of Qur'ān 7:172, adopted with slight changes from Abdullah Yusuf Ali's translation, *The Meaning of the Glorious Qurʾān* (London: Nadim and Co., 1975), 227–28, reads: "When your Lord drew forth from the children of Adam, from their loins, their descendants, and made them testify concerning themselves (saying): 'Am I not your Lord?' they said: 'Yes, we testify.' " Creative interpretation of this verse was a feature of Sufi

thought from its earliest phases; see Gerhard Böwering, *The Mystical Vision of Existence in Classical Islam: The Qurʾānic Hermeneutics of the Ṣūfī Sahl At-Tustarī (d. 283/896)*, 153–57.

38. Abdāl, fols. 8a and 50b.

39. Ibid., fol. 6b. On this *ḥadīth qudsī, awliyāʾī taḥta qibābī (qābāʾī) lā yaʿrifuhum ghayrī*, see Furūzānfar, *Aḥādīth-i Masnavī*, 52, no. 131; and Nūr al-Dīn ʿAbd al-Raḥmān Isfarāyinī, *Kāshif al-asrār*, ed. Hermann Landolt, 104, n. 144.

40. Abdāl, fols. 6b, 23a–b (on the "people of hospices"), 20a, 21b, 54b, 57b (on rejection of gifts).

41. For references on Sulṭān Şücāʿ and Ḥācī Bektāş, see chapter 5, n. 62, and chapter 6, n. 71, respectively.

42. Ḥācī Bektāş and Sulṭān Şücāʿ are mentioned in Abdāl, fol. 7b. On Bāyezīd Baba and Müʾmin Dervīş, see fol. 28b ff; on Maḥmūd Çelebi, fols. 112b–113a.

43. Ibid., fols. 11b and 32b.

44. Ibid., fols. 10b and 19b–21b.

5. DERVISH GROUPS IN FULL BLOOM, 1200–1500

1. Dhahabī, 398; idem, *al-ʿIbar fī khabar man ghabar*, ed. Ṣalāḥ al-Dīn Munajjid, 5:141–42; Ṣafadī, 293.

2. Ibn al-Kathīr, *al-Bidāyah wa-al-nihāyah*, 13:196; Nuʿaymī, 2:212. *Vilāyet-nāme*, 9–11, also refers to a period of captivity in Quṭb al-Dīn Ḥaydar's life. According to this work, Quṭb al-Dīn was held a prisoner by the "unbelievers of Badakhshān" (in present-day northeast Afghanistan), presumably the Ismāʿīlīs, and was saved from captivity by Ḥācī Bektāş.

3. Ibn al-Fūṭī ʿAbd al-Razzāq ibn Aḥmad, *al-Ḥawādith al-jāmiʿah* (Baghdad, 1351/1932), 342, as quoted in Michel M. Mazzaoui, *The Origins of the Safawids: Šīʿism, Ṣūfism and the Ġulāt*, 43, n. 3; also Meier, 500. A somewhat different version of the same story is found in ʿUbayd-i Zākānī, *Hajvīyāt va hazlīyāt*, 39; see also Edward Granville Browne, *A Literary History of Persia*, 3:251; and George Morrison, Julian Baldick, and Shafīʿī Kadkanī, *History of Persian Literature from the Beginning of the Islamic Period to the Present Day*, 66.

4. On al-Ḥarīrī, see note 17 below.

5. Ibn al-Kathīr, *al-Bidāyah*, 1:344; al-Maqrīzī, *al-Mawāʿiẓ*, 4:301–2.

6. Nuʿaymī, 2:209–10. On Qalandars and Ḥaydarīs in Damascus, see also Pouzet, 228–29.

7. Baṭṭūṭah, 1:61. Takrūr was the name given in particular to present-day Mauritania and Mali, though it was also used more generally to denote the Saharan region stretching from the Nile to the Atlantic; see Chouki El Hamel, "Fatḥ ash-Shakūr: Hommes de lettres, disciples et enseignement dans le Takrūr du XVIᵉ au début du XIXᵉ siècle," 74–75.

8. Al-Maqrīzī, *al-Mawāʿiẓ*, 4:301–2.

9. Mujīr al-Dīn al-ʿUlaymī al-Ḥanbalī, *al-Uns al-jalīl bi-taʾrīkh al-quds wa-al-khalīl*, 2:413–14. *See also* Huda Lutfi, *Al-Quds al-Mamlūkiyya: A History of Mamlūk Jerusalem Based on the Ḥaram Documents*, 115 (Zāwiyat al-Shaykh Ibrāhīm).

10. Jawbarī, fol. 18a, lines 4–6. On al-Jawbarī, see Brockelmann, *Geschichte der Arabischen Litteratur*, 1:655 (497) and Suppl. 1:910. A description of the contents of the work appears in Clifford Edmund Bosworth, *The Mediaeval Islamic Underworld: The Banū Sāsān in Arabic Society and Literature*, 1:106–18. I

follow Brockelmann in giving al-Jawbarī's personal name as ʿAbd al-Raḥmān; the Süleymaniye manuscript records it as ʿAbd al-Raḥīm.

11. Jawbarī, fol. 17a. This manuscript copy reads "Rifāʿīyah" instead of "Ḥaydarīyah" (followed by Bosworth, *The Mediaeval Islamic Underworld*, 113), yet the French translation of *Kashf al-asrār*, based on more copies, gives the name "Ḥaydarīyah": *Le voile arraché: L'autre visage de l'Islam*, trans. René R. Khawam, 83.

12. Taqī al-Dīn Aḥmad ibn Taymīyah, *Majmūʿat al-rasāʾil wa-al-masāʾil*, 1:33 and 64–65. Cf. Muhammad Umar Memon, *Ibn Taimīya's Struggle against Popular Religion, with an Annotated Translation of His* Kitāb iqtidāʾ aṣ-ṣirāṭ al-mustaqīm mukhālafat aṣḥāb al-jahīm, 61–62 and 65–66.

13. Muḥammad ibn Shākir al-Kutubī, *Fawāt al-wafayāt*, vol. 3, ed. Iḥsān ʿAbbās, 36–37; and Meier, 505–6, where the poem is given in German translation.

14. I read *julnak/jalnak/jilnak*, not *jilink* (Persian *jiling*, "a kind of silken stuff") as Meier does, and take this word to be an arabization of the Turkish *gönlek*, "shirt." The reading *jilink* does not make much sense in this context. The text reads: "nalbisu ʿiwaḍa hādhā al-kattān julnak min ṣūf al-khirfān aw dalaq aw nuṣbiḥu ʿuryān."

15. Vāʿiẓ Kāshifī, *Rashaḥāt ʿayn al-ḥayāt*, 2:460–61.

16. *Kitāb alf laylah wa-laylah*, ed. Muhsin Mahdi, 137; English translation: *The Arabian Nights*, trans. Husain Haddawy, 76 ("The Story of the Porter and the Three Ladies"). To the literary evidence documented above, one could also add Abū Ḥafṣ ʿUmar al-Suhrawardī's (d. 632/1234) discussion on Qalandars in his celebrated Sufi manual *ʿAwārif al-maʿārif* (Suhrawardī, 66), discussed in chapter 3 above. The Qalandars survived in Egypt well into the tenth/sixteenth century; see, for instance, Michael M. Winter, *Society and Religion in Early Ottoman Egypt: Studies in the Writings of ʿAbd al-Wahhāb al-Shaʿrānī*, 121, n. 52.

17. For a list of references on al-Ḥarīrī, see Meier, 507, n. 226. See also Köprülü 1, 301 (continuation of n. 2 from 300); Louis Massignon, "Ḥarīriyya," in *EI*, 3:222; Pouzet, 220–21; Aflākī, 2:640–41 (4/32), 2:677–78 (4/79); and Jawbarī, fols. 18a–19b. On other related dervish movements in Damascus, notably the *muwallahūn*, see Pouzet, 222–26. On Aḥmad al-Badawī, see K. Vollers and E. Littmann, "Aḥmad al-Badawī," in *EI*, 1:280–81. The most important compilation on his life is ʿAbd al-Ṣamad Zayn al-Dīn, *al-Jawāhir al-sanīyah fī al-karāmāt al-aḥmadīyah*, repeatedly printed; two modern studies on him are Saʿīd ʿAbd al-Fattāḥ ʿĀshūr, *al-Sayyid Aḥmad al-Badawī: Shaykh wa tariqatuh;* and ʿAbd al-Ḥalīm Maḥmūd, *al-Sayyid Aḥmad al-Badawī*. For a study of his cult in contemporary Egypt, see Edward B. Reeves, *The Hidden Government: Ritual, Clientalism, and Legitimation in Northern Egypt*. Cf. Alfred Le Châtelier, *Les confréries musulmanes du Hedjaz*, 161–82.

18. On Aḥmad al-Rifāʿī, see D. S. Margoliouth, "Al-Rifāʿī," in *The Encyclopedia of Islam*, first edition, 6:1156–57; the standard source on his life is Taqī al-Dīn ʿAbd al-Raḥmān al-Wāsiṭī, *Tiryāq al-muḥibbīn fī ṭabaqāt khirqat al-mashāyikh al-ʿārifīn*. That Rifāʿīs wore iron collars is attested in Ibn Taymīyah, *Majmūʿat al-rasāʾil*, 1:131–154. On Rifāʿīyah in Damascus during the seventh/thirteenth century, see Pouzet, 227; on Rifāʿīyah in general, see Trimingham, 37–40.

19. In this connection, it is possible to speculate that the initial Mongol intolerance forced the Qalandars to emigrate to other Islamic lands and generally discouraged them from entering Mongol territory. Muḥammad al-Khaṭīb, for

instance, writes, naturally with a good deal of exaggeration occasioned by his extreme hostility toward "heretics" (*zanādiqah*): "if it were not for the might of Mongol armies, practically all regions of the world would have been filled with these bands of irreligion" (Khaṭīb, 53b). More telling is the execution of a group of Qalandars at the orders of Hülegü in Ḥarrān in 658/1259–60; see chapter 1.

20. Fakhr al-Dīn Ibrāhīm Hamadānī ʿIrāqī, *Kulliyāt-i dīvān-i Shaykh Fakhr al-Dīn Ibrāhīm Hamadānī mutakhallaṣ biʾʿIrāqī,* ed. M. Darvīsh, "Muqaddimah-i jāmiʿ-i dīvān," 21–23.

21. Aflākī, 2:631 (4/28).

22. Rosenthal, 51.

23. Tavakkulī ibn Ismāʿīl, Ibn al-Bazzāz, *Ṣafvat al-ṣafāʾ* (Bombay, 1329/1911), 63; and Rashīd al-Dīn Faẓl Allāh, *Geschichte der Ilḫāne Abaġa bis Gaiḫatu 1265–95* (s'Gravenhage, 1957), 47 and 56, as cited in Hanna Sohrweide, "Der Sieg der Safaviden in Persien u. seine Rückwirkung auf die Schiiten Anatoliens im 16. Jh.," *Der Islam* 41 (1965): 103–4.

24. Tavakkulī ibn Ismāʿīl, Ibn al-Bazzāz, *Ṣafvat al-ṣafāʾ*, 31, as cited in Sohrweide, "Der Sieg der Safaviden in Persien," 103; also Meier, 498, n. 165; and Jean Aubin, "Shaykh Ibrāhīm Zāhid Gīlānī (1218?–1301)," *Turcica* 21–23 (1991): 41–43. Sohrweide notes that Shaykh Ṣafī too despised Qalandars, referring to *Ṣafvat al-ṣafāʾ*, 120, 214, and 258.

25. Khaṭīb, 52a–b. Awḥad al-Dīn Kirmānī himself was familiar with Qalandars; see Meier, 500, n. 179.

26. Abū Khālid is reported in al-ʿUqbarī, *Kitāb al-sawāniḥ,* as cited in Rosenthal, 51–53; and Ḥājjī Mubārak in Aflākī, 1:215 (3/123) and 467–68 (3/437).

27. Baṭṭūṭah, 3:79–80.

28. The text of Tāj al-Dīn ibn Bahā al-Dīn Jāmī (Pūr-i Bahā)'s work entitled *Kārnāma-yi awqāf* is given in transliteration and German translation in Birgitt Hoffmann, "Von falschen Asketen und 'unfrommen' Stiftungen," in *Proceedings of the First European Conference of Iranian Studies Held in Turin, September 7th–11th, 1987 by the Societas Iranologica Europaea,* part 2, *Middle and New Iranian Studies,* ed. Gherardo Gnoli and Antonio Panaino, 409–85 (text on 422–83). The description of the dervish and his young companion is on 444–45 (verses 130–37). Hoffmann mistakenly thinks that the beardless boy is the dervish's son, even though Pūr-i Bahā explicitly refers to the boy as the Ḥaydarī dervish's "witness" (*shāhid;* verse 133). I thank Professor J. T. P. de Bruijn for bringing the *Kārnāma-yi awqāf* to my attention.

29. Qazwīnī, 382–83.

30. "[Bābā Resūl] had gone to Iran along with others who were exiled from Anatolia during the campaign of Temür and had remained there. After a long period of religious education in those lands, he wanted [to join a] a Sufi order, *ṭarīḳat,* and became an Abdāl by spending many months and years at the *zāviyah* of Ḳuṭbeddīn Ḥaydar" (Ḥalvacıbaşızāde Maḥmūd Ḥulvī, *Lemeẓāt-i ḥulvīye ez lemeʿāt-i ʿulvīye,* Ms. Süleymaniye Kütüphanesi, Halet Efendi 281 [undated], fol. 186b).

31. Karbalāʾī, 1:467–68, where, however, Tūnī is said to be a Qalandar; and Shushtarī, *Majālis al-muʾminīn,* 36 and 267. For two differing views on the Ḥaydarīs of Tabrīz and the later Ḥaydarī-Niʿmatī conflict in major cities of Iran, see Zarrīnkūb, 85–87; and Mīr Jaʿfarī, "Ḥaydarī va Niʿmatī," 745ff.

32. Tācīzāde Saʿdī Çelebi, *Münşeʾāt,* ed. Necati Lugal and Adnan Erzi, 28; Mīr Jaʿfarī, "Ḥaydarī va Niʿmatī," 746. The person called Niʿmat Ḥaydarī, who

was responsible for bringing about the unpleasant incident that the poet Jāmī had to suffer through in Baghdad on his return trip from pilgrimage in 877–78/1472–74, also defies further identification, though in this case it is at least clear that, like the followers of Quṭb al-Dīn Ḥaydar, he had an unusually long moustache; see Vāʿiẓ Kāshifī, *Rashaḥāt ʿayn al-ḥayāt* 1:257–58; and Köprülü 1, 477.

33. Meier, 509 (based on the *Mazārāt-i Kirmān* of Miḥrābī, ed. Ḥusayn Kūhī Kirmānī [Tehran, 1330], 54–60; and Faṣīḥ al-Khvāfī, *Mujmal-i Faṣīḥī,* 3:147).

34. Jean Aubin, "Un santon quhistānī de l'époque timouride," *Revue des Etudes Islamiques* 35 (1967): 208; Meier, 510, n. 241. Aubin is quoting, without page references, from ʿAlī b. Maḥmūd Abīvardī Kūrānī's *Rawẓat al-sālikīn,* a biography of the Naqshbandī ʿAlāʾ al-Dīn Muḥammad Ābīzhī (d. 892/1487).

35. ʿAbd al-Ḥusayn Navāʾī, *Asnād va mukātabāt-i tārīkhī-i Īrān az Timūr tā Shāh Ismāʿīl,* 410–11; Meier, 505; n. 215.

36. Jāmī, *Nafaḥāt al-uns,* 14–15. It should be noted, however, that Jāmī bases his discussion mainly on al-Suhrawardī's *ʿAwārif al-maʿārif.* Further, see Najm al-Dīn ʿAbd Allāh ibn Muḥammad Rāzī "Dāyah," *The Path of God's Bondsmen from Origin to Return,* trans. Hamid Algar, index, s.v. "qalandar."

37. For the history of Qalandars in Iran during the Ṣafavid period and beyond, see Iskandar Bag Munshī, *History of Shāh ʿAbbās the Great,* trans. Roger M. Savory, 1:195; Adam Olearius, *Vermehrte Newe Beschreibung der Muscowitischen und Persischen Reyse,* ed. Dieter Lohmeier, 685; Raphael Du Mans, *Estat de la Perse en 1660,* ed. Ch. Schefer, 216; Muḥammad Ṭāhir Naṣrābādī, *Taẕkirah-i Naṣrābādī,* ed. Vaḥīd Dastgirdī, 264 (Bābā Sulṭān Qalandar, on whom see also Meier, 509, n. 2); Maʿṣūm ʿAlī'Shāh, *Ṭarāʾiq al-ḥaqāʾiq,* 2:354, quoting from *Riyāẓ al-siyāḥah* (comp. 1237/1821–22) of Zayn al-ʿĀbidīn ibn Iskandar Shīrvānī; the German translation of this passage appears in Meier, 510. One should also consult Gramlich, 1:70–82, who attempts to trace the early history of present-day Khāksār dervishes in Iran; cf. Zarrīnkūb, 92ff.

38. On Laʿl Shāhbāz, see Baranī, 67–68; Ghulām Sarvar Lāhūrī, *Khazīnat al-aṣfiyāʾ,* 2:46–47; Rizvi, 306 (relying on the *Maʿārij al-vilāyah* of Ghulām Muʿīn al-Dīn ʿAbd Allāh Khvashgī); Digby, 70–71, 78, 100, 102 (relying on Baranī, 67–68; and *Taẕkirah-i mashāʾikh-i Sivistān,* ed. S. H. Rashdī [Mihran, 1974], 205); Gramlich, 1:78 (note 48, relying on Lāhūrī, *Khazīnat al-aṣfiyāʾ,* 2:46–47); Zarrīnkūb, 89; Meier, 508–9; and N. B. G. Qazi, *Lal Shahbaz Qalandar: ʿUthman Marwandi,* where a few Persian poems attributed to Laʿl Shāhbāz are reproduced (39–44). There is also a pamphlet entitled *Qalandar Lal Shahbaz* published by the Department of Public Relations, Government of Sind, which is not devoid of interest.

39. See Nizami, 295; Rizvi, 304; and Digby, 63, 84–85. All three scholars rely on the *Akhbār al-akhyār fī asrār al-abrār* (comp. 999/1590–91) of ʿAbd al-Ḥaqq ibn Sayf al-Dīn al-Turk al-Dihlavī (d. 1052/1642–43); Rizvi also utilizes the *Mirʾāt al-asrār* (comp. 1065/1654) of ʿAbd al-Raḥmān al-Chishtī, Ms. British Library, for which see Charles Rieu, *Catalogue of the Persian Manuscripts in the British Museum,* 1:359b. To these, one could add the *Uṣūl al-maqṣūd* of Turāb ʿAlī Kākōravī (d. 1275/1858), as cited in Storey, 1035–37, no. 1378 (2).

40. See Khaliq Ahmad Nizami, "Abū ʿAlī Qalandar, Šaraf-al-Dīn Pānīpatī," in *EIR,* 1:258; Rizvi, 305; and Digby, 100–102.

41. When Bahāʾ al-Dīn refused to give alms to a group of Qalandars, they started to hurl bricks at the door of his *khānqāh;* see Digby, 87; and Nizami, 295. A solitary Qalandar, angered that he was not allowed to consume his hemp-

drink in peace, wanted at first to strike a certain disciple of Bābā Farīd by the name of Badr al-Dīn Isḥāq with his begger's bowl, but, at the intervention of Bābā Farīd himself, was content to crush his bowl against a wall; see Qalandar, 130–31; Digby, 88–89, and Nizami, 296. The same Bābā Farīd had another troublesome encounter with a Qalandar-like figure; see Digby, 92–93. Although Digby presents this incident as a murderous attack upon Bābā Farīd in keeping with the view expressed in his main source, it can certainly be interpreted as an innocuous visit by a dervish—most likely a Ḥaydarī.

42. Baranī, 91–92; Digby, 63 and 71; and Rizvi, 304. Since metal paraphernalia was the chief characteristic not of Qalandars but of Ḥaydarī dervishes, Baranī's use of the term Qalandar here is probably not accurate.

43. Qalandar, 6, 74, 112–13, 130–31, 250, 286–87; Digby, 71–72, 94–97. Ḥamīd Qalandar himself was a Qalandar who was "converted" at the time of Niẓām al-Dīn Awliyā'. Naṣīr al-Dīn Chirāgh-i Dihlī was possibly subjected to a murderous attack by a Qalandar, though the identification of his assailant as a Qalandar remains quite problematic (in spite of Digby's opinion to the contrary).

44. Digby, 69, 78–80. A more detailed account of Qalandars in Muslim India of the seventh–eighth/thirteenth–fourteenth centuries is found in this study by Digby. For later history of the Qalandars in India, see, other than Digby, 69–70, 77, 99, the following works cited in Storey: *Uṣūl al-masqṣūd* (comp. 1225–26/1810–11) of Turāb ʿAlī Kākōravī, Storey, 1036, no. 1378; *al-Rawẓ al-azhar fī maʿāṣīr al-Qalandar* of Taqī ʿAlī Kākōravī (d. 1290/1873), Storey, 1046, no. 1399; *Baḥr-i zakhkār* (comp. 1203/1788–89) of Wajīh al-Dīn Ashraf, Storey, 1031–32, no. 1374; *Taḥrīr al-anwar fī tafsīr al-qalandar* of ʿAlī Anwar Qalandar ibn 'Alī Akbar, Storey, 1047, no. 1400 (2).

45. Baranī, 212. On Abū Bakr Ṭūsī, see Bruce B. Lawrence, "Abū Bakr Ṭūsī Ḥaydarī," in *EIR*, 1:265. For later sources and detailed accounts of the Sīdī Muwallih affair, see Digby, 91–92; Nizami, 288–90; and Rizvi, 307–9. For other reports of Ḥaydarīs in Indian-Persian Sufi literature, see references in Ahmad, *Intellectual History*, 45; and Nizami, 286. Nizami reports from Ḥamīd ibn Faẓl Allāh Jamālī's *Siyar al-Ārifīn* (Delhi, 1311/1893), 67, that the Ḥaydarī practice of passing a lead ring through the urethra was konwn as *sīkh muhr*, "skewer or pin seal." On Jamālī, see Storey, 968–72.

46. Baṭṭūṭah, 2:6–7, 3:439, and 4:61; see also 3:309–11.

47. A. S. Bazmee Ansari, "Badīʿ al-Dīn," in *EI*, 1:858–59; ʿAbd al-Raḥmān al-Chishtī, *Mir'āt-i Madārī*, a full-scale sacred biography written in 1064/1654, for which see Rieu, *Persian Manuscripts*, 1:361a, 3:973a; and Storey, 1006; [Kaykhusraw Isfandiyār,] *Dabistān-i Maẕāhib*, ed. Raḥīm Riẓāzāda Malik, 1:190–91; H. A. Rose, ed., *A Glossary of the Tribes and Castes of the Punjab and North-West Frontier Province*, 3:43–44; Rizvi, 318–20; M. M. Haq, "Shāh Badiʿal-Dīn Madār and His Ṭariqah in Bengal," *Journal of the Asiatic Society of Pakistan* 12 (1967): 95–110. For Madārīs in recent times, see Marc Gaborieau, *Minorités musulmanes dans le royaume hindou du Nepal*, 122–27; and Kathy Ewing, "*Malangs* of the Punjab: Intoxication or *Adab* as the Path to God?" in *Moral Conduct and Authority: The Place of* (Adab) *in South Asian Islam*, ed. Barbara Daly Metcalf, 357–71. Cf. Jamini Mohan Ghosh, *Sannyasi and Fakir Raiders in Bengal*.

48. A. S. Bazmee Ansari, "Djalāl al-Dīn Ḥusayn al-Bukhārī," in *EI*, 2:392; Lāhūrī, *Khazīnat al-aṣfiyā'*, 2:35–38; *Dabistān-i Maẕāhib*, 1:191–92; Shīrvānī, *Būstān al-siyāḥah*, 152–53; Rizvi, 8, 277–82, and 320; Ahmad, *Intellectual History*, 44; Zarrīnkūb, 91–92; Baṭṭūṭah, 2:282; and Gramlich, 1:71–73.

49. Ebū'l Ḫayr Rūmī, *Ṣaltuḳnāme,* fols. 364b–65b, reports the presence of Qalandars in these towns during the time of Sultan ʿAlāʾ al-Dīn Kayqūbād (r. 616–34/1219–37).

50. Aflākī, 2:596 (3/581). Abū Bakr immediately ordered the bull to be sacrificed and distributed to the needy.

51. Ibid., 1:412 (3/355). Also Jalāl al-Dīn Muḥammad ibn Muḥammad Balkhī Rūmī, known as Mawlānā, *Mas̱navī-i maʿnavī,* ed. Reynold A. Nicholson, 1:18. For other references to Qalandars in the works of Rūmī, see Abdülbaki Gölpınarlı, *Mevlānā Celāleddīn: Hayatı, Felsefesi, Eserleri, Eserlerinden Seçmeler,* 61–63.

52. Aflākī, 1:215 (3/123) and 467–68 (3/437). Al-Aflākī also records an anecdote concerning Muḥammad Ḥaydarī, a disciple of Ḥājjī Mubārak, 2:773–74.

53. *Vilāyetnāme,* 64.

54. On the meaning of the word *baraḳ,* see Robert Dankoff, "Baraq and Burāq," *Central Asiatic Journal* 15 (1971): 111. For references on Ṣarı Ṣaltuḳ, to whom the *Ṣaltuḳnāme* is dedicated, see Machiel Kiel, "The Türbe of Sarı Saltık at Badabag-Dobrudja: Brief Historical and Architectonical Notes," *Güney Doğu Avrupa Araştırmaları Dergisi* 6–7 (1977–78): 205–25; a short biography of this figure is given in Ahmet T. Karamustafa, "Early Sufism in Eastern Anatolia," in *Classical Persian Sufism: From Its Origins to Rumi,* ed. Leonard Lewisohn, 193–96.

55. Algar, "Barāq Bābā," 3:754–55. Algar supplies copious references, to which should be added Abdülbaki Gölpınarlı, *Yunus Emre: Hayatı,* 39–47; and Donald P. Little, "Religion under the Mamlūks," *Muslim World* 73 (1983): 175–76; both Gölpınarlı and Little use additional Mamlūk sources not cited by Algar.

56. A description of Baraḳ Baba and his dervishes is given above in chapter 1.

57. The Persian original of Quṭb al-ʿAlavī's commentary along with a complete translation into Turkish is given in Abdülbaki Gölpınarlı, *Yunus Emre ve Tasavvuf,* 457–72 and 255–75, respectively.

58. On Yūnus Emre, see Gölpınarlı, *Yunus Emre ve Tasavvuf,* where Ṭaptuḳ Emre is also discussed, 41–43.

59. This information on the dervishes of Abdāl Mūsā is contained in a famous poem by Ḳayġusuz Abdāl; see Sadeddin Nüzhet Ergun, *Türk Şairleri,* 1:166; and Abdülbaki Gölpınarlı, *Kaygusuz Abdal, Hatayi, Kul Himmet,* 34–35. Cf. Ḳayġusuz Abdāl, *Kaygusuz Abdal'ın Mensur Eserleri,* ed. Abdurrahman Güzel, 23, which contains a slightly different version with some better readings; for instance "Alvan gölüñ" (a lake in Antalya, Ḳayġusuz Abdāl's hometown) instead of the usual "elvān gölüñ." There is also a short sacred biography of Abdāl Mūsā, reproduced in Ergun, *Türk Şairleri,* 1:166–69, which is not very informative.

60. See the poems of Ḳayġusuz in Gölpınarlı, *Kaygusuz Abdal,* especially nos. 6 (40–42), 7 (42–43), and 9 (46–48).

61. A list of Ḳayġusuz Abdāl's works is provided in Abdurrahman Güzel, *Kaygusuz Abdal (Alāaddin Gaybī) Bibliyografyası.* The summary of his views is based on his published prose works; see Ḳayġusuz Abdāl, *Mensur Eserleri.*

62. Orhan Köprülü, "Velāyet-nāme-i Sultan Şücaeddin," *Türkiyat Mecmuası* 17 (1972): 177–84, where other references on Sulṭān Şücāʿ can be found. To these one should add Abdāl, fol. 7b. On Ḥācī Bayram, see Fuat Bayramoğlu, *Hacı Bayram-i Veli: Yaşamı, Soyu, Vakfı.* Ümmī Kemāl is discussed in William C. Hickmann, "Who Was Ümmi Kemal?" *Boğaziçi Üniversitesi Dergisi* 4–5 (1976–77): 57–82. On Nesīmī, see Kathleen R. F. Burrill, *The Quatrains of Nesimī: Fourteenth Century Turcic Hurufi.*

63. For details of the Şeyḫ Şücāʿ complex, see Ayverdi, 2:420–21; also

Tayyib Gökbilgin, *XV–XVI. Asırlarda Edirne ve Paşa Livāsı: Vakıflar, Mülkler, Mukataalar,* 34.

6. DERVISH GROUPS IN THE OTTOMAN EMPIRE, 1450–1550

1. For previous surveys of the topic, see Ocak and Colin H. Imber, "The Wandering Dervishes," in *Mashriq: Proceedings of the Eastern Mediterranean Seminar, University of Manchester, 1977–78,* 36–50.

2. Theodoro Spandugino, *I commentari di Theodoro Spandvgino Cantacvscino Gentilhuomo Costantinopolitano, dell'origine de' principi turchi, & de' costumi di quella natione,* 193–94; contemporary French translation: *Petit traicté de l'origine des Turcqz par Théodore Spandouyn Cantacasin,* trans. Balarin de Raconis, ed. Charles Schefer, 224–28.

3. Menavino, 79–82; German translation, 36b–37b. The relevant passage is translated in full in chapter 1 above.

4. Vāḥidī, fols. 28a–31b. It should be pointed out that Vāḥidī himself was a respectable Sufi who did not approve of the Qalandarī path.

5. *Fatih Mehmed II Vakfiyeleri,* facsimile, 175–77; transliterated text, 259–60 (paragraphs 323–28). On closer scrutiny, it appears possible that this structure was a hospice for Mevlevīs. In any case, the building was soon converted into a religious college (*madrasah*) and a mosque; see the interpretation in Ayverdi, 3:428 (entries 456–58). Also Nejat Göyünç, "Kalenderhane Cāmii," *Tarih Dergisi* 34 (1984): 485–94; and Wolfgang Müller-Wiener, *Bildlexicon zur Topographie Istanbuls: Byzantion—Konstantinupolis—Istanbul bis zum Beginn des 17. Jahrhunderts,* 153–58.

6. Tayyib Gökbilgin, "XVI. asırda Karaman eyaleti ve Lārende (Karaman) vakıf ve müesseseleri," *Vakıflar Dergisi* 7 (1968): 38, no. 40.

7. For the *ḳalenderḫānes* in Birgi and Konya, of uncertain dates, see Ömer Lütfi Barkan, "Osmanlı İmparatorluğunda bir iskān ve kolonizasyon metodu olarak vakıflar ve temlikler: I, İstilā devirlerinin kolonizatör Türk dervişleri ve zāviyeler," *Vakıflar Dergisi* 2 (1942): 327; and Semavi Eyice, "Kırşehir'de Karakurt (Kalender Baba) Ilıcası," *İstanbul Üniversitesi Edebiyat Fakültesi Tarih Enstitüsü Dergisi* 2 (1971): 247–48, no. 40. The *ḳalenderḫāne* in Bursa is cited in Evliyā, 2:18, and the one in Erzincan is recorded in a pious endowment (*waqf*) document dated 937/1530; see İsmet Miroğlu, *Kemah Sancağı ve Erzincan Kazası (1520–1566),* 152.

8. Edirneli Mecdī, *Ḥadā'iḳü'ş-şaḳā'iḳ,* ed. Meḥmed Recā'ī under the title *Terceme-i şaḳā'iḳ-i nuʿmānīye,* 225.

9. Yūsuf ibn Yaʿḳūb, *Menāḳıb-i şerīf ve ṭarīḳatnāme-i pīrān ve meşāyiḫ-i ṭarīḳat-i ʿālīye-i ḫalvetīye,* 38–39.

10. Celālzāde Muṣṭafā, known as Ḳoca Nişāncı, *Geschichte Sultan Süleymān Ḳānūnīs von 1520 bis 1557 oder Ṭabāḳāt ül-memālik ve derecāt ül-mesālik von Celālzāde Muṣṭafā genannt Koca Nişāncı,* ed. Petra Kappert, 348b. Qalandars continued to exist in the Ottoman Empire after the mid-tenth/sixteenth century. Later European accounts rely mostly on Menavino (this is also true for other dervish groups). Nicolas de Nicolay, who was in Istanbul in 1551 (Nicolas, 189–91; English translation, 104–5; Salomon Schweigger, in Istanbul between January 1578 and May 1581 (*Ein newe Reyssbeschreibung auss Teutschland nach Constantinopel und Jerusalem,* 195–97); and Michel Baudier de Languedoc, whose work first appeared in 1625 (*Histoire générale de la religion des Tvrcs,* 386–96), all repeat

Menavino in either synoptic or extended versions. Sir Paul Rycaut (*History,* 258–60), who was in Asia Minor during the reign of Meḥmed IV (1058–99/1648–87), apparently based his description on his own observations. Barthélemy d'Herbelot (*Bibliothèque Orientale,* 244) is general and vague on Qalandars. A century later, Mouradja d'Ohsson (*Tableau général de l'Empire Othoman,* vol. 4, pt. 1, 684–85) seems to be the first to mention a certain "Youssouph Endeloussy" as the alleged founder of the Qalandars. His claim was taken over by some later authors; see, for instance, Rose's note to Brown's text in John Brown, *Darvisches,* 169–72, n. 1 (chapter 11 of this book is a reproduction of d'Ohsson's account of dervishes and Sufi orders); also Le Châtelier, *Les confréries musulmanes du Hedjaz,* 253–56; and Trimingham, 268–69. On the Ottoman side, the most significant source of recent times, Ḥarīrīzāde Meḥmed Kemāleddīn, *Tibyān wasā'il al-ḥaqā'iq fī bayān salāsil al-ṭarā'iq,* Ms. Süleymaniye Kütüphanesi, Ibrahim Efendi 430–32 (late 13th/19th century), 3:74b–77a, devotes a few pages to Qalandarīyah, where passages from Jāmī's *Nafaḥāt al-uns,* Tabrīzī's *Burhān-i qāṭiʿ,* Ibn Baṭṭūṭah's travelogue, and al-Maqrīzī's *al-Mawāʿiẓ* are quoted. The author himself thinks Qalandarīyah to be a branch of the Mevlevīye that was formed by Dīvāne Meḥmed Çelebi. For detailed information on this person, see Gölpınarlı, 101–22. Meḥmed Çelebi seems to have been not a Qalandar but a Shams-i Tabrīzī; see the section on Shams-i Tabrīzīs below in this chapter.

11. Spandugino, *Commentari,* 192; French translation: *Petit traicté,* 220 (read "Calenderi" in place of "Dynamies" in the French translation).

12. It is difficult to decipher the Turkish original of this sentence. The best I can offer here is "Geda olmak dilersen özini alçacık gör" (If you want to become a beggar, you should be humble).

13. Menavino, 75–76; German translation, 35a. Menavino's description is reproduced almost word by word in Nicolas, 182–83; English translation, 101.

14. Vāḥidī, fols. 53b–58a.

15. On the *tāj-i Ḥaydarī,* see Iskandar Bag Munshī, *History of Shāh ʿAbbās the Great,* 1:31; and Abdülbaki Gölpınarlı, "Kızılbaş," in *İslam Ansiklopedisi,* 6:789. Also cf. Adel Allouche, "The Origins and Development of the Ottoman-Safavid Conflict (906–962/1500–1555)," 118, n. 94.

16. Colin H. Imber, "The Persecution of the Ottoman Shīʿites according to the Mühimme Defterleri, 1565–1585," *Der Islam* 56 (1979): 245–73.

17. Gökbilgin, "Karaman eyaleti," 38, n. 41, where it is reported as "vaḳf-i zāviye-i ḥayderḫāne der nezd-i Alacaṣoluḳ" (in Lārende), with a total income of 3,265 *akçes;* and Miroğlu, *Kemah Sancağı,* 152.

18. Aḥmed Refīḳ, *Onuncu ʿaṣr-i hicrīde Istānbūl ḥayātı (961–1000),* 209; Suraiya Faroqhi, *Der Bektaschi-Orden in Anatolien (vom späten fünfzehnten Jahrhundert bis 1826*), 31–32. I follow Faroqhi's dating. It should be pointed out here that the *ḥaydarḫāne* in Lārende might conceivably not have been a hospice for Ḥaydarī dervishes but only named after its founder, a certain Ḥaydar. For examples of such cases, see Ḥāfıẓ Ḥüseyn ibn İsmāʿīl Ayvānsarāyī, *Ḥadīḳatü'l-cevāmiʿ,* 1:88, 89, 94, and 95; also Meḥmed Ṣüreyyā, *Sicill-i ʿOsmānī or Teẕkire-i meşāhīr-i ʿOsmānīye,* 2:442, on "Ḥayder Ḥüseyn Aġa," who is said to have founded a hospice (*dergāh*) in his name.

19. Oruç ibn ʿĀdil, *Tevārīḫ-i āl-i ʿOsmān,* ed. Franz Babinger, 138; German translation: *Der Fromme Sultan Bayezid: Die Geschichte seiner Herrschaft (1481–1512) nach den altosmanischen Chroniken des Oruç und des Anonymus Hanivaldanus,* trans. Richard F. Kreutel, 59–61. Oruç writes that the assassin had the appearance of a

Ḥaydarī, with earrings and an iron collar around his neck; he wore a felt coat. Later Ottoman chronicles, listed in Sohrweide, "Der Sieg der Safaviden," 138, are vague and refer to the assassin merely as a Qalandar.

20. "Do you, friends, know what a Ḥaydarī is? Getting intoxicated on a preparation of hashish, they roam the city and [its] markets, constantly reciting poems in couplets. Contented [to be] in the hospice of this world, some are hemp-addicts and others Abdāls" (Faḳīrī, *Taʿrīfāt,* Ms. İstanbul Üniversitesi Kütüphanesi, TY 3051 [undated], fol. 13b).

21. Nişānci, 234–37. The dervishes described by Küçük Nişāncı wear iron rings on their ears and around their necks as well as little bells on their shoulders and chests.

22. ʿĀşıḳ, fol. 270b. The accounts in other sources on Ḫayālī Beg are not as informative as ʿĀşıḳ Çelebi's; see Sehī Beg, *Heşt bihişt,* ed. Günay Kut, fols. 112a–b; Laṭīfī, 150–51; Ḳınalızāde, 1:354–60; ʿAhdī Aḥmed Çelebi, *Gülşen-i şuʿarā,* Ms. British Library, Add. 7876 (undated), fol. 72b; Muṣṭafā ʿĀlī, *Künhü'l-aḫbār,* Ms. British Library, Or. 32 (undated), fol. 278b; and Riyāżī Meḥmed, *Riyāzü'ş-şuʿarā,* Ms. British Library, Or. 13501 (dated 1337/1918–19, copyist Aḥmed ʿİzzet), fol. 65b.

23. For Ḥayderī, see Ergun 2, 1:73–76; and ʿĀşıḳ, fol. 90a. Cf. Ḳınalızāde, 1:314, though it is not clear if Ḳınalızāde is reporting on the same Ḥayderī. Meşrebī, who died in 962/1554–55, is said to have been a disciple of the same Bābā ʿĀlī Mest, the master of Ḫayālī; see Sehī, *Heşt bihişt,* fol. 116b; Laṭīfī, 311–12; ʿĀşıḳ, fol. 124a; and Ḳınalızāde, 2:903.

24. On the Arabic term *abdāl* (pl. of *badal,* literally "substitute") as used in Sufism, see Ignaz Goldziher, "Abdāl," in *EI,* 1:94–95; and Köprülü 2, 23–29. On the possible origins and meaning of the Turkish word *ışıḳ* ("bright, gleaming; brightness, gleam"; cf. Clauson, *Etymological Dictionary,* 977, col. 1), see Abdülbaki Gölpınarlı, *Yunus Emre Divanı: Metinler, Sözlük, Açılama,* 677–79. One could speculate that the usage of this term, at least initially, was not unrelated to the practice of *chahār ẓarb,* whereby "the sun that is the face" was made to "shine in all its brightness." However, an altogether different etymology that sees the Arabic word *shaykh* at the root of the Turkish *ışıḳ* has been proposed by Köprülü 2, 36. On Seyyid Baṭṭāl Ġāzī, see M. Canard and I. Mélikoff, "Baṭṭāl," in *EI,* 1:1102–4; and Pertev Naili Boratav, "Battal," in *İslam Ansiklopedisi,* 1:344–51.

25. Vāḥidī, fols. 41a–47a.

26. On the significance and origins of the hatchet of Abū Muslim in the Turko-Iranian cultural sphere, see Irène Mélikoff, *Abu Muslim, le "Porte-Hache" du Khorassan dans la tradition épique turco-iranienne.* The word *şücāʿī* (literally "serpent-like" or "relating to heroes, heroic") was used most likely in honor and memory of the early Abdāl master Sulṭān Şücāʿ; see the section on Anatolia in chapter 5.

27. Menavino, 76–79; German translation, 35b–36b. The assassination attempt in question was carried out against Bāyezīd II in the year 897/1492 by a dervish portrayed as a Ḥaydarī; see the section on Ḥaydarīs above in this chapter.

28. Nicolas, 185–88; English translation, 102–3.

29. Konstantin Mihailović, *Memoirs of a Janissary,* trans. Benjamin Stolz, 69. Even though Mihailović confuses the Abdāls with the Ḥaydarīs on two occasions (the sentences "And they gird themselves with chains in criss-cross fashion" and "And they sheathe their *instrumentum,* alias penis, in iron"), his "derwissler" are clearly the Abdāls.

30. In a well-known passage, ʿĀşıḳpaşazāde refers to Abdālān-i Rūm in passing as one of the four groups of travelers in Asia Minor: *Die Altosmanische Chronik der ʿĀšiḳpašazāde,* ed. Friedrich Giese, 201. Faḳīrī, *Taʿrīfāt,* fol. 13a, produces the following definition for *ışıḳ:* "An *ışıḳ* is one who has gone astray from the [right] path; all are sodomites, hashish-addicts, and outlaws. So burned and consumed are they with the love of ʿAlī that they have assumed eighteen different forms in this world. At their sides are hashish-containers; one would take them to be bitches of Kerbelā." In three further couplets (fol. 13b), Faḳīrī provides additional information on the *köçeks* (the youths mentioned in Menavino's account quoted above): "In the resting-place that is the world, *köçeks* are those who wait [in attendance] at the side of *babas.* Whenever [the *baba*] so wishes they go into a [special] state [an allusion to sexual intercourse] and become Abdāls with such humility. They are the lamps of the hospice of time; their beds are the sheepskin [seats] of the *babas.*" Köprülü 2, 31, gives the faulty reading "ışık oldur k'olamaz hep de hāriç" for the first verse of the first definition; the correct reading is "ışıḳ oldur k'ola mez̲hebden h̲āric." Nışāncı, 234, makes it known in two separate couplets that Abdāls shave their heads and do not wear any headgear. Cf. the first couplet of Küçük Nişāncı with Ḫayālī Beg, *Ḫayālī Bey Dīvānı,* ed. Ali Nihat Tarlan, 446, Muḳaṭṭaʿāt 9. Muṣṭafā ʿĀlī, *Ḫulāṣatü'l-aḥvāl,* ed. Andreas Tietze in "The Poet as Critique of Society: A 16th-Century Ottoman Poem," *Turcica* 9 (1977): 135, verses 138–39, contains two verses on *ışıḳs*: "If you are inclined to become an *ışıḳ,* you would be afflicted with fever and sighs from head to foot; wandering about barefoot and head uncovered in summer and winter, you would yearn after hemp-drink and hashish."

31. On Ḥasan Rūmī, see Laṭīfī, 131. On Seher Abdāl, see Ergun 1, 1:88–95; and Abdülbaki Gölpınarlı, *Alevī-Bektaşī Nefesleri,* 18. For Şirī, see Ergun 1, 1:116–25; and Gölpınarlı, *Alevī-Bektaşī Nefesleri,* 177–78. It seems possible that Seḥer Abdāl and Şirī lived later than the tenth/sixteenth century. Muḥyiddīn Abdāl was a disciple of Aḳyazılı Sulṭān, and Feyżī Ḥasan Baba of Otman Baba (on Aḳyazılı, see the section on Abdāls of Rūm below in this chapter); see Ergun 1, 1:141–55; and Gölpınarlı, *Alevī-Bektaşī Nefesleri,* 16.

32. Laṭīfī, 141–43; ʿĀşıḳ, fol. 175a; and Ḳınalızāde, 2:632. Cf. Ergun 2, 2:505–8.

33. ʿAhdī, *Gülşen-i şuʿarā,* fol. 149a; Ergun 1, 1:81–83, quoting from ʿAhdī. Kelāmī was alive and a resident of the Karbalāʾ hospice when ʿAhdī wrote his entry on him, which could have been any time between 971/1563–64, the first completion of the *Gülşen-i şuʿarā,* and 1001/1592–93, the date of ʿAhdī's latest addition to his work; see Agah Sırrı Levend, *Türk Edebiyatı Tarihi,* vol. 1, *Giriş,* 270–71. Apparently, Gelibolulu Muṣṭafā ʿĀlī appointed Kelāmī the administrator of his pious endowment at Karbalāʾ; see Cornell H. Fleischer, *Bureaucrat and Intellectual in the Ottoman Empire: The Historian Mustafa Āli (1541–1600),* 124, n. 38.

34. ʿĀşıḳ, fol. 95b.

35. Yemīnī. For a brief description of *Fażīletnāme*'s contents, see Charles Rieu, *Catalogue of the Turkish Manuscripts in the British Museum* 173–74, ms. Add. 19805. On Aḳyazılı Sulṭān, see this section below.

36. Şemsī is recorded in Laṭīfī, 209–10; ʿĀşıḳ, fol. 205a; and Ḳınalızāde, 1:521. According to Laṭīfī, he died before the end of the reign of Sultan Selīm I. For the relevant verses of the *Deh murġ,* see Şemsī, *Deh murġ,* (1) Ms. British

Library, Or. 7113, fols. 130b–50b (dated 998/1589–90, copyist ʿAbdülkerīm ibn Bākir ibn Ibrāhīm ibn Iskender ibn ʿAbdullāh), fols. 140a–b; and (2) Ms. British Library, Or. 7203, (undated), fols. 12b–14b, though the two copies consulted preserve only a very corrupt text. I could not consult İ. G. Kaya, "Derviş Şemsi ve 'Deh Murg,' " *Sesler* 19 (1983): 103–17.

37. On Ḥayretī, see the introduction to the critical edition of his collection of poems (*dīvān*) in Ḥayretī, *Dīvān: Tenkidli Basım,* ed. Mehmed Çavuşoğlu and M. Ali Tanyeri, X–XVII. Most important in connection with the *Abdāls* are *ḳaṣīde* no. 8 (19–21), entitled "Der beyān-i seyr ü sülūk-i abdāl-i Ḫüdā ve ʿuşşāḳ-i bī-ser ü pā," and *musammaṭs* nos. 11 through 15 (91–99).

38. See in particular *musammaṭ* no. 13, Ḥayretī, *Dīvān,* 94–95, entitled "Der keyfiyyet-i beng ve ḥālet-i esrār gūyed," with the refrain "Curʿadanı getür abdāl yine ḥayrān olalum."

39. Ḥayretī, *Dīvān,* 19, verses 8 and 4, respectively. Cf. verses 6 and 7. It could be added here that Köprülü, who first drew attention to some of the Abdāl poets mentioned above, was of the opinion that Ḥüseynī of Rumeli, noted by Laṭīfī, 132, was also an Abdāl. The more detailed entry on this poet in ʿĀşıḳ, fol. 88a, however, proves Ḥüseynī to have been a mere plagiarist.

40. The two poems in question can be found in Ergun 2, 1:234–39.

41. See ʿAṭā'ullāh ibn Yaḥyā Nevʿīzāde, *Ḥadāʾiḳü'l-ḥaḳāʾiḳ fī tekmileti'ş-şaḳāʾiḳ,* ed. Meḥmed Recāʾī, 56.

42. Vāḥidī, fol. 28b, 1.8, and elsewhere, consistently defines *müfred* as the disciple "who sits below the master, that is, the 'second-in-charge.' " See Dihkhudā, s.v. "Mufrad" for this meaning of the word.

43. ʿĀşıḳ, fol. 175a–b.

44. For details as well as references to earlier studies, see the thorough study of these documents in Suraiya Faroqhi, "Seyyid Gazi Revisited: The Foundation as Seen through Sixteenth Century Documents," *Turcica* 13 (1981): 90–122. The *tekke* is said to have been founded by Meḥmed ibn ʿAlī Miḫal in 917/1511; see Theodor Menzel, "Das Bektāšī-Kloster Sejjid-i Ghāzī," *Mitteilungen des Seminars für Orientalische Sprachen* 28 (1925): 113; and İ. Aydın Yüksel, *II. Bayezid-Yavuz Selim Devri* (continuation of Ayverdi), 317. Evliyā Çelebi's account is to be found in Evliyā, 3:13–14.

45. Faroqhi, "Seyyid Gazi Revisited," 94. The document in question contains the names and posts of forty-eight servants of the institution. Significantly, Faroqhi reads the document to mean that "there was no hereditary master, *şeyḫ,*" in the establishment and, relying on two further documents (dated 937/1530 and 938/1531–32, respectively), goes on to state that the resident "dervishes had the right to elect their own *şeyḫ,*" (95).

46. ʿĀşıḳ, fol. 175b; Nevʿīzāde, *Ḥadāʾiḳü'l-ḥaḳāʾiḳ,* 56; Nişāncı, 234–37; and Köprülü 2, 32.

47. Faroqhi, "Seyyid Gazi Revisited," 101–5.

48. Ibid., 113.

49. Individual Abdāls continued to exist during and after the eleventh/seventeenth century. Witness, for instance, the following report of Dr. John Covel, who was in Turkey between 1670 and 1679 C.E.: "I remember two Kalenderis abord the Viner . . . ; they had the caps of a wandering Dervise, but in all things else like the habit of the Kalenderi, in Mr. Rycaut, he makes them santons, but in good earnest they are meer Tomes of Bedlam. One had a horne tyed about his shoulders (like a wild goates but longer); he blew it like our sow

gelders, high to low. He had a great hand jar, a terrible crab-tree truncheon, a leather kind of petticoat about his middle, naked above and beneath. It was then in May or June. He had a coarse Arnout Jamurluck. He drank wine (like a fish water) which we gave him to blow his horne" (J. Theodore Bent, ed., *Early Voyages in the Levant: 1. The Diary of Master Thomas Dallam, 1599–1600; 2. Extracts from the Diaries of Dr. John Covel, 1670–1679,* 153). Cf. the observations of Adam Olearius, who saw Shīʿī Abdāls in Iran during his travels in that country in 1637 (*Newe Beschreibung,* 684–85). One could also draw attention to the confusing testimony of Sieur du Loir in a letter that he wrote from Istanbul in 1640 (*Les voyage du Sieur du Loir,* 149–59). For a much more recent report, see Brown, *Darvisches,* 93.

50. Menzel, "Das Bektāšī-Kloster," 120–25; Yüksel, *II. Bayezid-Yavuz Selim Devri,* 212.

51. Vāḥidī, fol. 42b, line 11. ʿUryān Baba, however, expressly pays allegiance to Otman Baba and Sulṭān Şücāʿ: fol. 42b, lines 7–8.

52. Filiz Aydın, "Seyitgazi Aslanbey köyünde 'Şeyh Şücaeddin' külliyesi," *Vakıflar Dergisi* 9 (1971): 201–25.

53. For a picture of this hospice, see Semavi Eyice, "Varna ile Balçık arasında Akyazılı Sultan Tekkesi," *Belleten* 31 (1967): 551–600, picture 20; for the location, ibid., 562. For historical attestations, see Barkan, "Türk dervişleri," 340–41, no. 178; Ayverdi, 4:45, no. 669; Evliyā, 8:766; and Sevim İlgürel, "Ḥibrī'nin 'Enīs'ül-müsāmirīn'i," *Güney Doğu Avrupa Araştırmaları Dergisi* 2–3 (1973–74): 146, no. 53 (reporting from Ḥibrī's *Enīsü'l-müsāmirīn,* comp. 1046/1636–37).

54. Yemīnī, 83.

55. For an architectural evaluation as well as references to primary sources, including Evliyā Çelebi, see Eyice, "Akyazılı Sultan Tekkesi"; also Ayverdi, 4:16–18, pictures 7–12. A short biography of Aḳyazılı Sulṭān himself appears in "Akyazılı Sultan," *TA,* 1:395 (probably by Gölpınarlı). It seems certain that Ḳıdemli Baba, whose *tekke* is still standing in Kalugerevo-Nove Zagora in Bulgaria, was also a disciple of either Otman Baba or Aḳyazılı Sulṭān. It is telling in this respect that the tomb of Ḳıdemli Baba, just like that of Aḳyazılı Sulṭān, is a heptagonal structure; see Machiel Kiel, "Bulgaristan'da eski Osmanlı mimarisinin bir yapıtı: Kalugerevo-Nova Zagora'daki Kıdemli Baba Sultan bektaşi tekkesi," *Belleten* 35 (1971): 45–60.

56. Franz Babinger, "Ḳoyun Baba," in *EI,* 5:283; Faroqhi, *Bektaschi-Orden,* 134, n. 3; Evliyā, 2:180ff. A hagiography of Ḳoyun Baba entitled *Manẓūme-i tercüme-i menākıb-i Ḳoyun Baba* exists in Çorum Merkez Genel Kütüphanesi, Ms. 1217, though this work could not be consulted in time for inclusion in the present study.

57. See, for instance, Klaus Kreiser, "Deñiz Abdāl—ein Derwisch unter drei Sultanen," *Wiener Zeitschrift für die Kunde des Morgenlandes* 76 (1986): 199–207.

58. Spandugino, *Commentari,* 192; French translation: *Petit traicté,* 220, where one should read "Diuami" in place of "Calender."

59. Vāḥidī, fols. 66a–70a.

60. Menavino, 72–74; German translation, 34a–b.

61. Nicolas, 178–80; English translation, 99–100. The only significant addition of Nicolas, other than his drawing reproduced in plate 4, was to state that the apparel of Jāmīs was "a little cassock without sleeves . . . made and fashioned untoo a deacons coate, so short, that it cometh but to aboue theyr knees." For other, less revealing, references to Jāmīs, see Faḳīrī, *Taʿrīfāt,* fol. 13b; Nişāncı, 235; and Celālzāde Muṣṭafā, *Geschichte Sultan Süleymān Ḳānūnīs,* 348b.

62. Fritz Meier, "Aḥmad-i Djām," in *EI,* 1:283–84, succinctly summarizes the earlier studies on Aḥmad of Jām, the most important of which are Wladimir Ivanow, "A Biography of Shaykh Ahmad-i Jam," *Journal of the Royal Asiatic Society* (1917): 291–365; and Fritz Meier, "Zur Biographie Aḥmad-i Ǧām's und zur Quellenkunde von Ǧāmī's Nafaḥātu'l-uns," *Zeitschrift der Deutschen Morgenländischen Gesellschaft* 97 (1943): 47–67. One should now consult the introductions to the following published works of Aḥmad of Jām: *Miftāḥ al-najāt,* ed. ʿAlī Fāẓil; and *Rawẓat al-muẓnibīn va jannat al-mushtāqīn,* ed. ʿAlī Fāẓil. His sacred biography is also available in print: Khvājah Sayyid al-Dīn Muḥammad Ghaznavī, *Maqāmāt-i Zhandah'Pīl,* ed. Hishmat Allah Muʾayyad Sanandajī.

63. On this collection of poems (*dīvān*), see Aḥmad of Jām, *Miftāḥ al-najāt,* 24–29; and Ghaznavī, *Maqāmāt-i Zhandah'Pīl,* 24–37. Fāẓil, the editor of *Miftāḥ al-najāt,* believes the greater part of the work to be authentic. Meier, "Aḥmad-i Djām"; H. Muʾayyad, the editor of *Maqāmāt-i Zhandah'Pīl;* and Zarrīnkūb, *Justujū,* 83, however, are highly suspicious of the attribution of the whole *dīvān* to Aḥmad. A rather ecstatic picture of Aḥmad of Jām is preserved in Qalandar, 177.

64. On Aḥmad's progeny, see Aḥmad of Jām, *Rawẓat al-muẓnibīn,* 25–57; and Ghaznavī, *Maqāmāt-i Zhandah'Pīl,* 37–38. The descendants of Aḥmad have been studied by Lawrence G. Potter, "The Kart Dynasty of Herat: Religion and Politics in Medieval Iran."

65. Vāḥidī, fols. 80b–84a.

66. Ibid., fols. 89a–94a.

67. See Gölpinarlı, 204–43. Ulu ʿĀrif Çelebi is discussed on 65–95, Dīvāne Meḥmed Çelebi on 101–22, Yūsuf Sīneçāk (the brother of the Abdāl poet Ḥayretī discussed in the section on Abdāls of Rūm in this chapter above on 124–27), and Şāhidī on 132–40. A summary of Gölpınarlı's account is available in Victoria Rowe Holbrook, "Diverse Tastes in the Spiritual Life: Textual Play in the Diffusion of Rumi's Order," in *The Legacy of Mediaeval Persian Sufism,* ed. Leonard Lewisohn, 99–120. On the Mevlevīye in general, see also Tahsin Yazıcı, D. S. Margoliouth, and Frederick De Jong, "Mawlawiyya," in *EI,* 6:883–88.

68. The institutional history of the order is studied in detail in Faroqhi, *Der Bektaschi-Orden,* which includes a comprehensive bibliography of modern studies. The most comprehensive study of Bektaşi belief and practice is still John Kingsley Birge, *The Bektashi Order of Dervishes.* Cf. also "Bektaşilik," in *TA,* 6:34–38 (probably by A. Gölpınarlı).

69. Vāḥidī, fols. 74a–80b.

70. The differences are outlined in Ahmet T. Karamustafa, "*Ḳalenders, Abdāls, Ḥayderīs*: The Formation of the *Bektāşīye* in the Sixteenth Century," in *Süleymān the Second [sic] and His Time,* ed. Halil İnalcık and Cemal Kafadar, 121–29.

71. For details on Janissary-Bektāşī relations, see Köprülü 1, 405–8; and İsmail Hakkı Uzunçarşılı, *Osmanlı Devleti Teşkilatından Kapıkulu Ocakları,* 1:147–50. A recent evaluation is Irène Mélikoff, "Un ordre des derviches colonisateurs, les Bektachis: Leur rôle social et leurs rapports avec les premiers sultans ottomans," in *Mémorial Ömer Lütfi Barkan,* 149–57. On Ḥācī Bektāş, see Karamustafa, "Early Sufism in Eastern Anatolia," 186–90. The earliest clear evidence for Janissary allegiance to Ḥācī Bektāş dates back only to the time of Meḥmed II (2d r. 855–86/1451–81); see Abdāl, fol. 93a, where the soldier accompanying Otman Baba to Istanbul at the orders of Meḥmed II declares that his headgear is modeled after that of Ḥācī Bektāş.

72. The argument for the formation of the Bektāşī order in the manner described here is presented in detail in Karamustafa, "*Ḳalenders, Abdāls, Ḥayderīs.*"

7. RENUNCIATION IN THE LATER MIDDLE PERIOD

1. Hodgson 2:1–151; Lapidus, *A History of Islamic Societies,* 137–224.

2. The only independent full-scale study of the subject is still Trimingham. Cf. Hodgson, 2:201–54.

3. Trimingham, 10–16.

4. Ibid., 166–217.

5. Reeves, *The Hidden Government,* 1. Cf. Hodgson, 2:217–18. Trimingham's description of the final stage in the organizational history of Sufism—the formation of *ṭā'ifahs*—has the disadvantage of concealing the analytical distinction between the *ṭarīqah* and the cult of saints; see Trimingham, 67–104.

6. Two recent studies on the history of the saint cult in Islam are Taylor, "The Cult of the Saints"; and Vincent Cornell, "Mirrors of Prophethood: The Evolving Image of the Spiritual Master in the Western Maghrib from the Origins of Sufism to the End of the 16th Century."

7. On Ayyūbid patronage of the Sufis, see Ramazan Şeşen, *Salāhaddīn Devrinde Eyyūbīler Devleti,* 263–66; on *khānqāhs* in Mamlūk Egypt, see Leonor Fernandes, *The Evolution of a Sufi Institution in Mamluk Egypt: The* Khanqah; Cf. Pouzet, 210–13; and Donald P. Little, "The Nature of *Khānqāhs*, *Ribāṭs*, and *Zāwiyas* under the Mamlūks," in *Islamic Studies Presented to Charles J. Adams,* ed. Wael B. Hallaq and Donald P. Little, 91–105.

8. Ernst, *Eternal Garden,* 200–26, demonstrates how the Khuldābād Chishtī shrines in the Deccan came to be associated with various political regimes from the mid-eighth/fourteenth century onward. The same process is documented for the Qādirīs as well as the Chishtīs in Bijapur during the late eleventh/seventeenth century in Richard M. Eaton, *Sufis of Bijapur 1300–1700: Social Roles of Sufis in Medieval India,* 203–42.

9. Gölpınarlı, 153–54; Hans Joachim Kissling, "Einiges über den Zejnīje-Orden im Osmanischen Reich," *Der Islam* 39 (1964): 143–79; idem, "Aus der Geschichte des Chalvetijje-Ordens," *Zeitschrift der Deutschen Morgenländischen Gesellschaft* 103 (1953): 233–89.

10. Hodgson, 2:220.

11. Cf. Eaton's study of the relationship between "landed" Sufis and *majdhūb* dervishes in Bijapur of the late eleventh/seventeenth century: *Sufis of Bijapur,* 203–81.

12. While the conclusion that conversion to dervish piety occurred primarily among male youth of the cultural elite is certainly justified, it must be admitted that the historical record on this issue is scanty. The sources naturally reported mostly on dervishes of socially prominent backgrounds. It is, however, highly unlikely that any hard evidence on the social composition of the deviant dervish groups will be forthcoming in the future. Under the circumstances, it remains to be observed here that comparative sociological observation supports the validity of the view adopted here. The Franciscan movement in Europe, for instance, provides us with a close parallel: "although they [the Franciscans] recruited members from all social groups, their chief attraction was understandably to the more affluent middle class and to the clerical intelligentsia" (Clifford

H. Lawrence, *Medieval Monasticism: Forms of Religious Life in Western Europe in the Middle Ages,* 200). On a somewhat different note, compare the following works on the counterculture movement of the 1960s in the United States: Timothy Miller, *The Hippies and American Values;* Edward P. Morgan, *The Sixties Experience: Hard Lessons About Modern America;* and Peter Clecak, *America's Quest for the Ideal Self: Dissent and Fulfillment in the 60s and 70s.*

13. Abū ʿAbd Allāh Musharrif al-Dīn ibn Muṣliḥ, known as Saʿdī, *Būstān,* ed. Muḥammad ʿAlī Furūghī, 196. The English translation is reproduced from *Morals Pointed and Tales Adorned: The Būstān of Saʿdī,* trans. G. M. Wickens, 195 (chapter 7, tale 129).

8. CONCLUSION

1. On Ibn Taymīyah, see Henri Laoust, "Ibn Taymiyya," in *EI,* 3:951–55; on Birgivī, see Kasım Kufrevī, "Birgewī," in *EI,* 1:1235.

2. Compare Richard F. Gombrich, *Theravāda Buddhism: A Social History from Ancient Benares to Modern Colombo,* 49–59; and Patrick Olivelle, *Samnyāsa Upaniṣads: Hindi Scriptures on Asceticism and Renunciation,* 29–33.

3. Lester K. Little, *Religious Poverty and the Profit Economy in Medieval Europe.*

4. See Janet L. Abu-Lugod, *Before European Hegemony: The World System A.D. 1250–1350.*

Bibliography

PRIMARY SOURCES

ʿAbd Allāh Ansārī Haravī. *Risālah-i Qalandar'nāmah*. In *Rasāʾil-i jāmiʿ-i ʿārif-i qarn-i chahārum-i hijrī Khvājah ʿAbd Allāh Ansārī*, edited by Vahīd Dastgirdī, 92–99. Tehran: Majallah-i Armaghān, 1347sh/1968.

ʿAbd al-Qādir al-Nuʿaymī. *Al-dāris fī taʾrīkh al-madāris*. Edited by Jaʿfar al-Ḥasanī. 2 vols. Damascus: Maktabat al-Thaqāfat al-Dīnīyah, 1988.

ʿAbd al-Raḥmān al-Dimashqī al-Jawbarī. *Kitāb al-mukhtār fī kashf al-asrār wa-hatk al-astār*. Ms. Süleymaniye Kütüphanesi (Istanbul), Karaçelebizade 253, dated 717/1317–18. French translation: *Le voile arraché: L'autre visage de l'Islam*. Translated by René R. Khawam. Paris: Phébus, 1979.

ʿAbd al-Rashīd al-Tattavī. *Farhang-i Rashīdī*. Edited by Ẕūlfiqār ʿAlī and ʿAzīz al-Raḥmān. 2 vols. Calcutta: Asiatic Society of Bengal, 1875.

Abū Saʿīd-i Abū al-Khayr. *Sukhanān-i manẓūm-i Abū Saʿīd-i Abū al-Khayr*. Edited by Saʿīd Nafīsī. Tehran: Kitābkhānah-i Shams, 1334sh/1955.

al-Aflākī, Shams al-Dīn Aḥmad al-ʿĀrifī. *Manāqib al-ʿārifīn*. Edited by Tahsin Yazıcı. 2 vols. Ankara: Türk Tarih Kurumu, 1956–61.

ʿAhdī Aḥmed Çelebi. *Gülşen-i şuʿarā*. Ms. British Library (London), Add. 7876, undated.

Aḥmad Amīn Rāzī. *Haft iqlīm*. Edited by Javād Fāẕil. 3 vols. Tehran: Kitābfurūshī-i ʿAlī Akbar ʿIlmī, 1340sh/1961.

Aḥmad-i Jām, Shihāb al-Dīn Abū Naṣr Aḥmad ibn Abī al-Ḥasan al-Nāmaqī al-Jāmī, known as Zhandah'Pīl. *Miftāḥ al-najāt*. Edited by ʿAlī Fāẕil. No. 40. Tehran: Bunyād-i Farhang-i Īrān, 1347sh/1968.

———. *Rawẕat al-muẕnibīn va jannat al-mushtāqīn*. Edited by ʿAlī Fāẕil. Tehran: Intishārāt-i Bunyād-i Farhang-i Īrān, 1355sh/1976.

Aḥmed Refīḳ. *Onuncu ʿaṣr-i hicrīde İstānbūl ḥayātı (961–1000)*. Tārīḫ-i ʿOs̱mānī Encümeni Külliyātı. Istanbul: Maṭbaʿa-i Orḫānīye, 1333/1914–15.

ʿAlī Şīr Nevāʾī. *Nesāyimü'l-maḥabbe min şemāyimi'l-fütüvve*. Edited by Kemal Eraslan. No. 2654. Istanbul: İstanbul Üniversitesi Edebiyat Fakültesi Yayınları, 1979.

Amīr Ḥasan Sijzī. *Favāʾid al-fuʾād*. Delhi: Maṭbaʿah-i Hindu Press, 1282/1865. English translation: *Nizam ad-Din Awliya: Morals for the Heart*. Translated by Bruce B. Lawrence. Classics of Western Spirituality. New York: Paulist Press, 1992.

ʿĀşıḳ Çelebi. *Meşāʿir üş-şuʿarā or Teẕkere of ʿĀşıḳ Çelebi*. Edited by G. H. Meredith-Owens. E. J. W. Gibb Memorial Series, new series, vol. 24. London: Luzac and Co., 1971.

ʿĀşıḳpaşazāde, Derviş Aḥmed. *Die Altosmanische Chronik der ʿĀšiḳpašazāde*. Edited by Friedrich Giese. Leipzig: Otto Harrassowitz, 1929.

ʿAṭṭār, Farīd al-Dīn Muḥammad Nīshābūrī. *Manṭiq al-ṭayr*. Edited by Sayyid Ṣādiq Gawharīn. Majmūʿah-i Mutūn-i Fārsī, no. 15. Tehran: Bungāh-i Tarjamah va Nashr-i Kitāb, 1342sh/1963.

Bābā Ṭāhir ʿUryān Hamadānī. *Dīvān-i Bābā Ṭāhir ʿUryān Hamadānī*. Edited by Manūchihr Ādamīyat. Tehran: Sāzmān-i Chāp va Intishārāt-i Iqbāl, 1361sh/1982.

Baranī, Ẓiyāʾ al-Dīn. *Tārīkh-i Fīrūz'Shāhī*. Edited by Saiyid Ahmad Khān. Calcutta: Bibliotheca Indica, 1862.

Baudier de Languedoc, Michel. *Histoire générale de la religion des Tvrcs*. Rouen: Jean Berthelin (dans la Cour du Palais), 1641.

Bent, J. Theodore, ed. *Early Voyages in the Levant: 1. The Diary of Master Thomas Dallam, 1599–1600; 2. Extracts from the Diaries of Dr. John Covel, 1670–1679*. Series 1, no. 87. London: Hakluyt Society, 1893.

al-Bukhārī, Muḥammad. *Ṣaḥīḥ*. Arabic-English bilingual edition by Muḥammad Muḥsin Khān. 9 vols. Beirut: Dār al-ʿArabīyah, 1405/1985.

Celālzāde Muṣṭafā, known as Ḳoca Nişāncı. *Geschichte Sultan Süleymān Ḳānūnīs von 1520 bis 1557 oder Ṭabāḳāt ül-memālik ve derecāt ül-mesālik von Celālzāde Muṣṭafā genannt Koca Nişāncı*. Edited by Petra Kappert. Verzeichnis der orientalischen Handschriften in Deutschland, Supplementband 21. Wiesbaden: Franz Steiner Verlag, 1981.

Dabistān-i Mazāhib. [By Kaykhusraw Isfandiyār?] Edited by Raḥīm Riẓāzāda Malik. 2 vols. Tehran: Kitābkhānah-i Ṭahūrī, 1362sh/1983.

Dawlat'Shāh ibn ʿAlāʾ al-Dawlah Bakhtī'Shāh al-Ghāzī al-Samarqandī. *Tadhkirat al-shuʿarāʾ*. Edited by Edward G. Browne. Persian Historical Texts, vol. 1. London: Luzac and Co.; Leiden: E. J. Brill, 1901.

al-Dhahabī, Shams al-Dīn Abū ʿAbd Allāh Muḥammad ibn ʿUthmān al-Dimashqī. *al-ʿIbar fī khabar man ghabar*. Edited by Ṣalāḥ al-Dīn Munajjid. 5 vols. al-Turāth al-ʿArabī, vols. 4, 5, 7, 10, and 15. Kuwait: Maṭbaʿah Ḥukūmat al-Kuwayt, 1960–66. Also vol. 3 of the edition by Abū Hājir Muḥammad al-Saʿīd ibn Bisyūnī Zaghlūl. Beirut: Dār al-Kutub al-ʿIlmiyah, 1405/1985.

———. *Taʾrīkh al-islām,* Part 63 (years 621–30). Edited by Bashshār ʿAwār Maʿrūf, Shuʿayb al-Arnaʾūṭ, and Ṣāliḥ Mahdī ʿAbbās. Beirut: Muʾassasat al-Risālah, 1408/1988.

d'Herbelot, Barthélemy. *Bibliothèque Orientale*. Paris: la Compagnie des Libraires, 1697.

d'Ohsson, Mouradja. *Tableau général de l'Empire Othoman*. Vol. 4, pt. 1. Paris: l'Imprimerie de Monsieur, 1791.

Du Mans, Raphael. *Estat de la Perse en 1660*. Edited by Ch. Schefer. Publications de l'Ecole des Langues Orientales Vivantes, 2d series, vol. 20. Paris: Ernest Leroux, 1890.

Ebū'l-Ḫayr Rūmī. *Ṣaltuḳnāme*. Edited by Fahir İz. 7 vols. Sources of Oriental Languages and Literatures 4, Turkic Sources 4. Cambridge, Mass.: Harvard University, Office of the University Publisher, 1974–84.

Edirneli Mecdī. *Ḥadāʾiḳü'ş-şaḳāʾiḳ*. Edited by Meḥmed Recāʾī under the title *Terceme-i şaḳāʾiḳ-i nuʿmānīye*. Istanbul: Dārü't-Ṭıbāʿati'l-ʿĀmire, 1269/1852–53.

Evliyā Çelebi. *Evliyā Çelebi Seyāḥatnāmesi*. Edited by Aḥmed Cevdet and Necīb ʿĀṣım. 6 vols. Istanbul: İḳdām Maṭbaʿası, 1314–18/1896–1901.

Faḳīrī. *Taʿrīfāt*. Ms. İstanbul Üniversitesi Kütüphanesi, TY 3051, undated.

Faṣīḥ al-Dīn Aḥmad ibn Muḥammad, known as Faṣīḥ al-Khvāfī. *Mujmal-i*

Faṣīḥī. Edited by Maḥmūd Farrukh. 3 vols. Mashhad: Kitābfurūshī-i Bāstān, 1341sh/1962.

Fatih Mehmed II Vakfiyeleri. Ankara: Vakıflar Umum Müdürlüğü, 1938.

Ghaznavī, Khvājah Sayyid al-Dīn Muḥammad. *Maqāmāt-i Zhandah'Pīl*. Edited by Hishmat Allah Mu'ayyad Sanandajī. Tehran: Bungāh-i Tarjamah va Nashr-i Kitāb, 1340sh/1961.

Giyās̱ al-Dīn ibn Humām al-Dīn Khvāndamīr. *Tārīkh-i ḥabīb al-siyar fī akhbār al-bashar*. Edited by Jalāl al-Dīn Humā'ī. 2d ed. Tehran: Khayyām, 1354sh/1975.

Ḥāfiẓ Ḥüseyn ibn İsmā'īl Ayvānsarāyī. *Ḥadīḳatü'l-cevāmiʿ*. 2 vols. Istanbul: Maṭbaʿa-i ʿĀmire, 1281/1864.

Ḥalvacıbaşızāde Maḥmūd Ḥulvī. *Lemeẓāt-i ḥulvīye ez lemeʿāt-i ʿulvīye*. Ms. Süleymaniye Kütüphanesi (Istanbul), Halet Efendi 281, undated.

Ḥamd Allāh Mustawfī Qazvīnī. *The Geographical Part of the Nuzhat-al-Qulūb Composed by Ḥamd-Allāh Mustawfī of Qazwīn in 740 (1340)*. Edited by Guy Le Strange. E. J. W. Gibb Memorial Series, vol. 23. London: Luzac and Co., 1915.

———. *The Tārīkh-i Guzīdah*. Edited by Edward G. Browne. 2 vols. E. J. W. Gibb Memorial Series, vol. 14. London: Luzac and Co., 1910–13.

Ḥamīd Qalandar. *Khayr al-majālis: Malfūẓāt-i Ḥaẓrat-i Shaykh Naṣīr al-Dīn Maḥmūd, Chirāgh-i Dihlī*. Edited by Khaliq Ahmad Nizami. Aligarh: Muslim University, 1959.

Ḥarīrīzāde Meḥmed Kemāleddīn. *Tibyān wasā'il al-ḥaqā'iq fī bayān salāsil al-ṭarā'iq*. Ms. Süleymaniye Kütüphanesi (Istanbul), Ibrahim Efendi 430–32 (late 13th/19th century).

Ḥayālī Beg. *Ḥayālī Bey Dīvānı*. Edited by Ali Nihat Tarlan. İstanbul Üniversitesi No. 3. Istanbul: Edebiyat Fakültesi Türk Dili ve Edebiyatı Yayınları, 1945.

Ḥayretī. *Dīvān: Tenkidli Basım*. Edited by Mehmed Çavuşoğlu and M. Ali Tanyeri. No. 2868. Istanbul: İstanbul Üniversitesi Edebiyat Fakültesi Yayınları, 1981.

Ibn Baṭṭūṭah. *Voyages d'Ibn Batoutah* [*Tuḥfat al-nuẓẓār fī gharā'ib al-amṣār wa ʿajā'ib al-asfār*]. Edited by C. Defrémery and B. R. Sanguinetti. 4 vols. Paris: Société Asiatique, 1853–58.

Ibn al-ʿImād, ʿAbd al-Ḥayy ibn Aḥmad. *Shadharāt al-dhahab fī akhbār man dhahab*. 8 vols. Cairo: Maktabat al-Qudsī, 1350–51/1931–32.

Ibn al-Jawzī, ʿAbd al-Raḥmān ibn ʿAlī. *Talbīs Iblīs*. Beirut: Dār al-Kutub al-ʿIlmīyah, 1368/1948–49.

Ibn Karbalā'ī, Ḥāfiẓ Ḥusayn Karbalā'ī Tabrīzī. *Rawẓat al-jinān va jannāt al-janān*. Edited by Jaʿfar Sulṭān al-Qurrā'ī. 2 vols. Majmūʿah-i Mutūn-i Fārsī, no. 20. Tehran: Intishārāt-i Bungāh-i Tarjamah va Nashr-i Kitāb, 1344–49sh/1965–70.

Ibn al-Kathīr, ʿImād al-Dīn Ismāʿīl ibn ʿUmar. *al-Bidāyah wa-al-nihāyah*. 14 vols. Cairo: Maṭbaʿat al-Saʿādah, 1351–58/1932–39.

Ibn Taymīyah, Taqī al-Dīn Aḥmad. *Majmūʿat al-rasā'il wa-al-masā'il*. 5 vols. in 2. Beirut: Dār al-Kutub al-ʿIlmīyah, 1403/1983.

ʿIrāqī, Fakhr al-Dīn Ibrāhīm Hamadānī. *Kulliyāt-i dīvān-i Shaykh Fakhr al-Dīn Ibrāhīm Hamadānī mutakhallaṣ biʿIrāqī*. Edited by M. Darvīsh. Tehran: Sāzmān-i Chāp va Intishārāt, n.d.

Isfarāyinī, Nūr al-Dīn ʿAbd al-Raḥmān. *Kāshif al-asrār*. Edited by Hermann Landolt. Lagrasse: Editions Verdier, 1986.

Iskandar Bag Munshī. *History of Shāh ʿAbbās the Great*. Translated by Roger M.

Savory. 2 vols. Persian Heritage Series, no. 28. Boulder, Colo.: Westview Press, 1978.

Jāmī, ʿAbd al-Raḥmān ibn Aḥmad. *Nafaḥāt al-uns min ḥaẓarāt al-quds*. Edited by Mahdī Tawḥīdī'Pūr. Tehran: Kitābfurūshī-i Saʿdī, 1337sh/1958.

al-Jullābī, ʿAlī ibn ʿUthmān al-Hujwīrī. *The Kashf al-Maḥjūb: The Oldest Persian Treatise on Sufism by al-Hujwīrī*. Translated by Reynold A. Nicholson. London: Luzac and Co., 1911.

Juvaynī, ʿAlā' al-Dīn ʿAtā Malik. *The History of the World-Conqueror* [*Tārīkh-i Jahān'gushā*]. Translated by John Andrew Boyle. 2 vols. Manchester: Manchester University Press, 1958.

Ḳayġusuz Abdāl. *Kaygusuz Abdal'ın Mensur Eserleri*. Edited by Abdurrahman Güzel. 1000 Temel Eser Dizisi, no. 97. Ankara: Kültür ve Turizm Bakanlığı Yayınları (no. 545), 1983.

Khaṭīb Fārisī. *Manāqib-i Jamāl al-Dīn Sāvī*. Edited by Tahsin Yazıcı. Ankara: Türk Tarih Kurumu, 1972. A later edition: *Qalandarnāmah-i Khaṭīb Fārisī yā Sīrat-i Jamāl al-Dīn Sāvajī*. Edited by Ḥamīd Zarrīnkūb. Tehran: Intishārāt-i Tūs, 1362sh/1983.

Khayyām, ʿUmar ibn Ibrāhīm Nīshābūrī. *Tarānahā-yi Khayyām*. Edited by Ṣādiq Hidāyat. 5th ed. Tehran: Kitābhā-yi Parastū, 1352sh/1973.

Ḳınalızāde Ḥasan Çelebi. *Tezkiretü'ş-şuʿarā*. Edited by İbrahim Kutluk. 2 vols. Ankara: Türk Tarih Kurumu Yayınları, 1978–81.

Kitāb alf laylah wa-laylah. Edited by Muhsin Mahdi. Leiden: E. J. Brill, 1984. English translation: *The Arabian Nights*. Translated by Husain Haddawy. New York: W. W. Norton and Co., 1990.

Küçük, Abdāl. *Velāyetnāme-i Sulṭān Otman Baba*. (1) Ms. Adnan Ötüken İl Halk Kütüphanesi (Ankara), no. 643, dated 1173/1759. Copyist Eş-Şeyḫ ʿÖmer ibn Dervīş Aḥmed. (2) Ms. Adnan Ötüken İl Halk Kütüphanesi (Ankara), nol 495, dated 1316/1899. Copyist Ḥasan Tebrīzī.

al-Kutubī, Muḥammad ibn Shākir. *Fawāt al-wafayāt*. Vol. 3. Edited by Iḥsān ʿAbbās. Beirut: Dār Ṣādir, 1974.

Lāhūrī, Ghulām Sarvar. *Khazīnat al-aṣfiyā'*. 2 vols. Lucknow, 1290/1873–74.

Laṭīfī, ʿAbdüllaṭīf Çelebi. *Tez̲kire*. Istanbul: İḳdām Maṭbaʿası, 1314/1896–97.

al-Maqrīzī, Aḥmad ibn ʿAlī. *al-Mawāʿiẓ wa-al-iʿtibār bi-dhikr al-khiṭaṭ wa-al-āthār*. 4 vols. Cairo: Maṭbaʿat al-Nīl, 1324–26/1906–8.

Maʿṣūm ʿAlī'Shāh ibn Raḥmat ʿAlī Niʿmat Allāhī al-Shīrāzī. *Ṭarā'iq al-ḥaqā'iq*. Edited by Muḥammad Jaʿfar Maḥjūb. 3 vols. Tehran: Kitābkhānah-i Bārānī, 1339–45sh/1960–66.

Meḥmed Ṣüreyyā. *Sicill-i ʿOs̲mānī or Tez̲kire-i meşāhīr-i ʿOs̲mānīye*. 4 vols. Istanbul: Maṭbaʿa-i ʿĀmire, 1308–14/1890–97.

Menavino, Giovan Antonio Genovese da Vultri. *Trattato de costumi et vita de Turchi*. Florence, 1548. German translation: *Türckische Historien: von der Türcken Ankunfft, Regierung, Königen und Kaisern, Kriegen, Schlachten, Victorien und Sigen, wider Christen und Heiden*. . . . Translated by Heinrich Müller. Frankfurt am Main, 1563.

Mihailović, Konstantin. *Memoirs of a Janissary*. Translated by Benjamin Stolz. Ann Arbor: University of Michigan, 1975.

Muḥammad Ḥusayn ibn Khalaf al-Tabrīzī. *Burhān-i qāṭiʿ*. Edited by Muḥammad Muʿīn. 5 vols. Tehran: Ibn Sīnā, 1342sh/1963.

Muḥammad ibn Bahādur al-Zarkashī. *Zahr al-ʿarīsh fī aḥkām (or taḥrīm) al-hashīsh*. In Franz Rosenthal, *The Herb: Hasish versus Medieval Muslim Society*, 176–97. Leiden: E. J. Brill, 1971.

Muḥammad ibn Manṣūr Mubārak'Shāh, known as Fakhr-i Mudabbir. *Ādāb al-ḥarb va al-shajāʿah*. Edited by Aḥmad Suhaylī Khvānsārī. Tehran: Intishārāt-i Iqbāl, 1346sh/1967.

Muḥammad ibn Muḥammad al-Khaṭīb. *Fusṭāṭ al-ʿadālah fī qavāʿid al-salṭanah*. Edited by Osman Turan, "Selçuk Türkiyesi din tarihine dair bir kaynak: Fusṭāṭ ul-ʿadāle fī ḳavāʿid is-salṭana," 553–64 (Persian text). In *60. Doğum Yılı Münasebetiyle Fuad Köprülü Armağanı*, 531–64. Istanbul: Ankara Üniversitesi Dil ve Tarih-Coğrafya Fakültesi, 1953.

Muḥammad Qāsim Hindū'Shāh Astarābādī, known as Firishtah. *Gulshan-i Ibrāhīmī*, usually called *Tārīkh-i Firishtah*. Lucknow: Nawal Kishore, 1281/1864–65.

Muʿīn al-Dīn Muḥammad Zamajī Isfizārī. *Rawẓāt al-jannāt fī awṣāf madīnah Harāt*. Edited by S. M. Kāẓim Imām. No. 535. Tehran: Intishārāt-i Dānishgāh-i Tihrān, 1338sh/1959.

Mujīr al-Dīn al-ʿUlaymī al-Ḥanbalī. *al-Uns al-jalīl bi-taʾrīkh al-quds wa-al-khalīl*. 2 vols. Cairo: Maṭbaʿat al-Wahbīyah, 1283/1866–67.

Muṣṭafā ʿĀlī. *Ḫulāṣatü'l-aḥvāl*. Edited by Andreas Tietze in "The Poet as Critique of Society: A 16th-Century Ottoman Poem." *Turcica* 9 (1977): 120–60.

———. *Künhü'l-aḫbār*. Ms. British Library (London), Or. 32, undated.

Muṣṭafā ibn ʿAbdullāh, known as Kātib Çelebi. *Kashf al-ẓunūn*. Edited by Şerefettin Yaltkaya and Kilisli Rifat Bilge. 2 vols. Istanbul: Maarif Matbaası, 1941–43.

Najm al-Dīn ʿAbd Allāh ibn Muḥammad Rāzī "Dāyah." *The Path of God's Bondsmen from Origin to Return*. Translated by Hamid Algar. Persian Heritage Series, no. 35. Delmar, N.Y.: Caravan Books, 1982.

Naṣrābādī, Muḥammad Ṭāhir. *Tazkirah-i Naṣrābādī*. Edited by Vaḥīd Dastgirdī. Tehran: Chāpkhānah-i Armaghān, 1317sh/1938.

Navāʾī, ʿAbd al-Ḥusayn. *Asnād va mukātabāt-i tārīkhī-i Īrān az Tīmūr tā Shāh Ismāʿīl*. Majmūʿah-i Īrānshināsī, no. 22. Tehran: Intishārāt-i Bungāh-i Tarjamah va Nashr-i Kitāb, 1341sh/1962.

Nevʿīzāde, ʿAṭā'ullāh ibn Yaḥyā. *Ḥadāʾiḳü'l-ḥaḳāʾiḳ fī tekmileti'ş-şaḳāʾiḳ*. Edited by Meḥmed Recāʾī. Istanbul: 1268/1851–52.

Nicolas de Nicolay Daulphinoys, Seigneur d'Arfeuille. *Les navigations, peregrinations et voyages, faicts en la Turquie, par Nicolas de Nicolay. . . .* Anvers: Guillaume Silvius, Imprimeur du Roy, 1576. English translation: *The Nauigations, Peregrinations and Voyages, made into Turkie by Nicholas Nicholay Daulphinois. . . .* Translated by T. Washington the Younger. London: Thomas Dawson, 1585. Facsimile edition, Amsterdam: De Capo Press and Theatrum Orbis Terrarum, 1968.

Nūr Allāh ibn Sayyid Sharīf Ḥusaynī Marʿashī Shushtarī. *Majālis al-muʾminīn*. Tehran: Sayyid Ḥusayn Tihrānī, 1268/1852.

Olearius, Adam. *Vermehrte Newe Beschreibung der Muscowitischen und Persischen Reyse*. Edited by Dieter Lohmeier. Tübingen: Max Niemeyer Verlag, 1971.

Oruç ibn ʿĀdil. *Tevārīḫ-i āl-i ʿOs̱mān*. Edited by Franz Babinger. Hannover: Orient-Buchhandlung Heinz Lafaire, 1925. German translation: *Der Fromme Sultan Bayezid: Die Geschichte seiner Herrschaft (1481–1512) nach den altosmanischen Chroniken des Oruç und des Anonymus Hanivaldanus*. Translated by Richard F. Kreutel. Graz: Verlag Styria, 1978.

Pūr-i Bahā, Tāj al-Dīn ibn Bahā al-Dīn Jāmī. *Kārnāma-yi awqāf*. In Birgitt Hoffman, "Von falschen Asketen und 'unfrommen' Stiftungen," 409–85 (text on 422–83). In *Proceedings of the First European Conference of Iranian Studies Held in Turin, September 7th–11th, 1987 by the Societas Iranologica Europaea*, part 2, *Middle and New Iranian Studies*. Edited by Gherardo Gnoli and Antonio Panaino. Rome: Istituto Italiano per il Medio ed Estremo Oriente, 1990.

al-Qazwīnī, Zakarīyā' Muḥammad. *Āthār al-bilād wa-akhbār al-ʿibād*. Beirut: Dār Ṣādir, 1380/1960.

Ramāẓānzāde Nişāncı Meḥmed, known as Küçük Nişāncı. *Tārīḫ-i Nişāncı Meḥmed Paşa*. Istanbul: Ṭabʿḫāne-i ʿĀmire, 1279/1862–63.

Riyāżī Meḥmed. *Riyāżü'ş-şuʿarā*. Ms. British Library (London), Or. 13501, dated 1337/1918–19. Copyist Aḥmed ʿİzzet.

Riẓā Qulī Khān Hidāyat. *Majmaʿ al-fuṣaḥā*. 2 vols. Tehran: n.p., 1295/1878.

Rūmī, Jalāl al-Dīn Muḥammad ibn Muḥammad Balkhī, known as Mawlānā. *Mas̱navī-i maʿnavī*. Edited by Reynold A. Nicholson. Vol. 1. E. J. W. Gibb Memorial Series, new series, no. 4. London: Luzac and Co., 1925.

Ruy Gonzales de Clavijo. *Clavijo: Embassy to Temerlane 1403–1406*. Translated by Guy Le Strange. London: George Routledge and Sons, 1928.

Rycaut, Paul. *The History of the Present State of the Ottoman Empire*. 4th ed. London: John Starkey and Henry Brome, 1675.

Saʿdī, Abū ʿAbd Allāh Musharrif al-Dīn ibn Muṣliḥ. *Būstān*. Edited by Muḥammad ʿAlī Furūghī. Tehran: Chāpkhānah va Kitābfurūshī-i Burūkhīm, 1316sh/1937. English translation: *Morals Pointed and Tales Adorned: The Būstān of Saʿdī*. Translated by G. M. Wickens. Persian Heritage Series no. 17. Toronto: University of Toronto Press, 1974.

al-Ṣafadī, Ṣalāḥ al-Dīn Khalīl ibn Aybak. *al-Wāfī bi-al-wafayāt*. Vol. 5. Edited by Sven Dedering. Wiesbaden: Franz Steiner Verlag, 1970.

Schweigger, Salomon. *Ein newe Reyssbeschreibung auss Teutschland nach Constantinopel und Jerusalem*. Nuremberg: Johann Lantzberger, 1608. Reprint. Graz: Akademische Druck- und Verlagsanstalt, 1964.

Sehī Beg. *Heşt bihişt*. Edited by Günay Kut. Sources of Oriental Languages and Literatures 5, Turkic Sources 5. Cambridge, Mass.: Harvard University Printing Office, 1978.

Şemsī. *Deh murġ*. (1) Ms. British Library (London), Or. 7113, fols. 130b–150b, dated 998/1589–90. Copyist ʿAbdülkerīm ibn Bākir ibn Ibrāhīm ibn Iskender ibn ʿAbdullāh. (2) Ms. British Library (London), Or. 7203, undated.

Shīrvānī, Zayn al-ʿĀbidīn. *Būstān al-siyāḥah*. Edited by Sayyid ʿAbd Allāh Mustawfī. Tehran: n.p., 1315/1897–98.

Sieur du Loir. *Les voyage du Sieur du Loir*. Paris: François Clouzier, 1654.

Spandugino, Theodoro. *I commentari di Theodoro Spandvgino Cantacvscino Gentilhuomo Costantinopolitano, dell'origine de' principi turchi, & de' costumi di quella natione*. Florence: Lorenzo, 1551. French translation: *Petit traicté de l'origine des Turcqz par Théodore Spandouyn Cantacasin*. Translated by Balarin de Raconis. Edited by Charles Schefer. Paris: Ernest Leroux, 1896.

al-Suhrawardī, Shihāb al-Dīn Abū Ḥafṣ ʿUmar. *ʿAwārif al-maʿārif*. Cairo: Maktabat al-Qāhirah, 1973. German translation: *Die Gaben der Entkenntnisse des ʿUmar as-Suhrawardī (ʿAwārif al-maʿārif)*. Translated by Richard Gramlich. Wiesbaden: Franz Steiner Verlag, 1978.

Tācīzāde Saʿdī Çelebi. *Münşe'āt*. Edited by Necati Lugal and Adnan Erzi. Istanbul: İstanbul Fetih Derneği, İstanbul Enstitüsü Yayınları, 1956.

Tarāshnāmah. (1) Ms. Süleymaniye Kütüphanesi (Istanbul), Hacı Mahmud 3843/3, fols. 7a–9b. (2) Ms. Süleymaniye Kütüphanesi (Istanbul), İzmir 793/5, fols.

90a–92a. (3) Ms. Süleymaniye Kütüphanesi (Istanbul), Pertev Paşa 635/3, fols. 22a–24b.

ʿUbayd-i Zākānī. *Hajvīyāt va hazlīyāt*. Tabriz: Intishārāt-i Ibn Sīnā, 1347sh/1968.

Vāḥidī. *Menāḳıb-i Ḫvoca-i Cihān ve Netīce-i Cān*. In Ahmet T. Karamustafa, *Vāḥidī's Menāḳıb-i Ḫvoca-i Cihān ve Netīce-i Cān: Critical Edition and Analysis*, 88–293. Sources of Oriental Languages and Literatures 17, Turkish Sources 15. Cambridge, Mass.: Department of Near Eastern Languages and Civilizations, Harvard University, 1993.

Vāʿiẓ Kāshifī, Fakhr al-Dīn ʿAlī ibn Ḥusayn. *Rashaḥāt ʿayn al-ḥayāt*. 2 vols. Edited by ʿAlī Aṣghar Muʿīniyān. Silsilah-i Intishārāt-i Bunyād-i Nīkūkārī-yi Nūriyānī, no. 15. Tehran: Bunyād-i Nīkūkārī-yi Nūriyānī, 1977.

Vilāyetnāme: Manāḳıb-i Ḥacı Bektāş-i Velī. Edited by Abdülbaki Gölpınarlı. Istanbul: İnkilap Kitapevi, 1958.

al-Wāsiṭī, Taqī al-Dīn ʿAbd al-Raḥmān. *Tiryāq al-muḥibbīn fī ṭabaqāt khirqat al-mashāyikh al-ʿārifīn*. Cairo: Maṭbaʿat Muḥammad Muṣṭafā, 1305/1888.

Yemīnī. *Fażīletnāme-i emīrü'l-mü'minīn ʿAlī*. Edited by Aḥmed Ḫıżır. Istanbul: Cihān Maṭbaʿası, 1327/1909.

Yūsuf ibn Yaʿḳūb. *Menāḳıb-i şerīf ve ṭarīḳatnāme-i pīrān ve meşāyiḫ-i ṭarīḳat-i ʿālīye-i ḫalvetīye*. Istanbul: n.p., 1290/1873–74.

SECONDARY SOURCES

Abu-Lugod, Janet L. *Before European Hegemony: The World System A.D. 1250–1350*. New York: Oxford University Press, 1989.

Adamec, Ludwig, ed. *Historical Gazetteer of Iran*. Vol 2, *Meshed and Northeastern Iran*. Graz: Akademische Druck- und Verlagsanstalt, 1981.

Ahmad, Aziz. *An Intellectual History of Islam in India*. Edinburgh: University of Edinburgh Press, 1969.

Ahmad, Muhammad Tagi. "Who Is a Qalandar?" *Journal of Indian History* 33 (1955): 155–70.

Algar, Hamid. "Barāq Bābā." In *Encyclopaedia Iranica*, 3:754–55.

Algar, Hamid, Frederick de Jong, and Colin Imber. "Malāmatiyya." In *The Encyclopaedia of Islam*, new edition, 6:223–28.

Allouche, Adel. "The Origins and Development of the Ottoman-Safavid Conflict (906–962/1500–1555)." Ph.D. diss., University of Utah, 1980.

Andrae, Tor. *In the Garden of Myrtles: Studies in Early Islamic Mysticism*. Translated by Birgitta Sharpe. Albany: State University of New York Press, 1987.

Ansari, A. S. Bazmee. "Badīʿ al-Dīn." In *The Encyclopaedia of Islam*, new edition, 1:858–859.

———. "Djalāl al-Dīn Ḥusayn al-Bukhārī." In *The Encyclopaedia of Islam*, new edition, 2:392.

———. "Al-Djazarī." In *The Encyclopaedia of Islam*, new edition, 2:522–23.

Arberry, Arthur John. *Sufism: An Account of the Mystics of Islam*. London: George Allen and Unwin, 1950.

Arjomand, Said Amir. *The Shadow of God and the Hidden Imam: Religion, Political Order, and Societal Change in Shi'ite Iran from the Beginning to 1890*. Chicago: University of Chicago Press, 1984.

ʿĀshūr, Saʿīd ʿAbd al-Fattāḥ. *Al-Sayyid Aḥmad al-Badawī: Shaykh wa tariqatuh*. Cairo: al-Dār al-Miṣrīyah li'l-Ta'līf wa-al-Tarjamah, 1966.

Aubin, Jean. "Un santon quhistānī de l'époque timouride." *Revue des Etudes Islamiques* 35 (1967): 185–216.

———. "Shaykh Ibrāhīm Zāhid Gīlānī (1218?–1301)." *Turcica* 21–23 (1991): 39–53.

Aydın, Filiz. "Seyitgazi Aslanbey köyünde 'Şeyh Şücaeddin' külliyesi." *Vakıflar Dergisi* 9 (1971): 201–25.

Ayverdi, Ekrem Hakkı. *Osmanlı Mimārīsinin İlk Devri*. 4 vols. Istanbul: İstanbul Fetih Cemiyeti, 1966–74.

Babinger, Franz. "Ḳoyun Baba." In *The Encyclopaedia of Islam,* new edition, 5:283.

Baldick, Julian. *Mystical Islam: An Introduction to Sufism*. New York: New York University Press, 1989.

Barkan, Ömer Lütfi. "Osmanlı İmparatorluğunda bir iskān ve kolonizasyon metodu olarak vakıflar ve temlikler: I, İstilā devirlerinin kolonizatör Türk dervişleri ve zāviyeler." *Vakıflar Dergisi* 2 (1942): 279–386.

Bausani, Alessandro. "Ḥurūfiyya." In *The Encyclopaedia of Islam,* new edition, 3:600–601.

Bayramoğlu, Fuat. *Hacı Bayram-i Veli: Yaşamı, Soyu, Vakfı*. 2 vols. Ankara: Türk Tarih Kurumu, 1983.

Bell, Catherine. "Religion and Chinese Culture: Toward an Assessment of 'Popular Religion.' " *History of Religions* 29 (1989): 35–57.

Bernand, M. "Idjmāʿ." In *The Encyclopaedia of Islam,* new edition, 3:1023–26.

Birge, John Kingsley. *The Bektashi Order of Dervishes*. Hartford, Conn.: Hartford Seminary Press, 1937.

Boratav, Pertev Naili. "Battal." In *İslam Ansiklopedisi,* 1:344–51.

Bosworth, Clifford Edmund. "Karrāmiyya." In *The Encyclopaedia of Islam,* new edition, 4:667–69.

———. *The Mediaeval Islamic Underworld: The Banū Sāsān in Arabic Society and Literature*. 2 vols. Leiden: E. J. Brill, 1976.

Böwering, Gerhard. "Baqāʾ and Fanāʾ." In *Encyclopaedia Iranica,* 3:722–24.

———. "Besṭāmī, Bāyazīd." In *Encyclopaedia Iranica,* 4:183–86.

———. *The Mystical Vision of Existence in Classical Islam: The Qurʾānic Hermeneutics of the Ṣūfī Sahl At-Tustarī (d. 283/896)*. Berlin: Walter de Gruyter, 1980.

Brockelmann, Carl. *Geschichte der Arabischen Litteratur*. 2 vols. (2d ed.) and 3 suppl. vols. Leiden: E. J. Brill, 1937–49.

Brown, John. *The Darvisches or Oriental Spiritualism*. Edited by H. A. Rose. London: Oxford University Press, 1927. Reprint, London: Frank Cass, 1968.

Brown, Peter. *The Body and Society: Men, Women, and Sexual Renunciation in Early Christianity*. New York: Columbia University Press, 1988.

———. *The Cult of the Saints: Its Rise and Function in Latin Christianity*. Chicago: University of Chicago Press, 1981.

Browne, Edward Granville. *A Literary History of Persia*. 4 vols. Cambridge: Cambridge University Press, 1928.

Bulliet, Richard W. *The Patricians of Nishapur: A Study in Medieval Islamic Social History*. Cambridge, Mass.: Harvard University Press, 1972.

Bürgel, Johann Christoph. "The Pious Rogue: A Study in the Meaning of *Qalandar* and *Rend* in the Poetry of Muhammad Iqbal." *Edebiyat* 4 (1979): 43–64.

Burrill, Katheen R. F. *The Quatrains of Nesimī: Fourteenth Century Turcic Hurufi*. The Hague: Mouton, 1972.

Canard, M., and Mélikoff, I. "Baṭṭāl." In *The Encyclopaedia of Islam*, new edition, 1:1102–4.
Chabbi, Jacqueline. "Khānḳāh." In *The Encyclopaedia of Islam*, new edition, 4:1025–26.
———. "Réflexions sur le soufisme iranien primitif." *Journal Asiatique* 266 (1978): 37–55.
———. "Remarques sur le développement historique des mouvements ascétiques et mystiques au Khurasan." *Studia Islamica* 46 (1977): 5–72.
Chodkiewicz, Michel. *Le sceau des saints: Prophétie et sainteté dans la doctrine d'Ibn Arabi*. Paris: Editions Gallimard, 1986.
Clauson, Gerard. *An Etymological Dictionary of Pre-Thirteenth-Century Turkish*. Oxford: Oxford University Press, 1972.
Clecak, Peter. *America's Quest for the Ideal Self: Dissent and Fulfillment in the 60s and 70s*. Oxford: Oxford University Press, 1983.
Cohen, Hayyim J. "The Economic Background and the Secular Occupations of Muslim Jurisprudents and Traditionists in the Classical Period of Islam (until the Middle of the Eleventh Century)." *Journal of the Economic and Social History of the Orient* 13 (1970): 16–61.
Constable, Giles. *Attitudes toward Self-Inflicted Suffering in the Middle Ages*. Brookline, Mass.: Hellenic College Press, 1982.
Cook, Michael. *Early Muslim Dogma: A Source-Critical Study*. Cambridge: Cambridge University Press, 1981.
Cornell, Vincent. "Mirrors of Prophethood: The Evolving Image of the Spiritual Master in the Western Maghrib from the Origins of Sufism to the End of the 16th Century." Ph.D. dissertation, UCLA, 1990.
Dabashi, Hamid. *Authority in Islam: From the Rise of Muhammad to the Establishment of the Umayyads*. New Brunswick, N.J.: Transaction Publishers, 1989.
Dankoff, Robert. "Baraq and Burāq." *Central Asiatic Journal* 15 (1971): 102–17.
De Bruijn, J. T. P. "The *Qalandariyyāt* in Persian Mystical Poetry, from Sanaʾī Onwards." In *The Legacy of Mediaeval Persian Sufism*, edited by Leonard Lewisohn, 75–86. London: Khaniqahi Nimatullahi Publications, 1992.
Digby, Simon. "Qalandars and Related Groups: Elements of Social Deviance in the Religious Life of the Dehlī Sultanate of the 13th and 14th Centuries." In *Islam in South Asia*, vol. 1, *South Asia*, edited by Yohanan Friedmann, 60–108. Jerusalem: Magnes Press/Hebrew University, 1984.
Dihkhudā, ʿAlī Akbar. *Kitāb-i amsāl va ḥikam*. 4 vols. Tehran: Maṭbaʿat-i Majlis, 1310sh/1931.
———. *Lughātnāmah*. Tehran: Dānishgāh-i Tihrān, Dānishkadah-i Adabīyāt, Sāzmān-i Lughātnāmah, 1327–60sh/1948–81.
Dols, Michael W. Majnūn: *The Madman in Medieval Islamic Society*. Edited by Diana E. Immisch. Oxford: Clarendon Press, 1992.
During, Jean. *Musique et extase: L'Audition mystique dans la tradition soufie*. Paris: Albin Michel, 1988.
Eaton, Richard M. *Sufis of Bijapur 1300–1700: Social Roles of Sufis in Medieval India*. Princeton: Princeton University Press, 1978.
Ergun, Sadeddin Nüzhet. *Bektaşi Edebiyatı Antolojisi: Bektaşi Şairleri ve Nefesleri*. 2d ed. 3 vols. in 2. Istanbul: Maarif Kitaphanesi, 1955–56.
———. *Türk Şairleri*. 3 vols. Istanbul: Bozkurt (and others), 1936–45.
Ernst, Carl W. *Eternal Garden: Mysticism, History, and Politics at a South Asian Sufi Center*. Albany: State University of New York Press, 1992.

———. *Words of Ecstasy in Sufism*. Albany: State University of New York Press, 1985.

Esin, Emel. " 'Eren': Les *dervīš* hétérodoxes turcs d'Asie centrale et peintre surnommé 'Siyāh-Ḳalam.' " *Turcica* 17 (1985): 7–41.

Ewing, Kathy. "*Malangs* of the Punjab: Intoxication or *Adab* as the Path to God?" In *Moral Conduct and Authority: The Place of* Adab *in South Asian Islam*, edited by Barbara Daly Metcalf, 357–71. Berkeley: University of California Press, 1984.

Eyice, Semavi. "Kırşehir'de Karakurt (Kalender Baba) Ilıcası." *İstanbul Üniversitesi Edebiyat Fakültesi Tarih Enstitüsü Dergisi* 2 (1971): 229–54.

———. "Varna ile Balçık arasında Akyazılı Sultan Tekkesi." *Belleten* 31 (1967): 551–600.

Faroqhi, Suraiya. *Der Bektaschi-Orden in Anatolien (vom späten fünfzehnten Jahrhundert bis 1826)*. Wiener Zeitschrift für die Kunde des Morgenlandes, Sonderband 2. Vienna: Verlag des Institutes für Orientalistik der Universität Wien, 1981.

———. "Seyyid Gazi Revisited: The Foundation as Seen through Sixteenth Century Documents." *Turcica* 13 (1981): 90–122.

Fehmi, Ḥüseyin. "Otman Baba ve Vilāyetnāmesi." *Türk Yurdu* 5 (1927): 239–44.

Fernandes, Leonor. *The Evolution of a Sufi Institution in Mamluk Egypt: The* Khanqah. Islamkundliche Untersuchungen, 134. Berlin: Klaus Schwarz Verlag, 1988.

Fleischer, Cornell H. *Bureaucrat and Intellectual in the Ottoman Empire: The Historian Mustafa Āli (1541–1600)*. Princeton: Princeton University Press, 1986.

Furūzānfar, Badīʿ al-Zamān. *Aḥādīth-i Ma̱snavī*. Tehran: Intishārāt-i Dānishgāh-i Tihrān, 1334sh/1955.

———. *Sharḥ-i aḥvāl va taḥlīl-i ā̱sār-i Shaykh Farīd al-Dīn Muḥammad ʿAṭṭār Nīshābūrī*. No. 41. Tehran: Intishārāt-i Anjuman-i Ā̱sār-i Millī, 1339–40sh/1960–61.

Gaborieau, Marc. *Minorités musulmanes dans le royaume hindou du Nepal*. Paris: Klincksieck, 1977.

Gellner, Ernest. "Flux and Reflux in the Faith of Men." In *Muslim Society*, 1–85. Cambridge Studies in Cultural Anthropology, no. 32. Cambridge: Cambridge University Press, 1981.

Ghanī, Qāsim. *Baḥ̱s dar ā̱sār va afkār va aḥvāl-i Ḥāfiẓ*. 2 vols. Tehran: Maṭbaʿah-i Bānk-i Millī-i Īrān, 1321–22sh/1942–43.

Ghosh, Jamini Mohan. *Sannyasi and Fakir Raiders in Bengal*. Calcutta: Bengal Secretariat Book Depot, 1930.

Goitein, Shelomo Dov. "The Rise of the Near-Eastern Bourgeoisie in Early Islamic Times." *Journal of World History* 3 (1956): 583–604.

Goldziher, Ignaz. "Abdāl." In *The Encyclopaedia of Islam*, new edition, 1:94–95.

———. "Asceticism and Sufism." In *Introduction to Islamic Theology and Law*, trans. Andras Hamori and Ruth Hamori, 116–34. Princeton: Princeton University Press, 1981.

———. "Veneration of Saints in Islam." In *Muslim Studies*, edited by S. M. Stern, translated by C. R. Barber and S. M. Stern, 2:255–341. London: George Allen and Unwin, 1971.

Gökbilgin, Tayyib. *XV–XVI. Asırlarda Edirne ve Paşa Livāsı: Vakıflar, Mülkler, Mukataalar*. No. 508. Istanbul: İstanbul Üniversitesi Edebiyat Fakültesi Yayınları, 1952.

———. "XVI. asırda Karaman eyaleti ve Lārende (Karaman) vakıf ve müesseseleri." *Vakıflar Dergisi* 7 (1968): 29–38.
[Gölpınarlı, Abdülbaki.] "Akyazılı Sultan." In *Türk Ansiklopedisi,* 1:395.
Gölpınarlı, Abdülbaki. *Alevī-Bektaşī Nefesleri*. Istanbul: Remzi Kitabevi, 1963.
[Gölpınarlı, Abdülbaki.] "Bektaşilik." In *Türk Ansiklopedisi,* 6:34–38.
———. *Hurufilik Metinleri Kataloğu*. Ankara: Türk Tarih Kurumu, 1973.
———. "Kalenderiye." In *Türk Ansiklopedisi,* 21:157–61.
———. *Kaygusuz Abdal, Hatayi, Kul Himmet*. 2d ed. Istanbul: Varlık Yayınevi, 1962.
———. "Kızılbaş." In *Islam Ansiklopedisi,* 6:789–95.
———. *Mevlānā Celāleddīn: Hayatı, Felsefesi, Eserleri, Eserlerinden Seçmeler*. Istanbul: İnkilap Kitabevi, 1952.
———. *Mevlānādan Sonra Mevlevīlik*. Istanbul: İnkilap Kitabevi, 1953.
———. *Yunus Emre Divanı: Metinler, Sözlük, Açılama*. 3 vols. in 2. Istanbul: Ahmet Halit Kitabevi, 1943–48.
———. *Yunus Emre: Hayatı*. Istanbul: Bozkurt Basımevi, 1936.
———. *Yunus Emre ve Tasavvuf*. Istanbul: Remzi Kitabevi, 1961.
———. *100 Soruda Türkiye'de Mezhepler ve Tarikatler*. Istanbul: Gerçek, 1969.
Gombrich, Richard F. *Theravāda Buddhism: A Social History from Ancient Benares to Modern Colombo*. London: Routledge and Kegan Paul, 1988.
Göyünç, Nejat. "Kalenderhane Cāmii." *Tarih Dergisi* 34 (1984): 485–94.
Gramlich, Richard. "Madjdhūb." In *The Encyclopaedia of Islam,* new edition, 5:1029.
———. *Die Schiitischen Derwischorden Persiens*. 3 vols. Deutsche Morgenländische Gesellschaft, Abhandlungen für die Kunde des Morgenlandes, nos. 26.1–4 and 45.2. Wiesbaden: Franz Steiner, 1965–81.
Güzel, Abdurrahman. *Kaygusuz Abdal (Alāaddin Gaybī) Bibliyografyası*. Kültür ve Turizm Bakanlığı Millî Folklor Araştırma Dairesi Yayınları 71, Biyografiler-Bibliyografyalar Dizisi 13. Ankara: Kültür ve Turizm Bakanlığı, 1986.
Hallaq, Wael B. "On the Authoritativeness of Sunni Consensus." *International Journal of Middle East Studies* 18 (1986): 427–54.
Hamel, Chouki El. "Fatḥ ash-Shakūr: Hommes de lettres, disciples et enseignement dans le Takrūr du XVIe au début du XIXe siècle." Ph.D. thesis, Université de Paris I–Panthéon-Sorbonne, 1992.
Hamori, Andras. "Ascetic Poetry (*Zuhdiyyāt*)." In *The Cambridge History of Arabic Literature: ʿAbbasid Belles-Lettres,* edited by Julia Ashtiany et al., 265–74. Cambridge: Cambridge University Press, 1990.
Haq, M. M. "Shāh Badiʿal-Dīn Madār and His Ṭariqah in Bengal." *Journal of the Asiatic Society of Pakistan* 12 (1967): 95–110.
Haravī, N. Māyil. *Sharḥ-i ḥāl va āṣār-i Amīr Ḥusaynī Ghūrī Haravī, mutavaffā 718*. Kabul: Vizārat-i Iṭṭilāʿāt va Kultūr, 1344sh/1965.
Hickmann, William C. "Who Was Ümmi Kemal?" *Boğaziçi Üniversitesi Dergisi* 4–5 (1976–77): 57–82.
Hodgson, Marshall G. S. *The Venture of Islam: Conscience and History in a World Civilization*. 3 vols. Chicago: University of Chicago Press, 1974.
Holbrook, Victoria Rowe. "Diverse Tastes in the Spiritual Life: Textual Play in the Diffusion of Rumi's Order." In *The Legacy of Mediaeval Persian Sufism,* edited by Leonard Lewisohn, 99–120. London: Khaniqahi Nimatullahi Publications, 1992.
Hourani, George F. "The Basis of Authority of Consensus in Sunnite Islam."

Studia Islamica 16 (1962): 13–40; reprinted in *Reason and Tradition in Islamic Ethics,* 190–226. Cambridge: Cambridge University Press, 1985.

Ibn Yūsuf Shīrāzī. *Fihrist-i Kitābkhānah-i Madrasah-i ʿĀlī-i Sipahsālār.* 2 vols. Tehran: Chāpkhānah-i Majlis, 1313–18sh/1934–39.

Ibrahim, Mahmood. *Merchant Capital and Islam.* Austin: University of Texas Press, 1990.

İlgürel, Sevim. "Ḥibrī'nin 'Enīs'ül-müsāmirīn'i." *Güney Doğu Avrupa Araştırmaları Dergisi* 2–3 (1973–74): 137–58.

Imber, Colin H. "The Persecution of the Ottoman Shīʿites according to the Mühimme Defterleri, 1565–1585." *Der Islam* 56 (1979): 245–73.

———. "The Wandering Dervishes." In *Mashriq: Proceedings of the Eastern Mediterranean Seminar, University of Manchester, 1977–78,* 36–50. Manchester: University of Manchester, 1980.

Ivanow, Wladimir. "A Biography of Shaykh Ahmad-i Jam." *Journal of the Royal Asiatic Society* (1917): 291–365.

İz, Fahir. *Eski Türk Edebiyatında Nesir: XIV. Yüzyıldan XIX. Yüzyıl Ortasına Kadar Yazmalardan Seçilmiş Metinler.* Istanbul: Osman Yalın Matbaası, 1964.

Kamali, Muhammad Hashim. *Principles of Islamic Jurisprudence.* Revised edition. Cambridge: Islamic Texts Society, 1991.

Karamustafa, Ahmet T. "The Antinomian Dervish as Model Saint." In *Modes de transmission de la culture religieuse en Islam,* edited by Hassan Elboudrari, 241–60. Cairo: Institut Français d'Archéologie Orientale, 1993.

———. "Early Sufism in Eastern Anatolia." In *Classical Persian Sufism: From Its Origins to Rumi,* edited by Leonard Lewisohn, 175–98. London: Khaniqahi Nimatullahi Publications, 1994.

———. "*Ḳalenders, Abdāls, Ḥayderīs*: The Formation of the *Bektāşīye* in the Sixteenth Century." In *Süleymān the Second [sic] and His Time,* edited by Halil İnalcık and Cemal Kafadar, 121–29. Istanbul: Isis Press, 1993.

Kennedy, Hughes. "From *Polis* to *Medina:* Urban Change in Late Antique and Early Islamic Syria." *Past & Present* 106 (1985): 3–27.

Kiel, Machiel. "Bulgaristan'da eski Osmanlı mimarisinin bir yapıtı: Kalugerevo-Nova Zagora'daki Kıdemli Baba Sultan bektaşi tekkesi." *Belleten* 35 (1971): 45–60.

———. "The Türbe of Sarı Saltık at Babadag-Dobrudja: Brief Historical and Architectonical Notes." *Güney Doğu Avrupa Araştırmaları Dergisi* 6–7 (1977–78): 205–25.

Kinberg, Leah. "Compromise of Commerce: A Study of Early Traditions concerning Poverty and Wealth." *Der Islam* 66 (1989): 193–212.

———. "What Is Meant by *Zuhd*?" *Studia Islamica* 61 (1985): 27–44.

Kissling, Hans Joachim. "Aus der Geschichte des Chalvetijje-Ordens." *Zeitschrift der Deutschen Morgenländischen Gesellschaft* 103 (1953): 233–89.

———. "Einiges über den Zejnīje-Orden im Osmanischen Reich." *Der Islam* 39 (1964): 143–79.

Kocatürk, Sadeddin. "Dar bārah-i firqah-i qalandarīyah va qalandar'nāmah-i Khaṭīb-i Fārisī, maʿnā-yi kalimah-i qalandar." *Doğu Dilleri* (Ankara Üniversitesi Dil ve Tarih-Coğrafya Fakültesi Doğu Dil ve Edebiyatları Araştırmaları Enstitüsü) 2 (1971): 89–121.

———. "İran'da İslamiyetten sonraki yüzyıllarda fikir akımlarına toplu bir bakış ve 'kalenderiye tarikatı' ile ilgili bir risale." *Ankara Üniversitesi Dil ve Tarih-Coğrafya Fakültesi Dergisi* 28 (1970): 215–31.

Köprülü, Mehmed Fuad. "Aḥmed Yesevī." In *İslam Ansiklopedisi,* 1:210–15.
———. "Anadolu'da İslāmīyet: Türk istilāsından soñra Anadolu tārīḫ-i dīnīsine bir naẓar ve bu tārīḫiñ menbaʿları." *Dārü'l-fünūn Edebīyāt Fakültesi Mecmūʿası* 2 (1922–23): 281–311, 385–420, 457–86. English translation: *Islam in Anatolia after the Turkish Invasion (Prolegomena).* Translated, edited, and with an introduction by Gary Leiser. Salt Lake City: University of Utah Press, 1993.
———. *Influence du chamanisme turco-mongol sur les ordres mystiques musulmans.* Istanbul: Mémoires de l'Institut de Turcologie de l'Université de Stanboul, 1929.
———. *Türk Edebīyātında İlk Mutaṣavvıflar.* Istanbul: Maṭbaʿa-i ʿĀmire, 1918.
———. *Türk Halkedebiyatı Ansiklopedisi.* Istanbul: Türkiyat Enstitüsü Yayınları, 1935.
Köprülü, Orhan. "Velāyet-nāme-i Sultan Şücaeddin." *Türkiyat Mecmuası* 17 (1972): 177–84.
Kreiser, Klaus, "Deñiz Abdāl—Ein Derwisch unter drei Sultanen." *Wiener Zeitschrift für die Kunde des Morgenlandes* 76 (1986): 199–207.
Kufrevī, Kasım. "Birgewī." In *The Encyclopaedia of Islam,* new edition, 1:1235.
Landolt, Hermann. "Khalwa." In *The Encyclopaedia of Islam,* new edition, 4:990–91.
———. "Walāyah." In *The Encyclopedia of Religion,* 15:316–23.
Lane, Edward William. *Manners and Customs of the Modern Egyptians.* London: J. M. Dent and Sons, 1908.
Laoust, Henri. "Ibn Taymiyya." In *The Encyclopaedia of Islam,* new edition, 3:951–55.
Lapidus, Ira M. *A History of Islamic Societies.* Cambridge: Cambridge University Press, 1988.
Lawrence, Bruce B. "Abū Bakr Ṭūsī Ḥaydarī." In *Encyclopaedia Iranica,* 1:265.
Lawrence, Clifford H. *Medieval Monasticism: Forms of Religious Life in Western Europe in the Middle Ages.* London: Longman, 1984.
Le Châtelier, Alfred. *Les confréries musulmanes du Hedjaz.* Bibliothèque Orientale Elzévirienne, no. 52. Paris: Ernest Leroux, 1887.
Levend, Agah Sırrı. *Türk Edebiyatı Tarihi.* Vol. 1, *Giriş.* Ankara: Türk Tarih Kurumu, 1973.
Little, Donald P. "The Nature of *Khānqāh*s, *Ribāṭ*s, and *Zāwiya*s under the Mamlūks." In *Islamic Studies Presented to Charles J. Adams,* edited by Wael B. Hallaq and Donald P. Little, 91–105. Leiden: E. J. Brill, 1991.
———. "Religion under the Mamlūks." *Muslim World* 73 (1983): 165–81.
Little, Lester K. *Religious Poverty and the Profit Economy in Medieval Europe.* Ithaca, N.Y.: Cornell University Press, 1978.
"Liwāṭ." In *The Encyclopaedia of Islam,* new edition, 5:776–79 (written by the editors).
Lorenzen, David N. *The Kāpālikas and Kālāmukhas: Two Lost Śaivite Sects.* Berkeley: University of California Press, 1972.
———. "Śaivism: Kāpālikas." In *The Encyclopedia of Religion,* 13:18–20.
Lutfi, Huda. *Al-Quds al-Mamlūkiyya: A History of Mamlūk Jerusalem Based on the Ḥaram Documents.* Islamkundliche Untersuchungen, no. 113. Berlin: Klaus Schwarz Verlag, 1985.
Lyons, M. C. "A Note on the *Maqāma* Form." *Pembroke Papers* 1 (1990): 115–22.
Macdonald, Duncan Black. "Darwīsh." In *The Encyclopaedia of Islam,* new edition, 2:164–65.

Madelung, Wilferd. "Murdji'a." In *The Encyclopaedia of Islam,* new edition, 7:605–7.

———. *Religious Trends in Early Islamic Iran.* Columbia Lectures on Iranian Studies 4. Albany: Bibliotheca Persica, 1988.

Maḥmūd, ʿAbd al-Ḥalīm. *Al-Sayyid Aḥmad al-Badawī.* Cairo: Dār al-Shaʿb, 1389/1969.

Makdisi, George. "Hanbalite Islam." In *Studies on Islam,* edited by Merlin L. Swartz, 216–74. Oxford: Oxford University Press, 1981.

Makdisi, George, Dominique Sourdel, and Janine Sourdel-Thomine, eds. *La notion d'autorité au Moyen Age: Islam, Byzance, Occident.* Paris: Presses Universitaires de France, 1982.

Margoliouth, D. S. "Al-Rifāʿī." In *The Encyclopaedia of Islam,* first edition, 6:1156–57.

Massignon, Louis. "Ḥarīriyya." In *The Encyclopaedia of Islam,* new edition, 3:222.

Mazzaoui, Michel M. *The Origins of the Safawids: Šīʿism, Ṣūfism and the Ġulāt.* Wiesbaden: Franz Steiner Verlag, 1972.

Meier, Fritz. *Abū Saʿīd-i Abū l-Ḫayr (357–440/967–1049): Wirklichkeit und Legende.* Acta Iranica, vol. 11. Tehran: Bibliothèque Pahlavi, 1976.

———. "Aḥmad-i Djām." In *The Encyclopaedia of Islam,* new edition, 1:283–84.

———. "Der Derwischtanz: Versuch eines Überblicks." *Asiatische Studien* 1–4 (1954): 107–36.

———. "Zur Biographie Aḥmad-i Ǧām's und zur Quellenkunde von Ǧāmī's Nafaḥātu'l-uns." *Zeitschrift der Deutschen Morgenländischen Gesellschaft* 97 (1943): 47–67.

Mélikoff, Irène. *Abu Muslim, le "Porte-Hache" du Khorassan dans la tradition épique turco-iranienne.* Paris: Adrien Maisonneuve, 1962.

———. "Un ordre des derviches colonisateurs, les Bektachis: Leur role social et leurs rapports avec les premiers sultans ottomans." In *Mémorial Ömer Lütfi Barkan,* 149–57. Bibliothèque de l'Institut Français d'Etudes Anatoliennes d'Istanbul, no. 28. Paris: Librairie d'Amérique et d'Orient Adrien Maisonneuve, 1980.

Memon, Muhammad Umar. *Ibn Taimīya's Struggle against Popular Religion, with an Annotated Translation of his* Kitāb iqtidā' aṣ-ṣirāṭ al-mustaqīm mukhālafat aṣḥāb al-jahīm. Religion and Society, no. 1. The Hague: Mouton, 1976.

Menzel, Theodor. "Beiträge zur Kenntnis der Derwisch-tāğ." In *Festschrift Georg Jacob,* edited by Theodor Menzel, 174–99. Leipzig: Otto Harrassowitz, 1932.

———. "Das Bektāšī-Kloster Sejjid-i Ghāzī." *Mitteilungen des Seminars für Orientalische Sprachen* 28 (1925): 92–125.

Michon, Jean-Louis. "Sacred Music and Dance in Islam." In *Islamic Spirituality: Manifestations,* edited by Seyyid Hossein Nasr, 469–505. World Spirituality: An Encyclopedic History of the Religious Quest, vol. 20. New York: Crossroad, 1991.

Miller, Timothy. *The Hippies and American Values.* Knoxville: University of Tennessee Press, 1991.

Mīnuvī, Mujtabā. "Az khāzā'in-i Turkīyah." *Majallah-i Dānishkadah-i Adabīyāt* (Tehran) 4 (1335sh/1956): 42–75.

Mīr Jaʿfarī, Ḥusayn. "Ḥaydarī va Niʿmatī." *Āyandah* 9 (1362sh/1983): 741–54. Earlier English version: "The Ḥaydarī-Niʿmatī Conflicts in Iran." *Iranian Studies* 12 (1979): 61–142.

Miroğlu, İsmet. *Kemah Sancağı ve Erzincan Kazası (1520–1566)*. Ankara: Atatürk Kültür, Dil ve Tarih Yüksek Kurumu Türk Tarih Kurumu Yayınları, 1990.

Molé, Marijan. "La danse extatique en Islam." In *Les danses sacrées,* 145–280. Sources Orientales 6. Paris: Editions du Seuil, 1963.

Morgan, Edward P. *The Sixties Experience: Hard Lessons about Modern America.* Philadelphia: Temple University Press, 1991.

Morrison, George, Julian Baldick, and Shafīʿī Kadkanī. *History of Persian Literature from the Beginning of the Islamic Period to the Present Day.* Handbuch der Orientalistik, pt. 1, vol. 4, sec. 2, no. 2. Leiden: E. J. Brill, 1981.

Müller-Wiener, Wolfgang. *Bildlexicon zur Topographie Istanbuls: Byzantion—Konstantinupolis—Istanbul bis zum Beginn des 17. Jahrhunderts.* Deutsches Archäologisches Institut. Tübingen: Verlag Ernst Wasmuth, 1977.

Munzavī, Aḥmad. *Fihrist-i nuskhahā-yi khaṭṭī-i Fārsī.* 6 vols. Tehran: Muʾassasah-i Farhang-i Minṭaqaʾī, n.d.

Nafīsī, Saʿīd. *Justujū dar aḥvāl va āsār-i Farīd al-Dīn ʿAṭṭār Nīshābūrī.* Tehran: Iqbāl, 1320sh/1941.

Nizami, Khaliq Ahmad. "Abū ʿAlī Qalandar, Šaraf-al-Dīn Pānīpatī." In *Encyclopaedia Iranica,* 1:258.

———. "Faḳīr." In *The Encyclopaedia of Islam,* new edition, 2:757–78.

———. *Some Aspects of Religion and Politics in India during the Thirteenth Century.* Bombay: Asia Publishing House, 1961.

Ocak, Ahmet Yaşar. *Bektaşi Menākıbnāmelerinde İslam Öncesi İnanç Motifleri.* Istanbul: Enderun Kitabevi, 1983.

———. "Kalenderīler ve Bektaşīlik." In *Doğumunun 100. yılında Atatürk'e Armağan,* 297–308. Istanbul: İstanbul Üniversitesi Yayınları, 1981.

———. *Osmanlı İmparatorluğunda Marjinal Sūfilik: Kalenderīler (XIV–XVII. Yüzyıllar).* Ankara: Atatürk Kültür, Dil ve Tarih Yüksek Kurumu Türk Tarih Kurumu Yayınları, 1992.

———. "Quelques remarques sur le rôle des derviches kalenderis dans les mouvements populaires et les activités anarchiques aux XVe et XVIe siècles dans l'empire Ottoman." *Osmanlı Araştırmaları* 3 (1982): 69–80.

Olivelle, Patrick. *Samnyāsa Upaniṣads: Hindi Scriptures on Asceticism and Renunciation.* New York: Oxford University Press, 1992.

Potter, Lawrence G. "The Kart Dynasty of Herat: Religion and Politics in Medieval Iran." Ph.D. dissertation, Columbia University, 1992.

Pouzet, Louis. *Damas au VIIe/XIIIe siècle: Vie et structures religieuses d'une métropole islamique.* Recherches (L'Université Saint-Joseph, Beirut), new series, A. Langue arabe et pensée islamique, vol. 15. Beirut: Dar al-Machreq Sarl Editeurs, 1988.

Qalandar Lal Shahbaz. Department of Public Relations, Government of Sind. Karachi: Ferozsons, n.d.

Qazi, N. B. G. *Lal Shahbaz Qalandar: ʿUthman Marwandi.* No. 26. Lahore: R. C. D. Cultural Institute Publications, 1971.

Radtke, Bernd. "The Concept of *Wilāya* in Early Sufism." In *Classical Persian Sufism: From Its Origins to Rumi,* edited by Leonard Lewisohn, 483–96. London: Khaniqahi Nimatullahi Publications, 1994.

Rahman, Fazlur. *Islam.* 2d ed. Chicago: University of Chicago Press, 1979.

———. *Major Themes of the Qurʾān.* 2d ed. Minneapolis: Bibliotheca Islamica, 1989.

Reeves, Edward B. *The Hidden Government: Ritual, Clientalism, and Legitimation in Northern Egypt.* Salt Lake City: University of Utah Press, 1990.

Reinert, Benedikt. "ʿAṭṭār, Farīd-al-Dīn." In *Encyclopaedia Iranica,* 3:21–25.
———. *Die Lehre vom* tawakkul *in der klassischen Sufik.* Berlin: Walter de Gruyter and Co., 1968.
Rieu, Charles. *Catalogue of the Persian Manuscripts in the British Museum.* 3 vols. and 1 suppl. vol. London: British Museum, 1879–95.
———. *Catalogue of the Turkish Manuscripts in the British Museum.* London: British Museum, 1888.
Ritter, Helmut. "Abū Yazīd al-Bisṭāmī." In *The Encyclopaedia of Islam,* new edition, 1:162–63.
———. "ʿAṭṭār." In *The Encyclopaedia of Islam,* new edition, 1:752–55.
———. *Das Meer der Seele: Mensch, Welt und Gott in den Geschichten des Farīduddīn ʿAṭṭār.* Leiden: E. J. Brill, 1955.
———. "Philologika XV: Farīduddīn ʿAṭṭār III. 7. Der Dīwān." *Oriens* 12 (1959): 1–88.
Rizvi, Saiyid Athar Abbas. *A History of Sufism in India.* Vol. 1. *Early Sufism and Its History in India to 1600 A.D.* New Delhi: Munshiram Manoharlal, 1978.
Rodinson, Maxime. *Islam and Capitalism.* Translated by Brian Pearce. New York: Pantheon Books, 1973.
Rose, H. A., ed. *A Glossary of the Tribes and Castes of the Punjab and North-West Frontier Province.* 3 vols. Punjab: Languages Department, 1970.
Rosenthal, Franz. *The Herb: Hashish versus Medieval Muslim Society.* Leiden: E. J. Brill, 1971.
Rossi, Ettore. " 'Torlak' kelimesine dair." *Türk Dili Araştırmaları Yıllığı—Belleten* (1955): 9–10.
Ṣafā, Ẕabīh Allāh. *Tārīkh-i Adabīyāt dar Īrān.* 5 vols. in 7. Tehran: Ibn Sīnā/ Intishārāt-i Dānishgāh-i Tihrān/Shirkat-i Muʾallifān va Mutarjimān-i Īrān, 1332–62sh/1953–83.
Ṣarrāf, Murtaẕā. "Āyīn-i qalandarī." *Armaghān* 52—dawrah-i sī-yu nuhum—(1349sh/1970): 705–15 and 53—dawrah-i chihilum—(1350sh/1971): 15–21.
Schimmel, Annemarie. *Islam in the Indian Subcontinent.* Leiden: E. J. Brill, 1980.
Şeşen, Ramazan. *Salāhaddīn Devrinde Eyyūbīler Devleti.* No. 2864. Istanbul: İstanbul Üniversitesi Edebiyat Fakültesi Yayınları, 1983.
Shoshan, Boaz. "High Culture and Popular Culture in Medieval Islam." *Studia Islamica* 73 (1991): 67–107.
Sohrweide, Hanna. "Der Sieg der Safaviden in Persien u. seine Rückwirkung auf die Schiiten Anatoliens im 16. Jh." *Der Islam* 41 (1965): 95–223.
Stillman, Yedida K., Norman A. Stillman, and T. Majda. "Libās." In *The Encyclopaedia of Islam,* new edition, 5:732–53.
Storey, Charles Ambrose. *Persian Literature: A Bio-bibliographical Survey.* Vol. 1, pt. 2. *Biography.* London: Luzac and Co., 1953.
Sviri, Sara. "Ḥakīm Tirmidhī and the *Malāmatī* Movement in Early Sufism." In *Classical Persian Sufism: From Its Origins to Rumi,* edited by Leonard Lewisohn, 583–613. London: Khaniqahi Nimatullahi Publications, 1994.
Taeschner, Franz. *Zünfte und Bruderschaften im Islam: Texte zur Geschichte der Futuwwa.* Zurich: Artemis Verlag, 1979.
Taylor, Christopher Schurman. "The Cult of the Saints in Late Medieval Egypt." Ph.D. dissertation, Princeton University, 1989.
Trimingham, J. Spencer. *The Sufi Orders in Islam.* Oxford: Oxford University Press, 1971.
Tyan, Emile. "Djihād." In *The Encyclopaedia of Islam,* new edition, 2:538–40.

Uzunçarşılı, İsmail Hakkı. *Osmanlı Devleti Teşkilatından Kapıkulu Ocakları*. 2 vols. Ankara: Türk Tarih Kurumu, 1943–44.
Vollers, K., and E. Littman. "Aḥmad al-Badawī." In *The Encyclopaedia of Islam*, new edition, 1:280–81.
Weber, Max. "Religious Rejections of the World and Their Directions." In *From Max Weber: Essays in Sociology*, translated and edited by H. H. Gerth and C. Wright Mills, 323–59. New York: Oxford University Press, 1946, 1977.
Wensinck, Arent Jan. "Khamr, I. Juridical Aspects." In *The Encyclopaedia of Islam*, new edition, 4:994–97.
Widengren, Geo. "Harlekintracht und Mönchskutte, Clownhut und Derwischmütze." *Orientalia Suecana* 2 (1953): 41–111.
Wilson, Peter Lamborn. *Scandal: Essays in Islamic Heresy*. Brooklyn, N.Y.: Autonomedia, ca. 1988.
Winter, Michael M. *Society and Religion in Early Ottoman Egypt: Studies in the Writings of ʿAbd al-Wahhāb al-Shaʿrānī*. New Brunswick: Transaction Books, 1982.
Yazıcı, Tahsin. "Ḳalandar." In *The Encyclopaedia of Islam*, new edition, 4:472–73.
———. "Ḳalandariyya." In *The Encyclopaedia of Islam*, new edition, 4:473–74.
Yazıcı, Tahsin, D. S. Margoliouth, and Frederick de Jong. "Mawlawiyya." In *The Encyclopaedia of Islam*, new edition, 6:883–88.
Yüksel, İ. Aydın. *II. Bayezid-Yavuz Selim Devri* [continuation of Ekrem Hakkı Ayverdi, *Osmanlı Mimārīsinin İlk Devri*. 4 vols. (Istanbul: İstanbul Fetih Cemiyeti, 1966–74)]. Istanbul: İstanbul Fetih Cemiyeti, 1983.
Zarrīnkūb, ʿAbd al-Ḥusayn. "Ahl-i malāmat va rāh-i Qalandar." *Majallah-i Dānishkadah-i Adabīyāt va ʿUlūm-i Insānī* (Tehran) 22 (1354sh/1975): 61–100. Reprinted in *Justujū dar taṣavvuf-i Īrān*, 335–79. Tehran: Amīr Kabīr, 1357sh/1978.
———. *Justujū dar taṣavvuf-i Īrān*. Tehran: Amīr Kabīr, 1357sh/1978.

[illegible]

Index